UNDERSTANDING REFORMS

'... a deep and fascinating account of the political economy of Indian economic reforms. Unlike many previous authors, it gives due weight to political debates and concerns, since in the vibrant democracy that India is, it is politics which is in command.'

Lord Meghnad Desai, Emeritus Professor,
London School of Economics

'A very thoughtful analysis of economic reforms in India. This pioneering work in the field of political economy will find an honoured place in the libraries of both informed and general reader.'

Vijay Kelkar, Former Chairman,
Thirteenth Finance Commission of India

'The book covers a wide range and gives an insightful review of the pushes and pulls of economic policymaking since independence. It is an important contribution to an understanding of this period and will, I am sure, become a standard reference on this subject.'

C. Rangarajan, Chairman,
Economic Advisory Council to the Prime Minister

'This one is different; it takes in both formal and informal structures, institutions and processes, to explain both the nature and speed of economic reforms ... an engaging work...'

T.N. Ninan, Editorial Director and Chairman,
Business Standard Ltd

To

long-time reformers by conviction

Manmohan Singh,

P.N. Dhar,

Jagdish Bhagwati, and

T.N. Srinivasan

UNDERSTANDING REFORMS

POST-1991 INDIA

SURESH D. TENDULKAR
T.A. BHAVANI

OXFORD
UNIVERSITY PRESS

OXFORD
UNIVERSITY PRESS

Oxford University Press is a department of the University of Oxford. It furthers the University's objective of excellence in research, scholarship, and education by publishing worldwide. Oxford is a registered trademark of Oxford University Press in the UK and in certain other countries

Published in India by
Oxford University Press
YMCA Library Building, 1 Jai Singh Road, New Delhi 110 001, India

First Edition published in 2007
Oxford India Paperbacks 2012

ISBN-13: 978-0-19-808558-4
ISBN-10: 0-19-808558-3

Typeset in Goudy 11.5/13.8
by Sai Graphic Design, New Delhi 110055

Contents

Tables and Figures

TABLES

FIGURES

Tribute to Suresh D. Tendulkar

Professor Tendulkar remained true to himself all through his life and strictly followed '*Manasa, Vacha, Karmana*' by doing what he spoke and speaking what he thought. As such he maintained scrupulous professional integrity throughout his career without any compromise. He was a perfect blend of intellect and humanness. I believe it was his intellectual bent of mind that chose academics as a profession since it allows learning on a continuous basis, while his humane nature was responsible for his single-minded focus on poverty and related issues in the Indian context. He was a committed teacher and a dedicated researcher and ever willing to learn. He was more of a '*Guru*' in a traditional sense and inspiring in every way—knowledge, dedication, simplicity, compassion, and caring. He was strongly positive in attitude and optimistic in outlook.

He viewed research as a means to understanding the real issues so as to find solutions for them. Hence, he focused on empirical research and tried to have an objective view of reality. As such he paid utmost attention to data, economic theory, and the context (socio-political and economic environment). His interest in truth-seeking was as strong as his interest in the real issues, which prompted him to focus on data. He not only took data limitations seriously into account in interpreting the reality but also took an interest in data collecting agencies such as NSSO and tried to improve the quality and adequacy of data. He refused to write anything without the support of hard facts revealed by data.

Professor Tendulkar was well aware of the fact that reality is too complex to be captured by one data set or theoretical model. So, he was always for an *eclectic* approach by integrating different but relevant data sets or models to have a meaningful idea about reality. By using simple statistics such as mean and standard deviation, and organizing them intelligently, he explained the reality sensibly.

While he was of the view that ideological commitment provides a sense of direction and at times helps in setting objectives, he was never dogmatic about ideology. He was of the view that specified ideology should be changed if it does not work in a given socio-political environment. For the same reason, he advocated that the new economic policy reforms as regulatory mechanism under the planning regime was inconsistent with the existing institutional framework and thus was not effective.

He was of a firm belief that knowledge is not something to be given and taken, but to be learnt and learning is individual-specific, and a teacher only facilitates the learning process. He played his role of research supervisor perfectly by facilitating a student's learning process through free and frank discussions. He always encouraged his students to think openly without restricting themselves to existing standardized interpretations.

Professor Tendulkar was a committed teacher and took his classes so seriously that he never missed one even when he was busy with high level committees. Rather, he accepted government assignments keeping his teaching responsibilities in mind. He was methodical and used to take his students step by step through the topic.

He never saw membership of high level committees as a symbol of greatness or source of power. Rather he considered them as a responsibility and took all the pains to deliver his responsibility in the best possible way. Neither did he use his positions for personal benefits.

T.A. Bhavani
Institute of Economic Growth, Delhi

Preface to the Paperback Edition

When Oxford University Press (OUP) approached us with the idea of bringing out a paperback edition in May 2010, we initially thought of revising the book as there have been major developments in political as well as economic domains after the first edition came out. We informed OUP about this and started collecting relevant material for the revision, while working on our (individual) prior commitments. We could actually sit together only in February 2011, after completion of our other commitments, to have a series of discussions about what we should include. As we had collected a lot of information, especially on the political front (including coalition politics, corruption, governance, and so on), and decided to confine ourselves to just updating of whatever was covered in the first edition. Instead of rewriting some of the chapters in the first edition, which a revised edition would have required, it was decided to add at the end one chapter on later developments and one appendix (Appendix II) to include supporting tables. We prepared the summary tables and started drafting with an aim of completing the draft before Professor Tendulkar left for Pune in the first week of April, but could not succeed. We thought of working independently while Professor Tendulkar was away and put the information together when he returned to Delhi. Unfortunately, he was destined not to come back and I had to take the responsibility of completing the draft. Professor Tendulkar was research supervisor for my MPhil and PhD theses and working with him was always a great learning experience, a fact that was responsible for my continuous association and research collaborations with him. His untimely demise has been a great shock and irreparable loss to me personally. It took some time and effort to come out of it and work on this draft. Words are not adequate to express my gratitude to Professor K.L. Krishna for his support without which things could have been worse for me. Professor Krishna went through this draft and gave valuable suggestions. I am also thankful to my friend Professor N.R. Bhanumurthy, who went through this draft carefully and gave useful suggestions. I would like to express my sincere thanks to the OUP editorial team. But for their persistence and patience, this edition could not have come out. However, I accept sole responsibility for the views and errors.

T.A. Bhavani
tatineni.bhavani@gmail.com

Preface and Acknowledgements

This book is our attempt to understand the ongoing post-1991 systemic economic reform process in India. We wholeheartedly support the growth-promoting direction of these reforms because we believe it would help achieve the long-cherished social objectives quickly and more effectively.

In our earlier years, we had enthusiastically embraced post-Independence India's socialist dream and the associated development strategy. The 1980s marked a watershed in our intellectual and professional lives. It became increasingly clear that efforts to create a utopia of establishing democratic socialism in a market economy, with public sector-dominated centralized industrial investment planning, fell between the two stools—inefficiencies generated by a virtually closed economy combined with stifled non-competitive domestic markets and private enterprise on the one hand and ineffectively operated and indiscriminately expanded public sector on the other. The end-result was slow economic growth during 1950–80 without any downward trend in the widely accepted index of poverty. In other words, we achieved neither improved living standards nor advancement of equity!

Simultaneously, academic research was highlighting technological stagnation in the USSR and other East European countries. Socialism was desperately 'in search of (technologically dynamic) economic system' as economists Brus and Laski from Poland put it. The spectacular growth performance of China's 'socialist market economy' indicated what socialism's search for economic system yielded—aggressively open market-driven economy! The underlying unpleasant irony was inescapable. When socialist China was pragmatically responding to the need of the hour India was trapped in the *closed and high-handedly regulated market economy* and that too in the name of socialism!

This was a process of learning by experience and observation—often described by our late colleague Raj Krishna as 'non-formal adult education'! Another basic fact struck us professionally. Any change in the mode of organizing the economic system has both positive *and* negative consequences inextricably linked to it and the choice can only be made on the basis of a judgement about the balance; as a famous quote from Deng Xiaoping puts it: 'when you open the window to get fresh air, some flies inescapably manage to smuggle themselves'. Our considered judgement is that the socially beneficial consequences of the ongoing growth-promoting reform process far outweigh the adverse ones. Consequently, a progressively competitive market-driven and globally integrated Indian economy would help attain social objectives of equity enhancement through faster rate of economic growth. The result—our unabashed and unrepentant support to the ongoing systemic reform process.

An uncomfortable question: Have we given up on our socialist dream?

We certainly believe, not. Internationally, equality of economic outcomes remained a mirage even in the ideologically committed long-time socialist countries. What the USSR and the East European countries achieved more successfully during their initial years than the capitalist countries was a more equitable distribution of basic necessities of life. Even this redefined socialist objective could not be sustained in the face of technologically stagnating economies, which eventually led to the collapse of their socialist polities. Sustaining socialism required a technologically dynamic growing economy, the search for which led China to the 'socialist market economy'. Another lesson in non-formal adult education followed. A capitalist instrumentality of Smithian invisible hand supported from the side by *responsible* state action can subserve the redefined socialist objective more effectively than public-sector-dominated economy.

Liberalization, globalization, and privatization are the terms used to characterize the ongoing reform process in India as well as in most developing countries. These terms are indeed *relative* to the initial situation prevailing in a specific country. On the eve of 1991 reforms, India was possibly the least open and most heavily—though not effectively— regulated market economy in the world. In this context, liberalization meant removing or loosening a variety of legislative and discretionary restrictions and withdrawal/adjustment of concessions that made suboptimal scale of operation profitable. Globalization meant opening up the economy to international trade in goods, services, and investment and, in turn, removal/loosening of a variety of complex and often internally inconsistent regulations on the current and capital account transactions in the balance of payments. In the context of indiscriminately expanded public sector, privatization meant withdrawal of public sector from all commercial activities to correct long-time inexcusable neglect of its core functions of supplying physical, social, and financial infrastructural facilities and services—indeed with public–private partnership.

We have a long way to go in the reform process.

We would like to acknowledge the intellectual debts, help, and assistance over the three-year duration of this project. We were prompted to undertake this project not only because of our unrepentant support to the reform process, but more importantly because of the inducement provided by generous financial assistance from the Global Development Network (GDN), then at the World Bank. The requirements of international comparison framework of GDN made us address institutional and political economy questions. We wish to express our grateful thanks to GDN for their financial support to undertake this task and in particular to Gary McMahon and Jose Fanelli for their helpful, detailed, and constructive criticisms and comments on the earlier drafts and for their tolerance of our overshooting their deadlines. The staff of the Centre for Development Economics, Delhi School of Economics where the project was housed, provided congenial administrative environment for research which we gratefully record. The helpful comments on the earlier drafts from T.N. Srinivasan, Isher J. Ahluwalia, Arvind Panagaria, Vijay Kelkar, Baldev Raj Nayar, and T.C.A. Srinivasa Raghavan are also gratefully acknowledged. Needless to say, we accept sole responsibility for the views, interpretations, and errors. We thank N.R. Bhanumurty for his help in finalizing the manuscript, Anup Pujari for supplying information on the FIPB clearances, and lawyers Ashok Desai and Ritin Rai for details of certain important court cases. We are also grateful for the competent research assistance provided by Kanupriya Gupta and Piyusha Mutreja. Finally, the editorial team at Oxford University Press deserves our special thanks for its efficiency. But for the editors, the book would not have seen the light of the day.

1

Questions in the Post-1991 Reforms Process

In July 1991, India initiated systemic changes in its economic policies after having remained a closed and heavily regulated market economy for more than three decades. These involved a major shift in the development strategy towards greater integration with the world economy and liberalization of restrictions on market transactions and private economic activities. At least two earlier attempts at piecemeal reforms had failed to take off. The first attempt was made in the year 1966 by then Prime Minister Indira Gandhi, consisting of devaluation combined with selective import tariff reductions and domestic investment liberalization. Prime Minister Rajiv Gandhi made the second attempt to liberalize domestic investment along with external trade during 1985–7.

The wide-ranging and systemic nature of the 1991 reforms can be seen in their extensive coverage and directional persistence for more than a decade and half—external sector (trade flows, exchange rate, capital inflows including private foreign direct investment), fiscal consolidation with reform on the revenue and expenditure side, monetary and financial sector (freeing of interest rates, reduction in statutory liquidity and cash reserve ratios, introduction of capital adequacy norms, reduction in directed lending, limited privatization, significant expansion in the variety of financial instruments of intermediation), industrial sector (virtual abolition of comprehensive investment licensing, abolition of restrictions on monopoly houses, significant opening up of activities previously reserved for the public sector), infrastructure (expansion of investment in roads, limited privatization of ports, privatization and introduction of competition in telecommunication), partial/full privatization of public-sector commercial enterprises, and so on. This is not to say that the reform process has been smooth, internally synchronized, complete, or fully successful but just to illustrate its *systemic, continuing, and wide-ranging* character.

The Indian case presents many prima facie paradoxical features that make it an unlikely candidate for *systemic* reforms. To start with, the reforms have been initiated and sustained in a low-income developing country democracy with mind-boggling social diversity where consensus building for systemic change poses a formidable challenge. Second, they have been taking place in an antithetical institutional environment where economic nationalism and socialism continue to have a stronghold and a volatile political environment of coalition politics that is deemed to be inimical to any kind of reforms. On top of this, the reforms have been spearheaded by political leaders with the most unlikely characteristics, namely they constitute a minority within their respective political parties, they do not command a numerically strong political support base, nor do they possess charismatic personalities! How has this leadership managed to maintain the directional consistency of reforms for a decade and a half and that too in an environment of coalition politics? Thus Indian economic policy reforms pose intriguing and challenging questions for political economy as well as institutional analysis.

In the political economy domain, Indian economic policy reforms constitute a unique case of systemic economic reforms in a *long-established developing country democracy* (Jenkins 1999). Given the proverbial aversion of democracy to systemic changes and the strong preference for status quo, how is it that a major shift in the development strategy and in the rules governing the economic system, which has the potential of disrupting the social and political fabric, has been initiated and sustained for more than a decade and a half? Even more important, how is it that such systemic change has been taking place in a *low-income country*[1] that has persisted with a democratic political framework for over half a century[2] where competitive populist pressures on polity for short-term quick-fix measures have been many and varied, and where frequent changes in governments and frequent elections have been taking place even before the constitutional term of five years that further narrow the horizon of elected representatives? The question becomes more intriguing given the added dimension of *stupendous diversity*—religious, ethnic, caste, regional, and linguistic—of the *second largest population* in the world where changing the status quo and forging a social consensus look prima facie near-impossible tasks.

In the institutional domain, certain deep-rooted path-dependent factors posed prima facie formidable obstacles to systemic reforms. The long-held beliefs in the ideologies of economic nationalism and Nehruvian socialism were firmly rooted in the suspicion of international trade, markets, and private capitalists and a naive faith in the benevolence and omniscience of state. They were responsible for the three-decade-long autarkic, public-sector-dominated, and basic and heavy industry-oriented development strategy of India till the end of the 1970s. This development strategy and the consequent economic policies resulted in a well-established and widely recognized feature of the Indian regulatory regime for three decades after Independence, namely heavy-handed regulation of the functioning markets and private economic activities. This is because India inherited limited but expanding functioning markets and private enterprise in modern industries,[3] which remained well entrenched due to the democratic political framework that provided constitutional sanctity to the private ownership of property. Unfortunately, however, going against the conventional wisdom of Adam Smith,[4] the potential positive contribution of these very features to economic development was never recognized by the political leadership inclined to establish a socialist pattern of society. Instead, centralized industrial investment planning through the expansion of the public sector and heavy-handed regulation of the long-scale private sector was deemed to be absolutely necessary for economic development. Valiant attempts were made to reconcile the latent tensions between the constitutional sanctity of private property and the consequent well-entrenched markets and private capitalists on the one hand and the egalitarian aspirations of the newly emerging nation state on the other by imposing a variety of direct discretionary restrictions on market transactions as well as on the activities of the modern private industrial sector. Thus on the eve of the reforms in 1991, India was possibly the most *comprehensively* regulated market economy. How were reforms possible given this formidable institutional legacy?

Finally, the more than a decade-and-a-half-long post-1991 reform experience throws up one more challenging question in the realm of political economy. The widely held belief in the iniquitous social outcomes of the markets provides the plausible reason why market-oriented globalizing reforms in India had to be introduced by stealth in 1991 (Jenkins 1999) by the Congress Party that had long been committed to the 'socialist pattern of society' since the mid-1950s under the charismatic leadership of the first Prime Minister Jawaharlal Nehru. In fact, this was the major electoral plank of the Congress Party in the general elections to the central parliament in 1957. The same Congress Party blamed the 1991–6 reform process that it had initiated for its allegedly inegalitarian consequences and held it responsible for its electoral defeats in the state elections in 1995 and central parliamentary elections in 1996 and 1999 and put them on the back burner.[5] However, the reforms were continued by the two left-of-centre coalition governments (formed on the basis of post-election alliances) during 1996–8, the two coalition governments headed by the Hindu Nationalist Bharatiya Janata Party (BJP) during 1998–2004 (formed on the basis of pre-poll alliances), and the current Congress-led United Progressive Alliance coalition government since May 2004. In other words, the macro-level direction of the reform process successfully survived all the permutations and combinations of political ideologies. Its spread in popular consciousness remained limited, however. A large-scale survey of political attitudes conducted between April and July 1996 found that hardly 19 per cent of the voters had even heard of economic reforms (Yadav and Singh 1996, cited in Sachs et al. 1999: 16). After pushing globalizing reforms for five years since 1999, the Hindu Nationalist BJP cleverly reformulated its earlier autarkic nationalism to make reform-based economic performance (in place of its traditional communal Hindutva agenda) as the election plank in its 'Vision Document' for the (April–May) 2004 central parliamentary elections. Not to be left behind in competitive electoral politics, this immediately prompted the Congress Party that had virtually disowned the 1991 reforms since

1996, to claim credit for initiating the economic reforms in its economic 'Vision Document' for the 2004 general election. Thus the two major contending parties in the coalition politics at the manifesto level have been vying with each other for openly owning up to economic reforms that had been introduced by stealth and bringing economic performance upfront on the political agenda. This convergence in economic policy transcending ideological lines appears to mark a welcome sea change in the approach to reforms by the two major contenders. Does this change in the major parties' viewpoint make reforms sustainable?

Our task is to offer a set of coherent and plausible clues towards unscrambling the puzzling features of the Indian reform process outlined in the preceding discussion while addressing the challenging questions in political economy and institutional analysis that they pose. The analytical framework that we have chosen with this end in view is that suggested by economic historian Douglass North, which we have supplemented with certain conceptual distinctions made by economist William Baumol. This framework is discussed in the next chapter. In this framework, the performance of economies over time is determined by path-dependent responses of individual entrepreneurs and organizations to the changing incentive structure generated by the evolving institutional matrix consisting of mutually interacting formal and informal rules of the game in the social, political, and economic domains. The critical role of path-dependence in this analytical framework prompts us to begin our discussion of the Indian case with the post-Independence economic development (strategy which itself was rooted in the pre-Independence period) that aimed at transforming an underdeveloped economy into a dynamically growing one with equitable distribution. This was reflected in the new formal regulatory rules of the game introduced by the activist political leadership. These rules along with their ideological and institutional origins form the subject matter of Chapter 3. Contrary to expectation, however, the interaction of the new regulatory formal rules with the existing institutional environment of expanding markets and private enterprise generated an incentive structure that resulted in a slow-growth distributional equilibrium that could be maintained for over two decades because of the numerically small size of the interest groups fostered by the incentive structure and availability of mechanisms of transfer that did not impinge on the exchequer (Chapter 4). The low-growth distributional equilibrium was disturbed despite a stepped-up growth rate of GDP in the 1980s by the entry of numerically large groups of farmers and small-scale industrialists/traders. Chapter 5 traces the origins of these major changes in polity and economy in the 1980s. The disturbed distributional equilibrium of the 1980s opened up a window of opportunity for the post-1991 reforms that form the theme of the remaining chapters along with the questions they raise.

Why were the reform initiatives of 1991 successful while earlier attempts had failed? To be specific, why were 1991 reforms successfully initiated by a minority government of the Congress Party with 227 seats in a house of 511 while the same party with an overwhelming 415 seats out of 543 could not sustain them just six years earlier? The explanation would revolve around the proximate role played by the external payments crisis, major changes in the Indian political economy in the 1980s that led to the surfacing of the more serious undercurrent of incipient fiscal crisis, changes in long-established public perceptions regarding public-sector enterprises, and, finally, some major international and domestic events that shook the long-held belief in the efficacy of planning and benign nature of the state. These questions are investigated in Chapter 6 in the backdrop of discussion of the fiscal and external payments crises of the 1980s that provided the context for the post-1991 reforms and other contingent factors that contributed to the timing of reforms.

While the crises can plausibly explain the timing of reforms, an all-important question of political economy remains. What explains the *directional persistence* of reforms by different coalition governments professing different ideological positions? Have the reforms brought about convergence in ideological positions or are the new entrants in the political economy game of the 1990s forcing the convergence in economic policy out of pragmatic considerations? We argue in Chapter 7 that it is more the latter than the former although both factors have been interacting with each other. This analysis also prompts some speculative suggestions about the sustainability and ownership of reforms.

The *macro-level* reform *process* whose context, timing and direction has been explored in the previous three chapters is basically the result of *interaction* amongst individual growth-promoting reform initiatives that seek to bring about *micro-level* structural adjustments in the economy. Chapter 8 discusses four selective specific reform initiatives to illustrate the evolving political economy of interest group politics that influences time path. Selectivity is dictated by the need to maintain sharp focus in view of the comprehensive and wide-ranging character of reforms described in the beginning. We select two procedural and two institutional reforms to bring out both the strengths and limitations of coalition politics that govern the feasibility and sustainability of individual initiatives. The procedural initiatives, which have progressed rapidly, include (i) liberalization of domestic and international private investment and (ii) liberalization of international trade in goods and services. The two institutional initiatives, which have proved difficult, include (iii) privatization of government-owned commercial enterprises—a story of partial success and (iv) organized labour market reforms where we observe emerging informal labour market flexibility in the face of formal legislative rigidity. Our focus will be entirely on reform moves by the central government. This is not to deny positive feedback and important moves from state politics in an increasingly strengthening federal polity in India. Our justification is twofold. One, our own inability to grasp and study the diversities and complexities in a large number of states in a tractable fashion. Two, given the stronger constitutional position of the centre vis-à-vis states, state-level reforms have critically depended on the centre's economic support. Consequently, the central government has been in the driver's seat in steering the overall pace as well as direction of reforms.

At the fundamental level, the hesitant economic policy reforms of the 1980s and wide-ranging systemic ones since 1991 have brought regulatory economic policies in line with the existing institutional environment. This has resulted in a remarkable transformation of the Indian economy from a slow-growing one till 1980 to ranking among the top ten fastest growing economies in the world since then. The Indian economy however, is, not alone in undertaking these reforms. Many other economies have also undertaken them for the same or similar reasons or in response to external shocks with varying success rates. The final chapter offers some general reflections on the reform process in the Indian perspective. It specifically, deals with the role to external influences, the reforming leaders, economic or political crises, and the all-important issue of ownership of reforms and the consensus-building.

NOTES

1. India's per capita GNP still hovered in the lowest third fractile group among 200 odd countries ranked according to GNP per capita in purchasing parity terms in the year 2000.
2. There was a brief interlude of emergency from 28 June 1975 to end December 1976 when fundamental civic rights were suspended by Mrs Indira Gandhi in the wake of high inflation and social agitations against her regime (see Dhar 2000 for a perceptive analysis and Jenkins 1999).
3. The jute and cotton textile mill industry in India emerged in the nineteenth century in a competitive fashion in the environment of laissez faire and free trade policy of the British colonial regime (Morris 1983). Other light industries came up during the inter-War period in response to limited tariff protection granted by the colonial regime in order to ensure indigenous supplies in the event of war. The estimated index of India's industrial production with 1913 as base was 239.7 in 1938, which was second only to Japan in international comparison among countries that included Canada, Chile, Italy, Germany, and the United States (Lall 1988: Table 8.5B). This is not to deny India remained predominantly agricultural in terms of labour absorption.
4. The consolation, if any, was that India was not alone in this as we note in the next chapter.
5. See Kumar (2004) for an interesting analysis of two nationwide opinion surveys in 1996 and 1998. Also see Chapter 7.

2

The Analytical Framework

Market-oriented economic reforms, by definition, seek to bring about a major change in the prevailing rules of the game and embedded incentive structure with a view to accelerating the pace of economic development. With this premise, the natural choice of broad framework for analysing the political economy and institutional questions in connection with the post-1991 systemic economic reforms in India is provided by the historical evolutionary approach to institutional change suggested by Douglass North (1990, 1994). Admitting that no 'theory of economic dynamics comparable in precision to general equilibrium theory' is available, North offers 'an initial scaffolding of an analytical framework that help us develop an analytical understanding of the way economies evolve over time' (North 1994: 359).

INSTITUTIONAL MATRIX, GOVERNANCE, AND INCENTIVE STRUCTURE

Central to North's framework is the notion of institutional matrix consisting of an interconnected web of informal and formal rules of the game in a society along with their enforcement characteristics. Informal rules include ideological beliefs, traditions, customs, conventions, widely accepted codes of conduct, and other behavioural norms. Formal rules cover general to specific rules such as constitution, statutes, common laws, individual contracts, and any formally binding procedures in the social, political, and economic domains. Rules in the political domain comprise those governing the structure of polity, its functioning, and basic decision-making processes. In the economic domain they fundamentally encompass rules relating to the ownership, exchange, and transfer of private property rights. Rules relating to inheritance of property, marriage, and family lie in the social domain.

Institutional matrix may be regarded as the society-specific, unique, path-dependent customized institutional software governing interaction among its members. Consequently, it also conveys the governance structure in the broader sense of generally predictable and legally or socially acceptable rules of interaction for cooperation and competition in the interconnected social, political, and economic domains. The term 'governance' refers to the organization, management, and development of the physical and human resources of society through social, political, administrative, and economic arrangements to meet the daily needs of people and ensure the development of society.[1] Traditionally, the term is restricted to the functioning of the formal constituents of the state, namely the legislature, executive, and judiciary. In a wider sense, the concept of governance has been extended to include the activities of local government bodies, business organizations, and civil society (that is the media, professional bodies, private voluntary organizations, sports, cultural and religious bodies, and so on). In this set up, institutionalization along with social acceptance of the rule of law including measures required for its enforcement and development activities of the government to promote the common welfare is taken to form the foundation as well as superstructure of governance while activities of the other decentralized organizations reinforce it. It is our understanding that in the framework of evolutionary institutional change, governance in the wider sense is the major determinant of economic change over time.

In this framework, the rules governing the formal organs of the state, namely the legislature, executive, and judiciary are taken to constitute the political contract accepted by the people for governance. The political contract, in turn, evolves from and is shaped by the ideology of the society as reflected in the commonly accepted set of shared beliefs, goals, and practices enshrined in what may be termed a social contract.

The government has a monopoly over legitimate coercive power for governance over the people. However, it assumes this power on their behalf in a fiduciary capacity that is derived from legitimacy and societal acceptance of government. In a democratic set up, this executive power is subject to countervailing checks and balances from the other two equally strong pillars of the state, legislature and judiciary, which are on par with the government. The government depends on the economy for its sustenance through revenues from economic activity and influences the economy's nature and development. This relationship is reflected in various fiscal, monetary, foreign trade, investment, and other economic policies. These policies may promote, prohibit, or interfere with economic activities and hence may be favourable or inimical to economic growth.

Institutions together with the standard constraints of economics define the choice set and determine the transformation (production) and transaction costs[2] and thus the feasibility and profitability of engaging in different economic activities. Thus, embedded in a given institutional matrix is the incentive structure in the society in terms of opportunities for gain in the social, political, and economic domains. Organizations and entrepreneurs emerge in these domains to reap the gains from the incentive structure. If the institutional framework rewards productive activities then economic organizations such as firms engage in productivity-enhancing activities like research and development. If the institutional framework offers gains from unproductive activities such as procuring licences to pre-empt competitors, firms spend their resources on these activities.

Organizations are nothing but groups of individuals bound together by some common purpose to achieve certain objectives. Organizations include political (political parties, regulatory agencies), economic (firms, trade unions), and social bodies (clubs, churches). Institutions are the rules of the game whereas organizations and entrepreneurs are the players in the game.

ENTREPRENEURS IN THE ECONOMIC, POLITICAL, AND SOCIAL DOMAINS

The institutional approach to economic change requires a wider definition of entrepreneurs than that in conventional economics. Following Schumpeter, economists generally recognize only productive entrepreneurship in the sense of devising innovative products, inputs, production processes, or organizations and methods of opening up new markets that help enhance profitability of economic activities and consequently increase productivity of resources and thus the welfare of society. Baumol (1990) widens this definition to include all those who use creative, novel, and ingenious methods to gain social recognition, power, prestige, or wealth. This definition has the advantage of covering unproductive (rent seeking or directly unproductive profit making) as well as destructive (discovering more deadly weapons) besides economically productive activities and includes entrepreneurs in the social and political domains as well. Given that we know little about the determinants of the supply of entrepreneurs, Baumol poses a more tractable and interesting problem of *allocation* of the available (unknown and ex ante unknowable) supply of entrepreneurs into three types—productive, unproductive, and destructive activities. This allocation is generated by the relative pay-offs to these activities, which are driven by the incentive structure that is embedded in the institutional matrix in North's sense. We interpret entrepreneurs in the Baumol sense not only to bring into existence innovative organizations to reap the gains from the existing incentive structure but also to be proactive agents who bring about a change in the institutional matrix itself so as to gain social recognition, prestige, power, or wealth. In this general framework, micro-level productive entrepreneurs may be taken to be those who respond to a *given* incentive structure to bring about shop-floor incremental improvements, major innovators are perceived to be those pushing the production technology frontier itself to earn supernormal profits, while reformist political, social, and industrial leaders are entrepreneurs attempting a change in the institutional matrix itself. Needless to add, depending on the incentive structure and the motivations of the leaders in different domains, they may push productivity in regressive directions as well.

INSTITUTIONS AND ECONOMIC PERFORMANCE

Institutions influence economic performance through (i) socially credible commitment to given rules and their enforcement mechanism; (ii) affecting costs and uncertainties associated with transacting; (iii) the allocation of entrepreneurial resources across productive, unproductive, and destructive activities; (iv) economic and political flexibility or otherwise in adapting to new opportunities; and (v) the incentive for innovation and learning in different domains. It should be obvious that if institutions show credible commitment, lower the costs and uncertainties associated with exchange, encourage productive entrepreneurship by making productive activities relatively more profitable, create incentives for learning, and impart economic and political flexibility to adapt to new opportunities, they foster higher economic growth.

It must be noted that it is the combination of formal rules, informal norms, and enforcement characteristics that shapes economic performance. That is why economies that adopt the formal rules of another economy will have very different performance characteristics from the first economy because of a different set of informal norms and enforcement characteristics with which the new formal rules interact.

Institutional change and technological change are two analytically distinct sources of economic growth. Technical changes directly affect transformation (production) costs and indirectly the transaction costs. For example, technical change in one industry, say telephone, not only reduces transformation costs in that industry but also leads to institutional change and lowering of transaction costs of communication in other industries. Institutional change, on the other hand, is expected to influence transaction costs directly and transformation costs indirectly. For instance, institutional change in the financial sector such as development banking altered the internal structure of firms in other industries by making it possible to raise capital through an external agency and enable them to go for technical change. It is the interplay of technology and institutions that contributes to or retards economic growth.

North and Wallis (1994) suggest a unified framework that incorporates technological and institutional changes as determinants of economic change through time. They offer an interesting redefinition of the term 'augmenting' (attenuating) in the literature on technological change to refer to a positive (negative) effect of a change in technology or institutions on the partial derivative of output with respect to an input. The total unit real resource cost for society is taken to be composed of transformation costs plus transaction costs. Micro-level entrepreneurs are taken to be those who bring about transformation augmenting technological change that saves on economic input costs subject to given transaction costs from slow-changing institutions. Social and political leaders, on the other hand, are those who bring about transaction-augmenting institutional change that reduces transaction costs of exchange or augments the supply of transaction inputs. Rapid economic growth results from a mutually reinforcing interaction between transformation-augmenting technological changes and transaction-augmenting institutional changes. There is no guarantee, however, that the two processes would be mutually reinforcing through time as we will have occasion to point out while interpreting the Indian growth process later. Transformation-augmenting technological change could be incremental (routine innovations) as well as proceeding in discrete large steps for a given firm or at best a group of firms. On the other hand, transaction-augmenting institutional change is necessarily an incremental process as it emerges from a complex interaction between formal and informal rules of the game involving society at large. Institutional change is consequently *path dependent* in the sense that the characteristics of the current institutional framework are shaped by previous institutional choices, which make it difficult to alter the direction of the economy once it is on a particular path. In North's words, 'The short-run profitable opportunities cumulatively create the long-run path of change' (1997: 8). North notes that the long-run effects of technological or institutional change are often unintended. This could be so for at least three reasons. One, in their single-minded pursuit of social recognition, power, prestige, or wealth, entrepreneurs are often impervious to consequences external to their motivating forces. Second, significant divergence between intentions and outcomes arises because of the intervention of unanticipated exogenous forces beyond the control of entrepreneurs. Third, the understanding of entrepreneurs regarding the complexity of interactions in the social, political, and economic domains is necessarily imperfect.

INTEREST GROUPS, DISTRIBUTIONAL COALITION, AND DISTRIBUTIONAL EQUILIBRIUM

As already mentioned, the institutional matrix in a given society at any given point of time gives rise to organizations and entrepreneurs to reap the benefits of the embedded incentive structure. Interest groups represent groups of individuals, organizations, or entrepreneurs that come together on the basis of commonality of interest in order to protect their turf, to promote their collective gains, or to mitigate collective losses[3] in the social, political, and economic domains. Kaviraj (1995) suggested an interesting analytical distinction between *horizontal* (based on commonality of economic interest but cutting across religious, linguistic, caste, or regional identities) and *vertical* mobilizations (based on commonality of identity in non-economic domains but cutting across economic interests). Interest groups seek to change the existing rules of the game to tilt them in their sectional favour in order to gain a more than proportionate share of public resources. In the political economy context, they may do this by influencing government policymaking, allocation of public revenues and expenditure, or claiming a share of directly unproductive profit-making activities such as rental income arising from market shortages. All the influential interest groups in society individually or together with other competing or non-competing interest groups[4] actively participate in pursuing common goals. A distributional coalition implies an unwritten informal implicit social contract that one can only infer from functioning. It continues so long as unwritten commitments to implicit distributional rules of the game are credibly practised by all the concerned partners within fuzzy budget constraints of sorts so that the distributional equilibrium may be deemed to be stable during its continual existence.

As regards share in the public exchequer, interest groups' claims are accommodated through various transfer mechanisms involving explicit and implicit subsidies. These basically include the unrecovered costs of publicly provided goods and services and affect the public expenditure, tax, and duty concessions. These inturn impact public revenues and the administered prices of the goods and services supplied by the autonomous public-sector entities and managerial posts that give extra perks along with pecuniary benefits.

These are introduced through various discretionary routes. When initially introduced, certain policy measures may serve a legitimate objective such as providing time-bound protection to small industries through some policy instruments like product reservation. This gives them time to attain competitiveness through technology upgradation, reorganization or overcoming other genuine handicaps. However, when these are continued even after realizing their unintended perverse incentive for small units to remain small, one can say that the policy-making process has been captured by the concerned interest groups.

As long as interest groups together do not take fiscal deficits to unsustainable levels through the earlier-mentioned transmission mechanisms and so long as partners in the distributional coalition honour the implicit contract regarding their individual agreed shares, the distributional coalition is viable. The coalition becomes unviable the moment it makes the public exchequer unsustainable in terms of huge fiscal deficits.

The interest groups generated by a particular institutional matrix are an important obstacle to any kind of change in this matrix over time.

NOTES

1. We draw on Hye (2001) for this discussion.
2. Transformation costs are production costs determined by technology and organization of economic activity. Transaction costs are non-economic costs incidental to but inextricably linked to a transaction between a buyer and a seller. They consist of costs of finding out alternative sources of exchange, working out an acceptable contract for exchange, and enforcing that contract. They absorb real resources that could otherwise have been devoted to enhancing production and productivity. See de Alessi (1988).
3. Because the rules of the game are determined by the initial bargaining position of influential segments of the population (North 1994) so that the adopted rules may turn out to be disadvantageous to some groups.
4. That non-competing groups can come together is intuitively obvious. Competing interest groups can and do come together when they perceive the gains from repetitive cooperative positive-sum game in the absence of which all of them perceive themselves to be losers.

3

The Development Strategy after Independence

THE ORIGINS

The pervasive belief of the Indian elite leadership in the ideology of economic nationalism and socialism dates back to the pre-Independence period, originating in the struggle against British colonial rule that ended in 1947. Economic nationalism was essentially a reaction to the colonial regime's laissez faire and free trade policy that was identified (wrongly, in retrospect) as the basic cause of India's economic underdevelopment by the pre-Independence political leadership (Srinivasan 1996; Srinivasan and Tendulkar 2003). In the process, other obstacles[1] to economic development that needed attention were neglected. Self-reliance under economic nationalism (Nayar 2001) was narrowly interpreted as self-sufficiency[2] and founded in a deep-rooted suspicion of international trade[3] and private capitalists[4] and belief in state activism to achieve self-reliance. Thus India's autarkic industrialization strategy[5] based on the ideology of economic nationalism predates and bore many similarities with import substitution-led industrialization by Nurkse, Prebisch, and Singer for the underdeveloped countries in the 1950s. This was reinforced by the then apparent success of state activism in two contrasting institutional environments. The first one was that of the centrally planned economy of the erstwhile USSR where centralized industrial investment planning had been bringing about rapid industrial transformation of an underdeveloped economy since the late 1920s under Communism. The second one was that of the capitalist United States of America where state intervention in a predominantly free-enterprise market economy helped recovery from the Great Depression of the 1930s. Both these were simplistically interpreted to establish the superiority of state activism over markets. Innocent faith in a benevolent state acting always in 'public interest' followed. The corollary was the trust reposed in the public sector to counter private capitalism[6] driven by profit (equated with 'greed') rather than social good. Consequently, expansion of the public sector (described as the temples of modern India by Nehru) became integral to the Nehruvian vision of the 'Socialist Pattern of Society' and was wrongly elevated to and equated with the socialist goal. The hold of socialist ideology had been very strong not only among the Indian intellectuals who were influenced by Nehru but also in the popular psyche in which markets operating for private gains were axiomatically assumed to produce socially unfair distributional outcomes in a traditional society and an underdeveloped economy. Stringent government regulations on private enterprise and functioning markets were generally applauded. Rudolph and Rudolph (1987: 26) in one of the first non-Marxist studies of the political economy of India's industrialization, describe how modern capitalists in India had to contend with pre-industrial cultural prejudices (heartless moneylenders, greedy merchants, and traders) as well as post-industrial ideological doctrines (anti-social profiteers and powerful exploiters).

At the time of Independence from British colonial rule in 1947, the culturally and socially diverse[7] Indian society was predominantly rural, traditional, and feudal with a few elements of modernity pervading the tiny urban-educated minority in interaction with the British colonial bureaucracy. Even though the economy was dominated by subsistence agricultural activities, functioning markets remained confined mostly to urban modern industries and isolated pockets of commercial crop production and plantations integrated with international markets. While efforts were made to eliminate feudal and semi-feudal structures by legislative abolition of absentee landlordism in the 1950s,[8] functioning markets and private capitalists remained well entrenched thanks to the democratic political framework.[9] In this environment, functioning markets gradually flourished with monetization and development. However, their potential positive contribution to economic development by alleviating scarcities was never recognized by the political leadership eager to usher in a socialist pattern of society.[10] Instead, centralized industrial investment planning through the expansion of the public sector and bureaucratic control over modern private capitalist enterprises were deemed necessary for economic development with equity. In this scheme of things, the enhancement of the socialist goal of equity was accorded much greater weight than dynamic efficiency and rapid economic growth, which was necessary to mitigate immediate shortages.

Thus an idealistic political leadership of post-Independence India embarked on a unique and historically untried and untested (and, in retrospect, utopian) experiment of democratic socialism in a low-income economy. The experiment started with the honest intention of 'governing' the believed iniquitous distributional outcomes of unregulated domestic and international markets. The idea was to establish a dynamic growing modern economy with equitable distribution on Soviet lines, not under communist dictatorship but in a democratic political framework. We interpret the vision of the 'Socialist Pattern of Society' of a charismatic leader like Jawaharlal Nehru in the analytical framework of North (Chapter 2) as social entrepreneurship seeking to bring about major changes in the formal rules of the game aimed at modernization of a traditional society and an underdeveloped economy. The new institutional matrix consisted of a regulatory regime comprising (i) public sector expansion; (ii) discretionary controls over markets and private economic activities; and (iii) stringent foreign exchange and import controls. The first two had their origin in the ideology of socialism and the last one was rooted in economic nationalism and the three together reflected activism of the newly established nation state. *Thus the firm grip of these two ideologies produced post-Independence India's economic development strategy of autarkic, public-sector-dominated, basic and heavy-industry-oriented, and centrally planned industrialization.* In North and Wallis's (1994) terminology,[11] the intention was to bring about transaction-augmenting institutional change, which was expected to interact with and reinforce transformation-augmenting technological change to establish a dynamically growing economy with equitable distribution. As we note shortly, the realized economic performance proved unsatisfactory for both equity and growth. We argue that this was the result of the adverse incentive structure that emerged from the new institutional matrix. Where did the expectations go wrong?

At a fundamental level, the reason lay in the inherent incompatibility between the *discretionary regulatory control* regime adopted by the activist state and the mixed economy institutional environment that the democratic Constitution dictated.[12] The basic incompatibility was further accentuated by the populist radicalization of Indian politics between the mid-1960s and end 1970s (more on this in the next section). The new institutional matrix had to contend and interact with the pervasive presence of the already established and gradually expanding markets and well-entrenched private enterprise. There existed an inherent and inescapable tension between the two that was sought to be resolved with centralized investment planning and the public sector reaching the '*commanding heights*'. The centralized planners naively believed that government commands backed by the coercive power of the state would prevail over markets driven by economic incentives and bring private investment in line with social priorities. In retrospect, it reflected inadequate understanding and appreciation of the strength of economic incentives driven by self-interest in the functioning markets.[13] Equally, the experience also brought out the ineffectiveness of the government machinery in monitoring in detail the decentralized actions of economic agents and the imperfect understanding of the complex interactions in the functioning markets. Both these handicaps proved formidable in effectively controlling what were perceived from the social point of view to be undesired outcomes in the market, which government commands sought to regulate. Consequently, the government could not effectively control the outcomes emanating from the markets nor could it prevent the emergence of underground or illegal markets when open markets were prohibited. The inherent incompatibility between the regulatory regime and the pre-existing institutional environment resulted in the wide divergence between government commands and their intended outcomes.[14]

We may note, however, that suspicion of markets was not confined to Indian political leadership that was not well versed in economics, interestingly, pervaded the mainstream economics profession at large in the 1950s. Following the trauma of the Great Depression of the 1930s, the profession had been grappling with and started theorising about market imperfections. It was also deeply influenced by the then evolving 'anatomy of market failure' (Bator 1958). Armed with these analytical developments, a group of eight leading American development economists of the 1950s made a strong plea to the United States Administration to give aid to support import-substitution-oriented *centrally planned* industrialization in India and other underdeveloped countries (Millikan and Blackmer 1961).[15]

RADICALIZATION OF INDIAN POLITICS SINCE THE MID-1960s

Major changes took place on the domestic political front in the 1960s. India had experienced single-party stable governments of the Congress Party at the centre as well as in the states till the mid-1960s spanning the first three general elections held in 1952, 1957, and 1962. This was primarily due to the continuing hold of the charismatic first Prime Minister Jawaharlal Nehru, an intellectual and a renowned thinker and writer, over the electorate with his appeal among the masses as well as elites. The Congress Party represented a loose coalition of various interest groups some of whom were committed to the dream of democratic socialism while most others stayed in its fold for opportunistic reasons to share the spoils of power. The Party provided an overarching organizational umbrella for sorting out the latent intra-Party conflicts among diverse interests. The period after the mid-1960s was marked by political instability. India lost two Prime Ministers in quick succession, Nehru in May 1964 and his successor Lal Bahadur Shastri in January 1966. There were many aspirants for prime ministership but none commanded the respect and confidence that Nehru had in the Party and outside. Some ambitious leaders left the Congress Party to establish independent political outfits. In the 1967 general election the ruling Congress Party lost its majority in many states while managing to retain a reduced majority at the centre. This was largely the consequence of the tussle for leadership in the Congress Party that eventually resulted in its split in 1969. Following Shastri's demise the consensus candidature of Mrs Indira Gandhi, Nehru's daughter, was reluctantly accepted by the major Party leaders competing for the top executive post in the hope of being able to exploit her inexperience to wield power by proxy. Other factors aggravating political instability and affecting the election results were social unrest caused by a steep price rise in foodgrains in the face of two back-to-back severe agricultural droughts in 1965 and 1966 with sharp declines in output and a rupee devaluation that had to be undertaken on 6 June 1966 which also became a politically contentious issue (more on this in Chapter 6). After the general election in 1967, Mrs Gandhi, uncertain of the organizational support from the established Party bosses, decided to bypass the Party organization and engage in plebiscitory mass politics exploiting the charisma of the Nehru family to establish and assert her leadership.

For the purpose of mass politics, Mrs Gandhi invoked the vote-catching slogan of 'Garibi Hatao' (Eradicate Poverty) and existing ideological prejudices against markets and private capitalists and in support of public sector. She nationalized the commercial banks in 1968 to establish her credibility among radical intellectuals as well as non-Congress Leftist and Left-leaning political parties. This was followed by indiscriminate expansion of the public sector that continued unabated till the 1980s. After her thumping victory in the 1971 general election and in the face of rising food prices following indifferent harvest in 1971–2 and a severe drought in 1972–3, she also resorted to an unsuccessful takeover of wholesale trade in wheat on the grounds of exploitation by private traders through profiteering by cornering food stocks. This argument was readily bought by radical intellectuals. Realizing that the government did not possess the organizational capability to put in place alternative machinery for moving food stocks from grain surplus to deficit areas, she revoked the decision a year later. Stringent restrictions were also placed through legislative measures on markets in 'essential' goods, on domestic large capitalists, and on private foreign investment. These measures were justified in the name of furthering the Nehruvian socialist dream. Appealing to economic nationalism, further tightening of restrictions on foreign exchange and imports (discussed later in this chapter) took place in the face of the first oil price hike in 1973. All these 'radical' measures made India possibly the *most comprehensively* (though *not necessarily most effectively*, as we discuss shortly) *regulated market economy* in the world.

These actions of Mrs Gandhi not only received mass support that helped her establish her supremacy within the Congress Party, but also elicited active political support in the parliament from Left-leaning elements within the Congress Party (the so-called 'young Turks') and the two Communist parties. They also enabled her to bypass the established but unwilling party organization. This period is described by P.N. Dhar (2003) as one of populist radicalization of Indian politics under which the traditional decentralized, federal organization of the Congress Party progressively weakened (termed 'deinstitutionalization' of the Congress Party by Rudolph and Rudolph 1987) and economic and political executive power was centralized in the charismatic 'Left-leaning' personality of Mrs Gandhi. Instead of evolving genuine but organizationally difficult solutions to the formidable economic problems facing the country, 'the so-called radicalism merely provided ideological justification for the structures of privilege and protection that excesses of politics created' (Dhar 2003: 152). The consequent tightening of the regulatory regime on ideological grounds without regard to its effectiveness in achieving the socialist goals further aggravated the basic incompatibility of the three elements of the new institutional matrix with the mixed economy institutional environment. We now turn to a discussion of these elements.

EXPANSION OF THE PUBLIC SECTOR

Immediately after Independence, the initial enthusiasm of the newly established activist state was tempered by the Constitutional guarantee of the fundamental right to private property. This was reflected in the Industrial Policy Resolution 1948 (1948 Resolution hereafter). It started by stating the goal and the means to achieve it.

> The nation has now set itself to establish a social order where justice and equality of opportunity shall be secured to all the people. For this purpose, careful planning and integrated efforts over *the whole field of national activity*

are necessary; and the Government of India propose to establish a National Planning Commission to formulate programmes of development and to secure its execution [Para 1].

It emphasized that a 'dynamic national policy must be directed to a continuous increase in production by all possible means side by side with *measures to secure its equitable distribution.*' Conscious that the fundamental right to property was guaranteed by the (forthcoming[16]) Constitution, it conceded that '*under the present conditions, the mechanism and resources of the State may not permit it to function forthwith in Industry as widely as may be desirable*', and underplayed 'acquiring and running existing units' presumably through nationalization and preferred 'concentrating on new units of production in other fields'. It assured private capitalists that should the State decide to acquire any unit, '*the fundamental rights guaranteed by the Constitution will be observed* and compensation will be awarded on a fair and equitable basis'. The state was to have exclusive responsibility for the establishment of new undertakings in an assortment of industries with public utility character and strategic importance such as defence production, atomic energy, coal, iron and steel, aircraft manufacture, shipbuilding, manufacture of telephone, telegraph and wireless apparatus, mineral oils, and generation and distribution of electric power. It declared that the remaining industries will '*normally* be open to private enterprise, individual as well as cooperative, [but] *the State will also progressively participate in this field; nor will it hesitate to intervene whenever the progress of an industry under private enterprise is unsatisfactory*' (emphases added).

The next landmark which again stated the intentions of an activist state was the Industrial Policy Resolution 1956 (1956 Resolution hereafter) that appeared after the parliament had accepted in December 1954 a *socialist pattern of society* as the objective of social and economic policy and Mahalanobis had expounded his famous model (Mahalanobis 1955). The Mahalanobis model stated in formal terms the critical importance of basic- and heavy-machine-producing industries for accelerating the tempo of growth under the autarkic industrialization strategy. Mahalanobis argued for basic and heavy industries to remain exclusively in the public sector. The justification was twofold. One, the private sector would be unable to raise adequate resources for these very capital-intensive industries and even if it could, it would command a monopolistic position that was deemed detrimental to social welfare. Two, by controlling the allocation of the output of basic and heavy industries in accordance with social objectives, it was hoped that the government would be able to channelize private sector growth according to social priorities. Not only were both the arguments in line with the then prevailing enthusiasm for state activism but they also merely formalized the dominant preference for basic and heavy industries among the political leadership since well before Independence (Paranjape 1985). Thus the Mahalanobis model merely provided the basic rationale in formal terms for the extension of the conventional boundaries of the public sector beyond public utilities which exhibit the characteristics of 'public goods'[17] in differing degrees such as electricity supply, roads, and bridges. Notice that basic and heavy industries are 'rival' and 'excludable' private goods.

Reflecting the then widely prevalent prejudice against private capitalists, the 1956 Resolution envisaged a much more expanded role of the public sector (than its 1948 predecessor) and strongly advocated, as a perceived socially superior alternative to large-scale private capitalism, a growing cooperative sector (to reap scale economies) and state support to cottage, village, and small-scale industries for decentralized industrialization. It stated that in order to realize the objective of a socialist pattern of society that gave 'more precise direction' to the Directive Principles of State Policy enshrined in the Indian Constitution adopted on 26 January 1950, 'it is essential to accelerate the rate of economic growth and to speed up industrialisation and, in particular, to develop heavy industries and machine making industries, to expand the public sector and to build a strong and growing co-operative sector'. With a view to generating increasing opportunities for gainful employment, improving living standards and working conditions of the masses, reducing disparities in income and wealth and preventing private monopolies, it stated that '*the State will progressively assume a predominant and direct responsibility* for setting up new industrial undertakings' in the specified fields. For this purpose, industries were divided into three categories: (i) those (listed in Schedule A to the Resolution) which were to be the *exclusive responsibility of the State*; (ii) those (listed in Schedule B) which were to be *progressively State-owned*; and (iii) all the remaining to be left to the initiative and enterprise of the private sector. Schedule A listed seventeen industries that included all those in the 1948 Resolution plus most minerals, metals, and heavy plant and machinery for machine tool production. Schedule B contained twelve industries including machine tools and basic and intermediate products required by the chemical industries.

The public sector was expanded mostly in physical infrastructure, iron and steel, and some machine-building industries in line with the Mahalanobis strategy till the mid-1960s, showing clear awareness of the Constitutional constraints on radical alternatives like nationalization and the limitations of transferring resources from private household to government. Populist radicalization of politics took over after the mid-1960s to extend the boundaries of the public sector well beyond what was envisaged in the Mahalanobis strategy, and public-sector enterprises were set up for building and running five star hotels and producing bread.

Figure 3.1 gives an idea of the indiscriminate expansion of the public sector as can be seen in the rapid rise in the number of central public-sector enterprises (PSEs) especially between 1968 and the commencement of the Eighth Five Year Plan in 1991. These are legally autonomous entities mostly incorporated under the Companies Act 1956 with 100 per cent equity capital owned by the central government. In addition, the central government also operate departmental enterprises like Railways and Posts and Telegraphs, which also employ a large number of workers but these are financed through the Central Budget. The legally autonomous PSEs have access to extra-budgetary sources of finance. Interestingly, the preference for legally autonomous entities appeared in the 1948 Resolution: 'Management of State enterprises will, as a rule, be through the medium of public corporations under the statutory control of the Central Government, who may assume such powers as may be necessary to ensure this' (para 4). The PSEs were used to fulfil multiple, often mutually conflicting, objectives of the government such as generating surpluses for investment, employment generation,[18] provision of goods and services at subsidized rates, and reducing regional imbalances in the name of 'socialism'. Conflict among multiple objectives often provided justification for operating without regard for commercial norms and camouflaging inefficiencies

FIGURE 3.1
Number of Central Public Sector Enterprises during Plan Periods 1951–2001

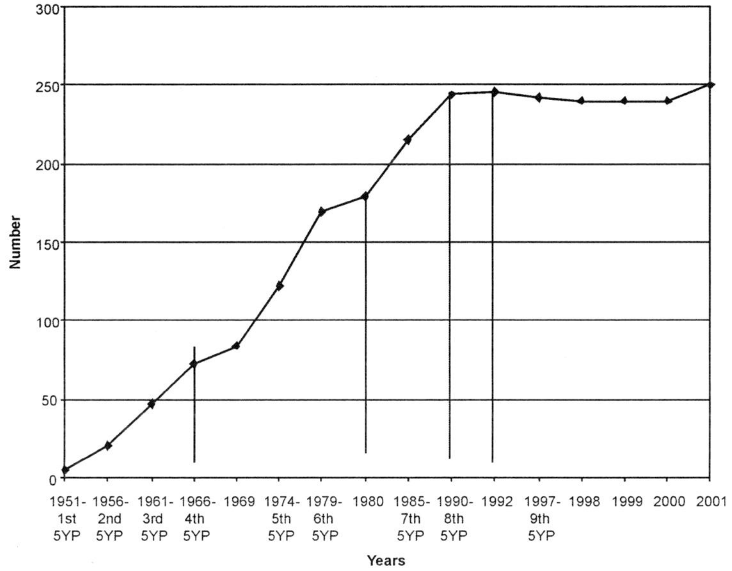

Source: Govt. of India, Ministry of Commerce and Industry (2002): Handbook of Industrial Policy and Statistics, 2001, Office of Economic Advisor, New Delhi, ch. VI, Table no. 37, p. 365.

under the specious excuse of serving often fuzzy social objectives. The PSEs operated under what Kornai has called a 'soft budget constraint'.[19] The PSEs were justified by appealing to Nehruvian socialist goals but in practice were used to serve certain interest groups, as we discuss shortly.

The Industrial Policy Resolution 1980 made an official reference to the undercurrent of popular disillusionment with the unsatisfactory state of the PSEs. While claiming the heredity of the 1956 Resolution, it noted 'the erosion of people's faith in the public sector' and announced the decision 'to launch a drive to revive the efficiency of the public sector undertakings through a time-bound programme of corrective action on a unit by unit basis'.

The first candid official admission of the indiscriminate expansion of and the serious problems afflicting the PSEs came at the beginning of the post-1991 reform period in the Statement on Industrial Policy July 1991 (July 1991 Statement hereafter). It mentioned 'serious problems' after 'initial exuberance' such as insufficient growth in productivity, poor project management, overmanning, lack of continuous technological upgradation, 'a very low rate of return on capital investment' that made the PSEs 'a burden rather than being a national asset', considerable dilution of the original concept of public sector reflected in the takeover of sick units from the private sector, and PSEs in consumer goods and services not fulfilling the 'original idea of public sector being at the commanding heights of the economy' (para 31). The 1991 Statement promised (para 31) a 'review of the existing portfolio of public investments with greater realism' in respect of public-sector units in those industries located in 'low technology, small scale and non-strategic areas, inefficient and unproductive areas, areas with low or nil social considerations or public purpose or areas where the private sector has developed sufficient expertise and resources'. We note later (Chapter 8) in our discussion of disinvestment that a hardheaded review promised in 1991 is still not in sight fifteen years down the line! A widespread mistaken and misguided view of public sector as a socialist goal rather than a mere instrument still persists in the irrational distinctions between PSEs such as being 'profit-making', 'loss-making', 'navaratnas', and 'mini-ratnas'. Grant of 'autonomy' promised from time to time since 1980 remains a far cry. The only major difference during the post-1991 reforms has been the entry of private players in areas earlier reserved exclusively for the public sector. In the face of competition, a few PSEs have managed to pull up their socks and improve operational efficiency, a few more that had been running well despite formidable constraints have been continuing to do so, but a large number have sunk deeper into the red.

DISCRETIONARY REGULATION OF MARKETS AND THE PRIVATE SECTOR

That markets and private economic activities have to be brought in line with social priorities was the conventional wisdom among the elite leadership with socialist ideological origins since well before Independence. Jawaharlal Nehru, as Chairman of the National Planning Committee (NPC)[20] circulated a memorandum on 4 June 1939 arguing that the state may own or *at least regulate and control* in public interest all public utilities, *large-scale industries* and also enterprises which were likely to be monopolistic in character. A resolution passed by the NPC on the same date specifically endorsed[21] the idea of *licensing for industries*. This was clearly the second best alternative to the predominant public ownership of means of production that existed in the Soviet Union, under the Indian conditions of predominant private ownership of property. The Handbook of the NPC also mentioned an assortment of other controls like fixation of prices, limitations of dividends, prescription of salaries and wages for labour, nomination of government directors on board of management, and others similar to war time economic controls like those on production and distribution of raw materials and capital goods, control of capital issues, and controls for foreign exchange conservation. The objective was to serve multiple social goals like prevention of monopolies, avoidance of overproduction, discouragement of establishment of uneconomic units, and some hazy *general economic interests*.

These pre-Independence ideas were given concrete shape with the establishment of the National Planning Commission in 1950 and enactment of the Industries (Development and Regulation) Act 1951 (IDRA hereafter) and nationalization of Life Insurance in 1956. In this section, we discuss only private-sector regulation.

The IDRA made government permission compulsory for private investment above a certain specified limit with a view to channellizing large-scale private investment in accordance with social priorities by preventing diversion of scarce resources into non-priority areas as also preventing overcapacity in priority areas (Marathe 1986: 63–4). The IDRA laid down elaborate rules for licensing. A licence was necessary for establishing a new industrial undertaking (Section 11); for manufacturing a new article by an existing undertaking (Section 11A); for substantial expansion of capacity of an undertaking in an existing line of manufacture (Section 13); for carrying on business of an existing undertaking to which licensing provisions of the Act did not originally apply; and for changing the existing location (Section 13). The First Schedule of the IDRA specified the industries to which the Act would apply (*Guidelines for Industries 1974–5*, Ministry of Industrial Development, Government of India, New Delhi: 3). Starting with a list of forty-two major industries, the First Schedule covered almost all the manufacturing activity by the middle of the 1960s (Bhagwati and Desai 1970: 250; Marathe 1986: 73).

The IDRA did not apply to all manufacturing units. It applied to all the *large* factories[22] employing fifty or more workers, if using power, or 100 or more workers, if not using power, thereby exempting all those units employing workers below the specified levels. Also exempted were those industries not appearing in the First Schedule of the IDRA and the small-scale and ancillary industries (as per official definition in terms of value of investment) and non-small-scale units with fixed investment lower than the specified limit, which was Rs 30 million by 1970 (*Guidelines for Industries 1974–5*: 3–4).

Further, to control the concentration of economic power, entry of large business houses defined in terms of the floor level of value of assets of interconnected undertakings (Rs 200 million initially) was restricted to only a subset of scheduled industries (specified in Annexure I of the Industrial Licensing Policy of 2 February 1973 [Annexure I industries hereafter]). Annexure I contained those industries where planned capacity was falling short of the plan targets.[23] The large industrial houses were otherwise controlled through the Monopolies and Restrictive Trade Practices (MRTP) Act 1969 (*Economic Survey* 1969–70: 20–1; *Guidelines for Industries 1974–5*: 74–5).

Foreign-owned companies came under the purview of the Foreign Exchange Regulations Act (FERA) 1973. They were permitted to operate only in Annexure I industries subject to specified conditions. FERA also imposed restriction on foreign direct investment (FDI) in India. Under the Act, Indian companies with more than 40 per cent foreign holdings and branches of foreign companies operating in India were required to obtain general/special permission from the Reserve Bank of India (RBI) for carrying on any activity or starting a new activity. Existing FERA companies were required to dilute their foreign equity stakes to no more than 40 per cent and raise the corresponding Indian participation (*Guidelines for Industries 1974–5*: 137–9).

Thus the legislated regulatory policy segmented Indian industry into compartments with different degrees of rigour in regulation and preference in government policy and without much scope for mobility from one segment to another. At one end were small-scale and ancillary units without much regulation and in addition enjoying promotional and protective government support. In the regulated segments, public-sector units were the most preferred and often enjoyed monopolistic positions. At the other end of the spectrum were the 'unwelcome' FERA and MRTP companies that bore the maximal rigour of government regulations. In between were those subjected to mandatory industrial licensing. Needless to add, there existed an unregulated segment outside the elaborate IDRA, MRTP, and FERA net. However, the scope was indeed limited at the upper end of the investment scale. Private units clearly preferred to be in the unregulated segment. Notice also that legislative clearances had to be obtained on a *case-by-case basis* leaving plenty of discretion in the hands of politicians and bureaucrats.

Legislative clearances under the IDRA were not the only hurdle to be crossed by prospective private investors. Technology and capital goods imports entered the chain of clearances as additional conditions in view of chronic foreign exchange shortages and the long-term policy of import substitution. Technology imports had to be approved by the office of the Directorate General of Technology Development (DGTD) for 'essentiality' and indigenous non-availability. Industrial units seeking investment licence had to report their timetable for procurement of their imported input requirements domestically under the Phased Manufacturing Programme. Foreign exchange requirement for raw materials was not to exceed specified limits. Distribution and price controls were also in place. There were industry-specific regulations in addition. Gradually, the range and depth of industrial regulations were extended well beyond the original objective of controlling industrial capacity and became more rigorous, rigid, and detailed involving administratively complex arrangements across numerous departments of government without any overarching coordinating mechanism (Bhoothalingam 1968: 26; Marathe 1986: 84; Mohan 1992: 96). Mohan (1992: 99) described the result graphically: 'No single department of government knows exactly what has been happening. Government lost control over the (controlling) mechanism and also the basic purpose of licensing.' T.N. Srinivasan (1991: 2143–5) has aptly characterized this as *anticipatory regulation*, that is a system designed to prevent *any* prospective deviation from policy *ever* occurring rather than to punish or cure any deviant behaviour as and when it occurs. He argued that no discretionary system involving case-by-case regulation can produce a set of rules to deal with all the myriad outcomes of, and responses to, the regulations and at the same time make them consistent with often conflicting multiple goals of industrial policy. It is humanly impossible to anticipate every eventuality, especially when it emerges from the complex interactions of a large number of decentralized decisions taken in the markets by economic agents whose activities and responses cannot be monitored by government. The pathology of the government's *discretionary* regulatory mechanism in a *market economy* should be obvious. The outcome was the emergence of a chronic shortage economy from demand–supply imbalances and the pattern of domestic production in the private sector followed the signals from these shortages in allocating investments by establishing units in the non-regulated segments of the industrial sector rather than follow the plan targets which had very little relationship with market demand. An even more pernicious consequence was reflected in the distorted responses of private units to comprehensive regulation. In order to escape the rigours of regulation, private entrepreneurs preferred to be in the unregulated segment and for this purpose resorted to fragmentation of capacity in multiple units, excessive diversification without regard to core competencies, and inefficient scales of operation.[24] These led to inefficient capacity creation in addition to inefficiencies resulting from protected, non-competitive markets.

IMPORTS AND FOREIGN EXCHANGE CONTROLS

We have already noted that self-reliance under the influence of the ideology of economic nationalism was (wrongly) equated with self-sufficiency. In implementation, the critical importance of foreign exchange was indeed recognized but the emphasis was placed on 'saving' foreign exchange from import-substitution much more than on 'earning' foreign exchange from exports.[25] The resulting policy was the same as that recommended by the then widely accepted import-substituting industrialization doctrine attributed to Nurkse, Singer, and Prebisch under the assumption of export pessimism. Because exports were axiomatically taken (without supporting empirical evidence) to be non-responsive to prices and incomes in the developed countries, the exchange rate was kept deliberately overvalued under the then prevailing fixed exchange rate system in order to keep foreign exchange 'cheap' for buying development imports. In order to contain the resulting excess demand for foreign exchange and prevent its diversion into non-development purposes, a variety of restrictions on 'non-essential' imports became necessary. These restrictions provided a protected domestic market for producers of non-essential products, raised their domestic profitability relative to exports, and in the process made exports internationally non-competitive thereby eroding the supply of foreign exchange. This prompted further tightening of import restrictions and led to a self-fulfilling prophesy of chronic foreign exchange shortages. Hence a complex administrative system of import and foreign exchange controls came into existence.

Given the acute shortage of foreign exchange most of the time, policymakers opted for direct allocation of foreign exchange among different users and uses through import licences. An import licence allowed a *specified amount* of a *specified item* to be imported by a *specified user* for a *specified purpose* sometimes even from a *specified* source of supply.[26] Quantitative restrictions (QRs) were selective in the sense that the specified ceiling limits were different for the imports of different items depending on their perceived importance in the development strategy. For instance, limits were high and liberal in the case of capital goods imports, and zero, low, and rigid for the imports of what government perceived to be 'non-essential' consumer goods.

The operational part of the specifications involved comprehensive details and a complex administrative mechanism. For the purpose, imports were divided into different categories, namely consumer goods, intermediate goods, and capital goods. Each category was subdivided into *non-permissible* (banned), *limited permissible* (with mandatory certification from another agency regarding essentiality as well as mandatory clearance from the Chief Controller of Imports and Exports [CCI&E]), *automatic permissible* (without mandatory certificate but with clearance from the CCI&E), and *open general licence* (OGL, without certification and without clearance of the CCI&E) groups. Licences were categorized further based on user type such as established importer, actual user, newcomer, ad hoc, export promotion schemes (like import replenishment licence), and others (like replacement licence). These licences were allotted sector-wise (public/private), industry-wise, and firm-wise. Grant of licence was considered on the basis of 'essentiality' and 'indigenous non-availability', which required separate agencies to authenticate these claims of the individual licence seekers. In most cases, the CCI&E was the licence-issuing authority and the Directorate General Technical Development (DGTD) was the authenticating agency. There were other agencies too like Iron and Steel Controller and individual firms had to approach more than one agency for obtaining licences. Some of the imports were allowed only through state trading agencies. Not surprisingly, the statement relating only to import policy for the period 1988–91 ran into 387 pages with twenty-three chapters and seventeen appendices (Srinivasan 2003: 584). *The transaction costs and uncertainties associated with these complexities in the procedures were perhaps responsible for the least resistance of industrialists to reforms in this area even at the cost of loss of protection from import competition.*

Grant of licence was decided on case-by-case examination that caused delays, which were further enhanced by the lack of coordination among the related multiple agencies. Delays coupled with changes in quota from time to time resulted in dislocation of and inflexibilities in production and made it difficult for the economy and industry to respond quickly to shocks and hence became vulnerable to crises (Joshi and Little 1996: 272–3).

Selective QRs were self-perpetuating because these provided complete protection from external competition to any domestic activity that was import substituting (Ahluwalia 1994: 294; Srinivasan and Tendulkar 2003: 33) and thus discouraged exports. Chronic foreign exchange shortages were inherent in this situation as increasing demand for imports and hence for foreign exchange could not be matched by export earnings, thus widening the scope for the vicious circle of further tightening of QRs.

Accompanying the relaxation of QRs in mid-1980s were high tariffs introduced partly to mop up higher import premia. Driven by chronic shortages of foreign exchange not only were average tariff levels high and unpredictably variable over time but so was the associated dispersion of rates, causing chaotic distortions[27] in the rates of effective protection[28] and resulting resource allocation. The consequent discrimination against exportables via reduced profitability was aggravated further by export taxes and/or quotas[29] in situations of domestic supply shortfalls. In order to offset the adverse effects of discrimination, various export incentive schemes such as cash assistance, duty drawbacks, and import replenishment licences had been introduced. These schemes too were so complex that the associated transaction costs discouraged small exporters from claiming assistance under them (Srinivasan 2003: 588).

Analytically, exchange rate adjustment is considered a better option than import controls to manage balance of payments (BOP) deficits as it affects all tradables uniformly without discriminating against any sector. Thus it does not lead to any type of distortion in resource allocation nor does it require any complex administrative mechanism to implement. Yet exchange rate adjustment was never used as an instrument to manage the repeated BOP crises under the presumed non-responsiveness of exports to prices.[30] The exchange rate remained overvalued for most part of the pre-reform period. An overvalued rupee made imports cheaper and exports unprofitable and further contributed to current account imbalances. The complex administrative mechanism of import and export controls remained more or less intact till 1990 but for piecemeal deregulation measures in 1980s. This is apparent from the fact that 60 per cent of all imports and 90 per cent of manufacturing imports were subject to QRs in 1990 (Srinivasan and Tendulkar 2003: 33).

In concluding this discussion, it may be noted that we chose to spell out the three basic elements of the post-Independence institutional matrix in detail basically for two reasons. One, it reflected a major effort by the activist leadership to bring about a major *centrally directed* institutional change that had never earlier been tried anywhere and that proved utopian in retrospect despite the widespread consensus it enjoyed. Second, it also throws into sharp relief the remarkable institutional transformation *in reverse* that has been taking place during the last fifteen years that forms the theme of the present volume.

NOTES

1. These included heavy reliance on monsoon-dependent agriculture for livelihood of three-fourth of the population and other weaknesses in the economic structure and caste-based socio-occupational division of society that came in the way of economic mobility.
2. We note in Chapter 6 the redefinition of self-reliance by Finance Minister Dr Manmohan Singh while unfurling economic reforms in the 1990s.
3. The first Prime Minister Nehru (1946: 403) who was at the forefront in the Independence movement observes: 'The objective for the country as a whole was the attainment as far as possible of *national self-sufficiency*. International trade was certainly not excluded, but we were anxious to avoid being drawn into a *whirlpool of economic imperialism*. We wanted neither to be victims of imperial power, nor to develop such tendencies ourselves.' (emphasis added).
4. Nehru (1946: 417) while mentioning the prosperity in the textile mill industry that came up in competition with the British mills, disapprovingly brackets the prosperous mill owners with 'war contractors, hoarders and profiteers' while making (justifiably) laudatory references to the Tatas who established the first steel mill in India in 1909. We quote Nehru not only as the most influential political leader of pre- and post-Independence India but also because of his tremendous hold over the Indian intelligentsia.
5. There was widespread social consensus on this strategy from the pre-Independence period among intellectuals, businessmen, as well as trade unions (Srinivasan 1996).
6. Whose existence could not be wished away by the Indian state because of the Constitutional sanctity accorded to private ownership of property and means of production in a democratic framework.
7. The multi-religious, multi-ethnic, and multi-lingual character of Indian society is well known. The multiplicity of castes and sub-castes in the Hindu community further added to the diversity.
8. See Kaviraj (1995) on how this legislation was pushed by the lawyer-dominated parliament while its implementation at state level was sabotaged by the landed interests that dominated the state units of the ruling Congress Party.
9. Notice that the democratic political framework, by sanctifying private ownership of property, necessarily implies capitalist economy. The converse is NOT true.
10. See Tendulkar (1991) for elaboration. For sound and persuasive arguments bringing out the positive role of the market mechanism as a practical instrument of development policy in underdeveloped countries, interested readers may refer to Myint (1971).
11. See Chapter 2 in this volume.
12. It is argued (Tendulkar 1993) that the mixed economy institutional environment (consisting of the co-existence of the private and public sectors) in the Indian context could be rationalized as an effort by an activist state to reconcile the capitalist and pre-capitalist institutions inherited at the time of Independence with the socialist aspirations in a democratic framework.
13. This was recognized more than two centuries ago by Adam Smith, the father of modern economics, in his classic *The Wealth Of Nations* (1776). He coined the term invisible hand to describe the dynamic function of the markets in

coordinating large number of decentralized economic activities motivated by economic incentives. He provided a convincing rationale for how self-interest can be harnessed to enhance social welfare through an invisible hand.

14. Why did government commands succeed at least in the early phase in the centrally planned economy of the erstwhile Soviet Union? It is argued elsewhere (Tendulkar 1993) that the tighter control required for success could be attributed to the predominant state ownership of the means of production, unchallenged presence of a single cadre-based party ideologically committed to socialism, and the single-minded pursuit of rapid industrialization. These conditions could not be replicated in the mixed economy institutional environment of India.
15. The group included W.W. Rostow and Paul Rosenstein-Rodan.
16. This was being discussed in the Constituent Assembly then and was later adopted on 26 January 1950.
17. In public economics, public goods are mostly those that are collectively consumed (legally or physically non-excludable in technical term) and consumption by one person does not preclude consumption by others (non-rival in technical jargon). 'Private goods' such as cars are, in contrast, 'rival' and 'excludable'. Public goods provide the conventionally accepted minimal analytical rationale for their public provision even in predominantly market economies where production and supply of 'private goods' is entirely left to private enterprise.
18. In economic terms, this does not simply mean creating posts, employing people, and paying salaries as is commonly understood. At firm level, *additional productive* employment is said to be generated *only when* the revenue from output produced by additional workers exceeds their wage bill *and* leaves a surplus that is at least as high as that which can be earned by invested capital in the next best alternative. Whenever revenue falls short, additional employment is said to be *featherbedding* in character because it does not make a net addition to real national product.
19. This term was coined by the Hungarian economist Janos Kornai in connection with the problems of public enterprises under centrally planned economies of East Europe and the erstwhile Soviet Union. A privately owned enterprise faces a 'hard budget constraint' in the sense that it has to strive continuously to remain economically viable or face bankruptcy in a situation of making persistent losses. In contrast, a PSE is said to face a 'soft budget constraint' because it does not go bankrupt even after turning persistently loss-making and hence economically unviable. It survives with government support from budgetary and extra-budgetary avenues.
20. Appointed by the Indian National Congress, the pre-Independence incarnation of the present-day Congress Party.
21. We draw on Paranjape (1985) for this discussion.
22. It may be noted that the coverage of factories under the IDRA was different from that under the Factories Act 1948. Under the Factories Act, a factory is defined as an establishment employing ten or more workers, if using power or twenty or more workers, if not using power.
23. This appeared to be a reluctant concession under compulsion because plan targets were perceived to be not attainable with public-sector investment plus non-MRTP private investment.
24. Goyal et al. (1984) provide numerous examples of the presence of large industrial houses including MNCs (multinational corporations) in the small-scale sector.

25. This contrast was sharp in rewards offered in India and South Korea during this period. In India, the entrepreneurs were felicitated for import-substitution for saving foreign exchange without much regard to resource costs or productivity, whereas in South Korea they were honoured for their export performance in internationally competitive markets.
26. From specified countries with bilateral barter trade arrangements.
27. By way of clarification of this technical term, note that producers, in their resource allocation, respond to changes in relative sectoral profitabilities, which, in turn, are determined by relative sectoral prices. Distortion in resource allocation is a deviation from efficient resource allocation across sectors that result from a single uniform rate of indirect tax on all sectors because a uniform rate leaves the *relative* sectoral prices unchanged. In contrast, dispersion in sectoral rates of indirect taxes brings out differential changes in relative (sectoral) market prices and hence affects relative profitability across sectors and consequently resource allocation.
28. Rate of effective protection reflects protection to primary (non-produced) factors employed in a sector after netting out the impact of import tariffs on intermediate inputs.
29. Export taxes were imposed under the presumed non-responsiveness of demand for exportable commodities to prices in foreign (receiving) markets. Export quotas were also imposed on raw material exports like cotton when domestic cotton output fell short of domestic demand from the textile industry due to bad harvest.
30. However, experience proved otherwise during the post-1972 floating exchange rate regime as we discuss later.

4

The Slow-growth Phase: 1950–1 to 1980–1

INCENTIVE STRUCTURE AND ECONOMIC PERFORMANCE

The framework of evolutionary institutional change suggested by Douglass North maintains that the incentive structure embedded in any institutional matrix consisting of formal and informal rules of the game is the key determinant of economic performance. The activist state in India sought to bring about major changes in the formal rules of the game through the three elements of the New Institutional Matrix discussed in Chapter 3 with a view to bring economic growth accompanied by equitable distribution. The formal rules in the three elements, be they relating to public-sector functioning, industrial investment licence, or acquisition of import licence, had to interact with the rules operating in the existing institutional environment of expanding markets and constitutionally guaranteed private ownership of means of production. The activist leadership genuinely believed that the interaction would be positive and lead to a dynamically growing economy while furthering the equity objective. As mentioned in Chapter 3, it underestimated the strength of economic incentives embedded in the existing environment and overestimated the effectiveness of the coercive power of the state to curb those incentives. In this chapter we examine the resultant incentive structure that emerged from the interaction of the three elements of the new institutional matrix with the existing environment.

Foreign Exchange and Import Controls

We start with one overarching factor that emerged from the import and foreign exchange regulation element of the new institutional matrix. We argued that the perennial shortages of foreign exchange resulted mainly from the adopted policies themselves that made them a self-fulfilling prophecy and not due to some kind of 'foreign exchange constraint' beyond the control of the policymakers that was postulated in some widely used 'two-gap' models like Chenery and Strout (1966) in the 1960s. The shortages led to progressive tightening of *differentiated* import controls consisting of variable quota restrictions across users/commodities/purposes and slabs of tariffs rates in accordance with perceived social priorities of the policy makers that sounded prima facie reasonable but had consequences that were perverse and hence inimical to the social objectives. Notice that quotas provided unlimited protection to domestic producers irrespective of costs whereas tariffs provided protection to domestic producers with cost in proportion to or lower than the level of tariff.[1] Topmost priority was given to capital goods imports as they were critical for long-term growth and to keep them relatively cheap they were placed in the lowest tariff slab. Next in importance were imports of intermediate inputs that were put in a higher tariff slab. Consumer goods imports were deemed least essential and hence were either banned or put in a very high tariff slab sometimes combined with tight quota restrictions. Tariffs and quotas restricted imports that were sought to be controlled in social interest. However, the signal they conveyed to the domestic producers and importers was totally opposite because, by curtailing imports, they led to shortages in the domestic market and provided protection to domestic producers of import-competing products or generated premia for importers. Consequently, the producers of capital goods where plan targets emphasized import-substitution for attaining self-reliance were the least protected and profitability was highest for domestic producers of least essential consumer goods. As a result, private-sector resource allocation based on profitability went in a socially unplanned direction in favour of consumer goods along with the capital goods and intermediate inputs required to produce them! Thus, for private domestic producers of import-competing products, the incentive was to divert resources to non-priority areas rather than fall in line with plan priorities. Because of foreign exchange shortages, a large premium existed on imported commodities in the domestic market that was appropriated by the importers especially when it was humanly impossible for the bureaucracy to monitor all the transactions in the market. As a result, even if the initial allocation of import licences was according to plan priorities, it was eventually mediated by the markets. The incentive import controls generated was to seek import licences to appropriate premia rather than use imports in production.

Controls on Markets and the Large Private Capitalist Sector

Next, we turn to the incentive effects of the regulation of markets and the private sector including the industrial investment licensing mechanism, the second element of the new institutional matrix. We have noted that this regulation was discretionary and anticipatory in nature. Srinivasan (1991) who provided this characterization has drawn an interesting analogy of this regulation with *preventive* health care in comparison with a *curative* approach to the delivery of health care services. Notice that the causes of major epidemics and their seasonal occurrences are scientifically well established in a unique cause and effect relationship and hence are easily preventable so that preventive rather than curative medicine is more effective in less developed countries. This is, however, not the case in the regulation of markets because outcomes to be controlled in markets emerge from complex interactions of a variety of decentralized economic decisions that cannot be captured in a unique cause-and-effect relationship. Consequently, regulation tended to be blunt, heavy-handed, and complex in the illusory search for effectiveness. If the prices of essential commodities rose, apprehending social unrest, the response of the activist government was to ban the operation of the open market and to resort to administered distribution (rationing) of the commodity in short supply at lower than market prices. This was no doubt prima facie a reasonable short-run solution. However, it was usually not accompanied by simultaneous efforts to enhance the supply of the commodity in question through imports or inducements for higher domestic output. The result was continued shortages and hence rationing leading to malpractices in administered distribution and diversion of rationed supplies to underground markets.

The case of regulation of private industrial capacity through industrial investment licensing was worse with far-reaching consequences for the behaviour of private industrial investors and entrepreneurs and hence for the evolving industrial structure in the economy. Clearly, any rational investor would put money where the expected pay-off from investment was most lucrative. The pathology of a discretionary regulatory system in a market economy that we described in the last chapter unintentionally generated incentives for unproductive rent-seeking activities[2] and diverted resources away from productive uses. How did it happen? We briefly discuss some mechanisms. A potential industrial investor in a given activity had the choice of seeking industrial licence or escaping regulation by choosing a scale of investment in an unregulated zone. Going through the regulatory channel involved transaction costs of obtaining government clearances of various kinds (capacity licence, foreign exchange, import) that consumed resources including time spent by investors in pushing mandatory sanctions through bureaucracy that could otherwise be devoted to taking legitimate business decisions. The regulated segment became increasingly exhaustive in terms of coverage of industries but there was always scope for escaping regulation at the lower end of the scale of investment, which also attracted concessions of various kinds in order to encourage decentralized industrialization (Chapter 3). The prospective investor would then be expected to compare return on prospective investment in the regulated segment after netting perceived transaction costs associated with clearances with return in the unregulated segment at the lower end of the scale of investment. The decision would go in favour of where the rate of return was higher, often in the unregulated segment, at the cost of fragmentation of optimum scale. In the regulated segment, the hassle of obtaining an investment licence was a precondition for applying for lucrative import licence with handsome scarcity premia. Follow-up of investment licences, once granted, in terms actual capacity creation and utilization, was virtually non-existent because it was administratively and organizationally costly. This led to a variety of malpractices. Not intending to establish additional capacity, an investment licence was often used as an entry barrier to competitors, the resulting shortage being used to earn scarcity rents. For this purpose, there was bunching of applications at the beginning of the plan period when additional plan capacity creation was announced. The plan targets were used as industry-level ceiling limits by the licence-disbursing bureaucracy for granting investment licences. Derived from the long-term growth scenario, the targets had little connection with market conditions. In certain consumer goods industries where they happened to reflect market scarcities, there was excess demand for investment licences and licence seeking became a profitable activity earning rents for the bureaucracy. Even in areas where the targets did not reflect demand pressures, the demand for licences was either for pre-empting capacity by existing producers to block entry of competitors or for earning premia on associated lucrative import licences. A phased manufacturing programme limited imports irrespective of the domestic costs of import substitutes thereby leading to internationally non-competitive high-cost domestic manufacturing capacity. This would still enable existing producers to earn profits when the shortages persisted. Where the market conditions were unfavourable, the existing producers tended to diversify into totally unrelated areas where shortages persisted. Thus the idea of 'governing' the market and large private capitalists in public interest through discretionary controls ended up generating generally higher pay-offs to unproductive rent-seeking activities than productive investment. Productive investment, wherever profitable, was driven by perceived shortages rather than plan priorities. Shortages were generated in an environment where the economy was insulated from foreign competition by elaborate import and foreign exchange controls and industrial investment licensing unintentionally created non-competitive oligopolistic markets at the upper-end of the scale of operation. In this environment, industrial units in the public as well as private sector turned inefficient but still privately profitable in a persistent shortage economy. The result was a high-cost low-quality industrial structure not quite in line with plan priorities that were followed more in the public than private sector. However, the remarkable degree of diversification of an internationally non-competitive industrial structure was not found in other countries with same level of per capita income as India's.

Indiscriminate Expansion of the Public Sector

Generally, the activities of the public sector in the economic sphere are undertaken in *fiduciary capacity*, that is in trust on behalf of society to serve certain socially agreed objectives. In these fiduciary activities, commercial profit earning is *not* the primary objective but efficient cost-effective operation is still important to justify the spending of public money. Cost-effective supply of public-sector activities to serve social objectives in the non-commercial domain poses a formidable challenge. However, cost-effectiveness is not the strong point of public-sector activities in most countries. Consequently, commercial activities are left to the private sector in usually competitive markets where profit-earning efficient operation becomes the driving force in the face of actual or potential competition from domestic producers or imports or what economists call contestable markets. Public-sector activities are generally confined to areas where markets are known to fail or, what economists call public goods.[3] However, Minhas (1991) had pointed out (i) that diagnosis of market failure in particular contexts was often not an easy task; and (ii) existence of market failure provided only a *necessary condition* for *some* form of government intervention but *not necessarily* through government production/provision of the relevant goods. He argued for what he called the 'double-market failure criterion':

> First, one must establish sound evidence of market failure. Second, one must also search for evidence that a *less intrusive policy* cannot be utilized, or effective contracts for private production of public provision cannot be devised. Whenever double-market failure criterion is fulfilled, the case for public sector production/provision is *usually* strong.

Even when the double-market failure criterion was satisfied, it was necessary to take careful account of uncertain administrative costs and harmful side effects of government intervention, which might often overwhelm the potentially harmful social consequences of market failure so that it would still be desirable to leave the situation to the market. In other words, he argued for market failure to be weighed against government failure to design economic organization and systems of incentives and disincentives to promote necessary control of costs and quality in public services. His cautious approach was clearly shaped by the Indian experience where, he argued, corrective action to mend the behaviour of public-sector enterprises did not emerge because either (i) competitive market criteria could not be applied as in the case of public goods or (ii) market criteria got lower priority than so-called public interest criteria as in the case of private goods and services being produced in the public sector. Mahalanobis recommended pushing the conventional boundaries of the public sector beyond public goods in terms of basic and heavy machine-making industries being exclusively reserved for the public sector. Populist radicalism pushed the boundaries further into a variety of commercial areas as noted in the last chapter. A multiplicity of social objectives in the non-economic domain provided a convenient excuse for covering up inefficiencies in the PSEs operating in the commercial domain. These were often public monopolies or very large units with dominant market share. They survived on the strength of a soft-budget constraint.[4] These provided a convenient vehicle for featherbedding,[5] patronage distribution, and other malpractices in addition to persistent inefficiencies in operation.

To recapitulate the discussion so far, persistent foreign exchange shortages resulting from a deliberately maintained overvalued exchange rate provided a self-fulfilling justification for stringent quantitative controls on foreign exchange and imports that protected domestic producers of import-competing goods and generated shortage-induced large rents on imported products. This clearly reflected the influence of the ideology of economic nationalism. Note that the domestic markets insulated from external competition encouraged inefficiency *both* in public- *and* private-sector units. Heavy-handed regulation of markets and private industrial activity generated ample opportunities for politicians and bureaucracy (that exercised discretionary powers from case-by-case disposal) and large private industrialists (to seek discretionary favours in a chronic shortage economy) to earn rents. Indiscriminately extended PSEs, with a legal identity distinct from that of government, became what

Minhas (1991: 6) described as private trading posts in which 'jobs, favours, policies and contracts are freely traded for money and private gains, and rents on political and bureaucratic power are collected in most transactions'. Thus the three elements of the new institutional matrix introduced by the activist government in interaction with the existing institutional environment where private enterprise and markets had been gradually expanding, considerably reduced the scope for competition in terms of costs, quality and productivity, opened up avenues for unproductive profit-seeking activities, and stifled the creative dynamism of private enterprise and functioning markets while fostering inefficiency in the expanding PSEs. In the process, the Indian economy became, as already mentioned, one of the most heavily but ineffectively regulated market economies in the world by combining (unintentionally, to begin with) the worst of both planning as well as markets. This regime continued with varying intensity till the end of the 1970s and was reflected in economic performance.

Growth Performance

The aggregate GDP growth (at constant 1993–4 prices) remained, between 1950–1 and 1980–1, stuck at 3.6 per cent per annum on the average (Table 4.1, col. 6). Notice that this was *despite* successful efforts of the activist government at mobilizing domestic savings. The rate of gross domestic savings doubled from 8.8 per cent during the first quinquennium of the 1950s to 18.7 per cent during 1973–4 and 1979–80, the period marked by two steep oil price hikes and shift of the international economy to a volatile floating exchange rate regime that derailed the growth process in many other oil-importing developing countries. The rate of gross domestic investment (at current prices) too more than doubled from 9.0 per cent to 18.5 per cent over the same period. This meant that investment was not utilized effectively, which can also be seen in high and increasing incremental capital–output ratios (ICORs) (Table 4.1), a measure of efficiency of utilization of mobilized capital. Consequently, the constraints on growth in the Indian context arose from the development strategy and the incentive structure generated by the new institutional matrix and not from the shortage of '*resources*' as

Table 4.1: Growth Performance and Macroeconomic Indicators 1950–1 to 2002–3

(Period Averages in Per Cent)

Time Period	Rate of GDCF current prices	Rate of GDS at current prices	Rate of Net Capital Inflow (+) (current prices)	Rate of GDCF (1993–4 prices)	Rate of Growth of GDP(fc) (1993–4 prices)	Implicit ICOR Col. (5)/(6)	AV– WPI – All Commo-dities	AV – CPI – Industrial Workers	GFD/ GDP – Centre	GFD/ GDP – Centre + States	RD/ GDP	CAD/ GDP
(1)	(2)	(3)	(4)	(5)	(6)	(7)	(8)	(9)	(10)	(11)	(12)	(13)
1950–1 to 1954–5	9.04	8.76	0.28	13.90	3.88	3.59	–0.43	–1.42	N.A	N.A	N.A	0.0
1955–6 to 1959–60	13.30	11.18	2.12	17.98	3.36	5.34	3.88	4.54	N.A	N.A	N.A	–1.8
1960–1 to 1964–5	14.26	12.04	2.22	18.26	4.99	3.66	5.55	5.11	N.A	5.7	N.A	–1.8
1965–6 to 1972–3	15.23	13.84	1.39	20.44	2.54	8.04	6.90	6.19	N.A	5.4	N.A	–1.4
1973–4 to 1979–80	18.54	18.69	–0.14	21.61	3.39	6.37	9.81	8.73	3.94	5.9	–0.41	0.24
1980–1 to 1984–5	19.76	18.44	1.32	21.16	5.64	3.75	9.28	10.12	5.92	7.2	1.04	–1.52
1985–6 to 1989–90	22.70	20.38	2.32	22.44	5.96	3.77	6.66	7.96	7.73	8.9	2.43	–2.16
1990–1	26.30	23.10	3.20	25.40	5.57	4.56	10.30	11.16	7.85	9.4	3.26	–3.10
1991–2	22.60	22.00	0.60	22.00	1.30	16.95	13.70	13.50	5.56	7.0	2.49	–0.30
1992–3 to 1996–7	24.80	23.48	1.32	24.94	6.69	3.73	8.74	9.36	5.61	7.1	2.85	–1.2
1997–8 to 2002–3	23.97	23.38	0.58	25.90	5.25	4.93	4.63	5.90	5.92	9.1	3.87	–0.53

Notes: 1. GDCF = Gross Domestic Capital Formation 2. GDS = Gross Domestic Savings 3. GDP (fc) = Gross Domestic Product at factor cost 4. ICOR = Incremental Capital-Output Ratio 5. AV–WPI = Average Annual Variation (%) in Wholesale Price Index 6. AV–CPI = Average Annual Variation (%) in Consumer Price Index 7. GFD = Gross Fiscal Deficit 8. RD = Revenue Deficit 9. CAD = Current Account Deficit

Source: 1. Central Statistical Organisation, *National Accounts Statistics* Back series 1950–1 to 1992–3 (2001).

2. Central Statistical Organisation, *National Accounts Statistics* 2002.

3. *Handbook of Statistics on the Indian Economy 2003–4*, Tables No. 224–6, 230, pp. 478–80, 486 Reserve Bank of India, Mumbai.

4. *Handbook of Industrial Policy and Statistics 2001*.

5. Vijay Joshi and I.M.D. Little (1994), *India: Macroeconomics and Political Economy*, World Bank, Washington D.C.

the development literature of the 1950s would have us believe.[6] In this literature, with labour being abundant in low-income economies, the primary resource constraints on growth were basically taken to be two: foreign exchange arising from perceived inelastic demand for exports and limited capacity to save at low levels of per capita income. Of these, the foreign exchange shortages flowed directly from the pervasive influence of the ideology of economic nationalism. The doubling of the ex post rate of gross domestic savings indicated remarkable success of the government in mobilizing domestic savings so that capacity to save could not be deemed to be a constraint. Thus, while constricting growth, the resulting incentive structure from the development strategy provided fertile ground for nurturing powerful economic interest groups that emerged to reap gains from that incentive structure. We now turn to the discussion of these interest groups during the slow-growth phase.

ECONOMIC INTEREST GROUPS AND DISTRIBUTIONAL EQUILIBRIUM

With skew distribution of earnings from economic activities partly in proportion to economic contributions and partly in line with gains from the incentive structure, powerful economic interest groups are expected to be numerically small but well connected to the levers of political and economic power so as to make more than proportionate claims on the national output. We start by listing the interest groups that emerged during the phase of slow growth from 1950–1 to 1980–1 on the basis of commonality of economic interests. These were the beneficiaries of autarkic industrialization and indiscriminate expansion of PSEs and were located in the organized segment of the economy with much higher than average productivity per worker. They included: (i) the bureaucracy; (ii) large private industrialists; (iii) mostly white-collar employees of the public sector; and (iv) blue-collar workers of the organized factory manufacturing segment.

BUREAUCRACY

Case-by-case discretionary controls over private-sector activities and the persistent regime of shortages that they induced, earned scarcity rents for the overcrowded bureaucracy in public administration that exercised the discretionary powers. It earned rents in disbursing import and investment licences and administering controlled prices of products as well as specified inputs including capital.[7] Central PSEs got top-level bureaucracy rents in terms of top managerial positions, the associated perks and privileges, power to offer jobs, and trading favours and contracts. In the state PSEs, these benefits were expropriated by state-level politicians. Quasi-government entities with legal identities distinct from government have been politically preferred by the governments at different levels to departmental entities for the following plausible reasons. Operations and accounts of the quasi-government bodies are not subject to as much legislative scrutiny and interference as those of the departmental enterprises. They are, therefore, more amenable to covert influences of various kinds by politicians and bureaucrats than departmental enterprises. More importantly, these entities can access the capital markets in addition to government loans and public revenues, the sources to which departmental enterprises are mostly confined. Finally, subsidies to the departmental enterprises invariably have to go through the budget and hence are open to greater public scrutiny. Quasi-government entities can be subsidized in extra-budgetary fashion including setting discretionary administered prices, enhancing equity (by increased public debt), and writing-off of accumulated loans and interests. Their continuing losses are supported by the public exchequer through various devices leading to the 'soft budget constraint'.[8] In addition, PSEs offer considerable opportunities for patronage and corruption in bulk purchases of materials and equipment, in recruitment, in directed credit, in shipping and trading contracts, and so on. Rules that govern travel and daily expenses in PSEs are more generous than those in the government thereby giving scope for extending privileges to the politicians and bureaucrats (Desai 1999). These avenues revealed themselves over time but gathered momentum in the 1980s.

Large Private Industrialists

A virtually closed economy resulting from stringent import and foreign exchange controls coupled with the policy-induced entry barriers to domestic markets (such as mandatory government sanction through industrial licences) offered protected markets to large private industry (Tendulkar 1993) that earned it super normal profits in a perennial shortage economy. These profits were further boosted by using cheaper capital from the public financial institutions.[9] Capacity-linked import licences provided another source of sure shot profit or rents in terms of the premium they commanded.

White-collar Employees of the Public Sector

The public sector was also looked upon as a major source of featherbedding (or labour absorption without reference to productive contribution at the margin). This can be seen from employment in the public sector by branch of government in Figure 4.1. In this chart, employment in quasi-government entities indicates the absorption of labour in PSEs owned by all three branches of government, namely the central government, state governments, and local bodies. This category shows a very rapid rise particularly between 1970 and 1981. Table 4.2 shows total (mostly wage and salary earning, contractual, non-casual) employment in the organized segment of the economy, its public- and private-sectors breakdown, and the disaggregation of public-sector employment for selected years. Several interesting facts

FIGURE 4.1
Employment in Public Sector by Branch 1960–2001

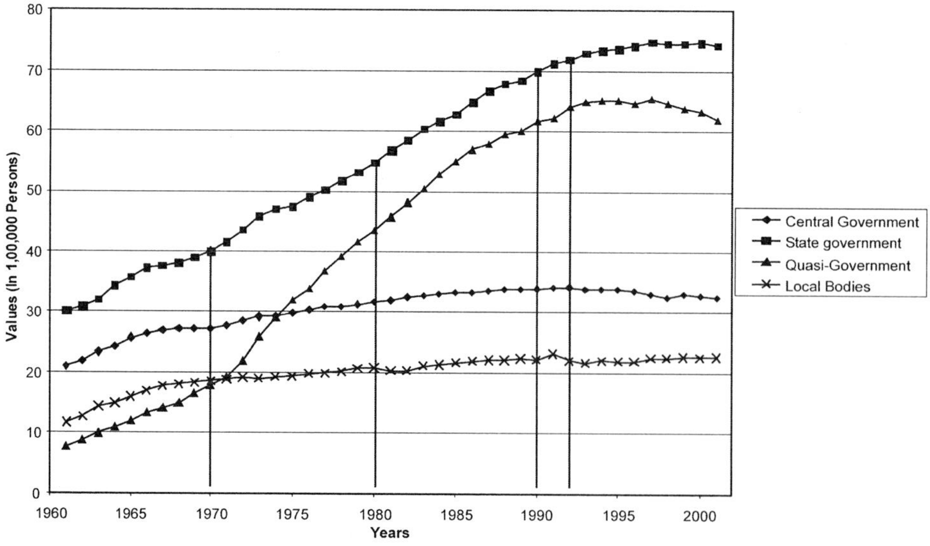

Source: Economic Survey, Ministry of Finance-GOI (Various Issues)

Table 4.2: Organized Employment in India 1961, 1966, 1981, 1991, 2001

(Millions)

		1961	1966	1981	1991	2001
1.0	Public sector total	7.050	9.476	15.484	19.057	19.139
		(58)	(58)	(68)	(71)	(69)
1.1	Central government	2.090	2.636	3.195	3.410	3.261
1.2	State government	3.014	3.723	5.676	7.112	7.425
1.3	Quasi-government	0.773	1.318	4.576	6.222	6.192
		(11)	(14)	(30)	(33)	(32)
1.4	Local bodies	1.173	1.701	2.037	2.313	2.261
2.0	Private sector	5.04	6.81	7.395	7.677	8.652
3.0	Total organized (1.0+2.0)	12.090	16.286	22.879	26.734	27.791
	Memo: Total workforce	188.167	N.A.	302.703 *	374.124 **	397.928 ***

Notes: *: For the year 1983; **: For the year 1993–4; ***: For the year 1999–2000. Figures in row 1.0 in parentheses are percentage shares in total organized employment given in row 3.0. Figures in row 1.3 in parentheses are percentage shares in total public-sector employment given in row 1.0.

Sources: Directorate General of Employment and Training (DGE&T) Ministry of Labour and Employment, Government of India for the main table. National Sample Surveys on Employment and Unemployment for 1983, 1993–4 and 1999–2000, and Population census 1961 for total workforce figures in Memo.

stand out. One, the share of the public sector in total organized employment rose from 58 per cent in 1961 (the earliest year for which data are available) to 68 per cent in 1981 and further to 71 per cent in 1991. Over the same period, the share of quasi-government entities in total public-sector employment nearly trebled from 11 per cent in 1961 to 30 per cent in 1981 and 33 per cent in 1991. The major part of the increase came during the period of populist radicalization of politics from the mid-1960s to the mid-1970s.[10] In comparison, over the same period, private-sector employment in the organized segment increased only marginally. In other words, the activist government also turned aggressive employer mostly in the form of featherbedding. Finally, and most importantly, elite organized-sector employment with much greater than national average productivity per worker accounted for a miniscule single-digit share of the total workforce in India. This reflected total failure of the adopted industrialization strategy to improve the working conditions of an overwhelming proportion of the total workforce.

Professional employees in the public sector, like those in public administration, enjoyed secure high-wage employment with more generous social security packages and time-bound promotions—all without much reference to performance. They improved their bargaining positions further using the strategic sectoral location in the public sector (such as banks, insurance, and electricity supply) where a strike could disrupt the economy badly (Tendulkar 2004). The recent one-week-long strike (3–9 April 2006) by the employees of the government-owned State Bank of India, the largest commercial bank with a more than 55 per cent share in deposits and lending, provides an eloquent case in point. In this context, it may be noted that all public-sector bank employees receive *either* provident fund *or* pension in addition to gratuity. The employees of the State Bank of India are already privileged in receiving *all the three* benefits. The strike was for raising the magnitude of pension. The employees succeeded in forcing the government to accept their exorbitant demands after causing a week-long disruption in banking transactions.

Blue-collar Workers of the Organized Manufacturing Sector

The blue-collar workers in the organized factory manufacturing segment—in both public and private sectors—were the *passive* beneficiaries[11] of autarkic industrialization with the support of the activist state. They mainly benefited from regular long-term contractual employment with reasonable job security without much regard to their productivity levels, thanks to the comprehensive labour legislation that was enacted and enforced by the activist state with supplementary support from the judiciary.

Two deliberate omissions from above listing are worth noting. The first group is that of modern small enterprises (initially confined to manufacturing but later extended to services) which was given a host of promotional and protective concessions to further the Gandhian ideal (Tendulkar and Bhavani 1997). These enterprises, being small and dispersed, took until the 1980s to get organized to assert their common economic interests. The second category is that of surplus-producing peasants. Agriculture did not receive adequate attention under the centrally planned autarkic industrialization strategy of the 1950s. Rather, stringent import controls on industrial products as part of the import-substituting industrialization provided a boost to industrial profits in insulated domestic markets vis-à-vis those in agricultural products and turned the terms of trade against potentially exportable agricultural products in the first fifteen years of planning resulting in disprotection (implicit tax) of agriculture. It required two severe back-to-back agricultural droughts of 1965 and 1966 to force the policymakers to pay attention to agriculture and provide impetus for the introduction of chemical-biological technology in agriculture (described in common parlance as the green revolution) in the second half of the 1960s. It was more than fifteen years before farmers started getting organized and participated in the terms-of-trade politics of the 1980s. These two numerically large and dispersed groups were in their formative stages and hence weak during the slow-growth phase and thus have not been considered here. They became influential in the 1980s and will be discussed in Chapter 5.

Distributional Coalition of Interest Groups during the Slow-Growth Phase

The aggregate numerical magnitude of the powerful interest groups of the slow-growth period was small. Bureaucrats in public administration and professional employees of the PSEs together formed 70 per cent of the well-paid regular wage and salary earning organized workers but accounted for less than 4 per cent of the total 302 million employed workers in 1983.[12] Blue-collar workers contributed another 2 per cent while large private industrial capitalists remained miniscule and industrially segmented, seeking case-by-case discretionary favours.[13] All of them were located in the organized segment of the economy that was characterized by much greater than average national productivity per worker and well connected to the levers of political and bureaucratic power.

How did the interest group constellation affect the public exchequer in the slow-growth phase? There was an internal nexus among private industrialists, bureaucrats, and blue-collar factory workers. The claims of the bureaucrats (and often politicians) were met out of the scarcity rents generated by shortages caused by import-control-distorted domestic prices and delays in implementing/granting investment licences.[14] These rents accrued to the industrialists who passed on part of them to the exchequer in the form of indirect taxes, another part to the blue-collar factory workers enjoying generous state-mediated wage settlements, and were still left with handsome margins on low-volume businesses. *This redistribution of scarcity rents contributed to rather than making direct claims on the public exchequer*. The claims of the white-collar professional employees were met partly out of exploiting the monopoly position of PSEs through administered prices wherever possible (for example in telecommunications) and partly through budgetary transfers of discretionary types.

How was the momentum of even slow growth maintained with the predominantly rent-seeking incentive structure? The slow tempo of growth was basically maintained by raising the rate of investment faster than deterioration in efficiency of utilization of capital.[15] This was also the case in the erstwhile Soviet Union from the late 1920s to the 1950s. Investment requirements for the indiscriminate expansion of the PSEs were met out of the mobilization involved in near doubling of the rate of gross domestic savings from 8.8 per cent in the first quinquennium of the 1950s to 18.7 per cent during 1974–80 (Table 4.1). Household deposits in monopolistic public-sector banks and mostly indirect (import and excise) taxes were used as instruments of savings mobilization while allocation of imports and private investment were sought to be influenced through discretionary controls. There was a nexus between budgetary mobilization through taxes and scarcity rents in a low-growth regime. Mobilized household deposits were diverted through cash reserve ratios and statutory liquidity ratios to finance public-sector investments and government-approved large private investment through term loans from public-sector financial institutions at administered (low) interest rates.

A distributional coalition with internal nexuses thus evolved over time in the form of implicit social contract and apparently remained stable over the first three decades of Independence. This social contract among the powerful interest groups operated in the modern formal or organized segment of the economy with much higher than national average productivity per worker, a lion's share in output, and close connections with the levers of political and bureaucratic power. This formal segment of the economy that has been the driving force of economic growth had been increasing its share of GDP during the period of public-sector-dominated and autarkic industrialization. However, its share of labour absorption remained limited to single digit figures in relation to total Indian workforce because the inherently higher *technical capital intensity*[16] of modern industry rose further due to widespread inefficiencies in capital utilization fostered by lack of competition. An overwhelming majority of workers were residually absorbed in the remaining unorganized or informal part of the economy that operated with traditional technology with considerably lower than average productivity per worker and poor organizational links with formal-sector financial institutions. Although this unorganized segment remained predominantly rural and agricultural in character, consisting of mostly self-employed and dispersed enterprises, its non-agricultural and urban informal component had been growing in terms of contribution to GDP. With its poor connectivity to the levers of power, the informal segment had no option but to passively accept whatever came its way after the prior claims of the powerful interest groups were met. In the absence of government-funded social security, this overwhelming majority had no other alternative than to work in order to earn subsistence-level livelihood irrespective of very low productivity of work. In a virtually closed economy, its role in the growth process remained confined to supplying labour and a market for the formal segment. Its economic performance remained autonomous but subject to weather-induced shocks.

It appeared that the distributional equilibrium to accommodate the claims of the interest groups could be sustained in a low-growth trajectory of 3.5 per cent per annum with responsible fisc and reasonable balance-of-payments deficits for the following reasons. One, scarcity rents in a perpetual shortage economy generated by an overall protected non-competitive environment provided a convenient vehicle for transmitting gains to powerful interest groups without impinging on the public exchequer. Second, a redistributional nexus existed among the interest groups for sharing the scarcity rents. Third, the numerical magnitude of the interest groups remained very small. Finally, the successful mobilization of domestic savings out of gains from the incentive structure was combined with foreign assistance for raising the rate of investment faster than the rate of deterioration in efficiency of utilization of capital, so that the low-growth momentum could be maintained.

To cite empirical support on fiscal and current account deficits, we have to limit ourselves to the decade of the 1970s, as fiscal data are not available for the earlier years. For the decade from 1970–1 to 1979–80, central government subsidies averaged about 0.75 per cent of GDP, gross fiscal deficit averaged 3.8 per cent of GDP, and there were revenue account surpluses in most of the years. Similarly, the consolidated gross fiscal deficit of state governments averaged 2 per cent of GDP with revenue account surpluses in most of the years. (RBI 2003: Tables 221 and 222). Current account deficits averaged 0.4 per cent of GDP with current account surpluses in three out of ten years of the decade marked by two steep oil price hikes (RBI 2003: Table 225). GDP growth averaged around 3 per cent during the decade. We interpret this to be a case of low-growth equilibrium with fiscal and balance-of-payments stability albeit with distorted prices. Low growth despite doubling of the rate of gross domestic savings was the combined result of competition-limiting policies and growth-constricting direct discretionary controls and distorted prices arising out of differentiated excise and customs duties and other quantitative controls that managed to maintain fiscal and external payment stability.

NOTES

1. Often, the height of tariff exceeded the cost of the highest cost domestic producer. This situation is described as having 'water' in the tariff.
2. In standard economic terminology, rent is a return on any resource in fixed supply. For example, land, being in fixed supply, earns rent because of its scarcity. Rent-seeking activities are generally those that seek quick profits by exploiting genuine or artificially created shortage by cornering fixed supplies. These activities use up resources that could otherwise be used for productive investment. They are also alternatively described as directly unproductive profit-seeking activities.
3. See n. 17 in Chapter 3.
4. See n. 19, Chapter 3.
5. See n. 18, Chapter 3.
6. Chenery and Strout (1966) exemplify this dominant view of the period.
7. This was recognized and noted in an official report in the early 1960s itself. The Santhanam Committee Report (Report of the Committee on Prevention of Corruption 1964) states: 'Where there is power and discretion, there is always the possibility of abuse, more so when power and discretion have to be exercised in the context of scarcity and controls and pressure to spend public money' (p. 9), cited in Myrdal (1968: 945).

8. See n. 19, Chapter 3.
9. Markets for short-term (for working capital) and long-term institutional credit operated under the administered interest rates, which were deliberately pegged much lower than market clearing rates in order to encourage investment. Government-owned public financial institutions not only provided term loans to industry for investment but also subscribed to its equity thereby also sharing risk. Nationalized banks and other state-owned financial institutions often held as much as 40 to 45 per cent of corporate equity and also provided almost all long-term debt (Goswami 1996: 68)). Rudolph and Rudolph (1987: 20) term this as '[state] 'dependent [private] capitalism'.
10. It is possible to divide total quasi-government employment into that in the central and non-central government (state governments plus local bodies)-owned quasi-government entities from 1971. This exercise (not reported here) indicated that these two components had about equal (nearly 1.5 million) employees in 1974. By 1991, employment in central government entities had started declining slowly and stood at a little above 2 million. In the same year, the non-central component had reached nearly 4.5 million, showing unabated increase. In other words, state governments and local bodies had raced ahead of the central government in their employment expansion drive.
11. Passive because, as we argue later (Chapter 8), trade unionism has been extremely fragmented and weak.
12. A clarification of our choice of the year 1983 may be useful at this point. Reasonably reliable data on total workforce are availably only from the quinquennial National Sample Surveys (NSS) on employment and unemployment. The 1983 NSS was the closest to 1981, the year we use to mark the end of the slow-growth phase.
13. See Chapter 3 for discussion of the segmentation of industries for policy purposes.
14. Investment licensing was also used as a device to pre-empt a large share of planned capacity and hence deter entry of rival producers.
15. In a well-known economic growth identity, the rate of growth is a ratio of rate of investment and incremental capital-output ratio that reflects efficiency of utilization of capital.
16. Technical capital intensity represents that level of capital–labour ratio when both capital and labour are utilized efficiently (i.e. without any underutilization) at a given level of output.

5

The Decade of the 1980s

EMERGENCE OF VERTICAL MOBILIZATIONS

The 1980s marked the watershed decade in India's polity and economy. There were two major changes in polity with their origin in the populist radicalization of politics since the mid-1960s (Chapter 3). Social mobilizations on vertical lines cutting across economic interests and based on religion, language, region, and caste emerged as important pressure groups that could not be ignored by mainstream elite politics. Second, two numerically large economic interest groups of farmers and small industrialists/traders—became organized and forced their way into the distributional coalition. The economy did emerge out of a thirty-year-long slow-growth phase but even the stepped-up GDP growth of 5.7 per cent per annum proved inadequate to maintain the distributional equilibrium in the 1980s. However, the decade ended with fiscal and external payments crises that provided an opportunity for reforms.

Historically, the Congress Party had provided from pre-Independence days when it was Indian National Congress, a federal umbrella for diverse social and economic interest groups to unite first for liberation from colonial rule and after Independence for reconciling and ironing out diverse inter-group conflicts in the politico-economic realm. After Nehru's death in 1964, the single-party dominance of the Congress Party started getting eroded by the ensuing intra-party tussle for succession which failed to arrive at an effective consensus. This resulted in weakening of the party organization, loss of electoral majority in several states in the 1967 general elections, and the eventual split of the party in 1969. Even after the split that was engineered by Mrs Gandhi, she was unsure of support from the party organization for her leadership. She, therefore, resorted to populist radicalization of politics in an effort to widen her mass base and centralize power and control in her charismatic personality. This process has been described by Rudolph and Rudolph (1987: 6) as deinstitutionalization of the Congress Party and state organizational structures by systematically isolating and naturalizing actual or potential rivals in the party. It considerably weakened the earlier federal structure of the Congress Party that had permitted reasonable autonomy for diverse interest groups. Kaviraj (1995) makes an interesting observation in this context. Indira Gandhi made herself and the Congress Party more powerful by regaining legislative majorities at the centre and in most states in the 1971 general elections through engaging in direct mass politics based on her charisma and bypassing the party organization. Ironically, however, in this process, the political system dramatically reduced its effectiveness in terms of institutional ability to achieve complex policy objectives without excessive conflict and violence to meet the rising social aspirations from the radical rhetoric. Despite legislative majority of the Congress Party in most states, the state governments failed to provide policy stability, with 'one faction of the party chasing another out of office, mostly with the central approval' (Kaviraj 1995: 110). The continual turnover of state party leaders generated an undercurrent of instability despite apparent political stability in state legislatures so that radical rhetoric and short-term quick-fix solutions became substitutes for effective implementation. Commenting on this period, Rudolph and Rudolph (1987: 6) noted the depletion of political capital as 'the independence of professional standards and procedural norms of the parliament, the courts, the civil service and the federal system gave way to centralisation based on personal loyalty'. Electoral majorities and centralization of power resulted in increasing intolerance on the one hand, and increasing intra-party dissidence due to erosion of intra-party democracy on the other hand created a political space for alternative avenues for popular mobilizations in a society as diverse as India's. Consequently, localized and sectional mobilizations emerged to give vent to their grievances on the streets to exert pressure on the elected politicians such as the Gorkhaland agitation in West Bengal.[1] There has been a fundamental shift in the basis of formation and organizational modalities of these groups with respect to tangible and intangible assets deployed in democratic politics (Kaviraj 1995:115). In the earlier period, the pressure groups in the polity were based on the harmony of economic interests, were numerically small but economically powerful in terms of linkages to levers of power, and operated in formal elite politics. In contrast, the social agitations of the 1980s were based on religious, ethnic, caste-group, and linguistic identities cutting across economic interests and in the process managing to combine numbers with financial muscle and they operated in the realm of mass politics. The growing importance of regional and sectional parties in national politics in the 1990s (discussed in Chapter 7) has its inspirations or origins in the institutionalization of these spontaneous agitations, movements, and mobilizations in the 1980s that initially arose without any alignment to organized political parties.

ENTRY OF FARMERS AND SMALL INDUSTRIALISTS/TRADERS

The origins of peasant farmers as an interest group can be traced to the green revolution that was initiated in the second half of the 1960s as a response to the back-to-back agricultural droughts of 1965 and 1966, and the politically perceived urgent need[2] to attain self-sufficiency in food production to feed the growing population. The agricultural transformation strategy consisted of effective training and visit extension system and giving incentive prices combined with subsidies on modern inputs such as fertilizers, high-yielding varieties of seeds, pesticides, irrigated water and preferential subsidized institutional credit to finance these modern inputs. The subsidies were initially meant to popularize the new technology. With the diffusion of modern technology especially in the assured irrigation areas of the north-west, the marketed surplus-producing farmers reaped huge profits in the 1970s. The widely quoted study on barter terms-of-trade for agriculture vis-à-vis non-agriculture by Thamarajakshi (1990) suggests fluctuations without trend from 1950–

1 to 1965–6, a positive trend of 2 per cent per annum in favour of farmers between 1965–6 and 1973–4, and a reversal to a negative 2.4 per cent trend growth from 1973–4 to 1979–80. The negative growth in the last phase had its origin in rising energy costs in the wake of the oil price hikes in the 1970s. This led to a pressure on the large profit margins[3] that grain-surplus-producing farmers in the north-western areas had been enjoying till 1973–4.

Non-party mass organizations of farmers seeking higher producer prices and farm input subsidies have been strong in Maharashtra, Gujarat, Punjab, Karnataka, and Tamil Nadu. Producer prices mattered initially only for large surplus-producing farmers. With the diffusion of technology in assured irrigation areas, small farmers also started producing surpluses for sale. All categories of farmers irrespective of size benefited from input subsidies. Marginal farmers and agricultural labourers were net buyers of grains. On economic considerations, their support depended on the extent to which higher producer prices were translated into higher agricultural wages. This was a doubtful proposition. This was where identity politics based on caste groups (like other backward castes) played a critical role and large farmers and middle peasants managed to make a common cause with small and marginal peasants and agricultural labourers to set up formal and non-formal organizations that were strong in terms of money as well as numbers.

In organized party politics, the 1970s saw the emergence of the peasant-dominated Bharatiya Lok Dal (BLD) under the leadership of farmer-leader Chowdhary Charan Singh, a stout defender of private proprietorship in agriculture since his earlier incarnation in the Congress Party till 1967. He was a staunch opponent of large-scale industrialization, attacked urban bias in development, and advocated the Gandhian economic policy of decentralization.[4] There had also been a change in the political stance of all the national political parties including the two Communist parties towards agriculture, which can be seen in their election manifestos for the 1980 mid-term general elections (Varshney 1995: 138–9). This was prompted by the efforts of the major political parties with predominantly urban base to extend their support base to rural areas. It was reflected not only in the political support farmers received across party lines for policies favouring agriculture but also in choice of candidates that resulted in a rising number of agriculturists among members of parliament.[5]

Using their political clout and the argument that the domestic prices of rice and wheat were much lower than the international prices and that agriculture was implicitly taxed because of a variety of protective import taxes on industrial inputs and the ban on exports of agricultural products (Pursell and Gulati 1993), farmer leaders started pressurizing the government to raise the Minimum Support Prices (MSP) and input subsidies in the 1980s. The decade of the 1980s thus also emerged as the decade of the terms-of-trade politics.

Gulati and Narayanan (2000: Table 6.1) estimate that input subsidies on power, fertilizer, and irrigation as per cent of agricultural and total GDP rose steeply from 1.8 per cent and 0.62 per cent respectively in 1980–1 to 8.6 per cent and 2.45 per cent in 1990–1. On a per hectare of gross cropped area basis, the input subsidies increased seven times between the two points of time at 1981–2 constant prices. While it is difficult to estimate the full magnitude of impact of these measures on the public exchequer, two explicit subsidies, namely food and fertilizer, provide a partial reflection of the transfer of state revenues to agriculture sector. These two subsidies show a rising trend in the 1980s (Figure 5.1).

The second group that became politically important in this period was that of small traders and industrialists. This group has traditionally been favoured by the Gandhian policy of decentralized, dispersed industrialization, which was postulated as a counter to large private capitalists and complementary to large-scale, public-sector-dominated industrialization. It comprises modern 'small-scale industry' (SSI), defined initially by a ceiling level on original value of plant and machinery (which has been rising overtime) with later further subdivision into 'tiny' and 'small' units. These industries have been the beneficiaries of a variety of promotional and protective measures (Tendulkar and Bhavani 1997). The promotional measures were meant to impart competitive strength to small units by helping them offset the genuine handicaps of small scale of operation. They included provision of infrastructure like industrial estates, consultancy and training services, common facilities for industry like tool rooms and quality testing stations, supply of machines on hire purchase,

FIGURE 5.1
Explicit Subsidies in Central Budget 1979–1990

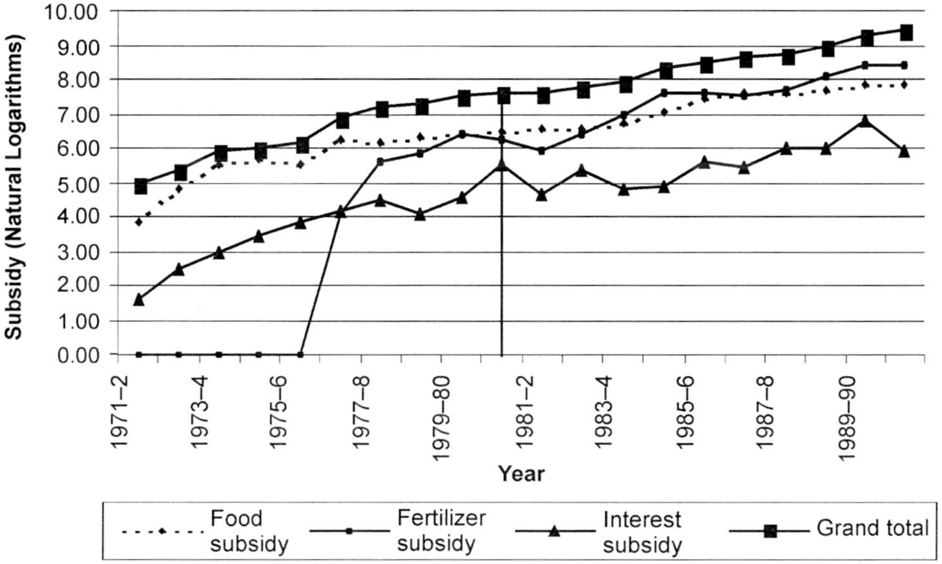

Source: D.K. Srivastava and Tapas K. Sen (1997). *Government Subsidies in India*, National Institute of Public Finance and Policy, Delhi, Annexure I, for 1971–2 to 1996–7.

and easier access to credit and raw materials. While legitimate, the discretionary character of many of these promotional measures opened up avenues for rent seeking. Protective measures, on the other hand, sought to protect small units from competition with large-scale domestic units through a variety of preferential treatment involving explicit or implicit subsidies. In addition to their discretionary character, the indefinite continuation of these measures for political gains enabled these units to remain profitable despite being inefficient. Apart from the inequity in practice of relatively larger units among the eligible ones mopping up the discretionary promotional and protective measures and prompting unproductive profit-seeking activities, these measures also fostered inefficiency by making it profitable to remain 'small' (Abid Hussain Committee Report 1997: 119; Mohan 2002: 259, 261). The benefits of concessions often outstripped the perceived profits from a higher and more efficient scale of investment that would make the unit ineligible for concessions. In the high tariff regime of the 1980s, 'small' scale producers often found it more profitable to turn traders by selling the preferentially allocated imported inputs in short supply at a premium to larger units in the domestic market rather than using them in their own production. In the post-liberalization lower tariff phase, it is not uncommon to find inefficient producers importing the cheaper imported commodities for sale in domestic grey markets for products such as watches and toys (Krishna 2001). Protective concessions of various kinds enabled reasonable returns despite inefficiencies (Bhavani and Tendulkar 2000). One of our recent studies (Bhavani 2001, 2006) confirmed the widely reported phenomenon of the domination of the urban-based better-off segment of small enterprises by traders and professionals who were in a better position to get organized into a pressure group. An idea of the political clout of this group can be had from some seemingly innocuous but important policy shifts brought about through notifications. They are: the subdivision of small-scale industry into 'tiny' and non-tiny residual with 'more' preferential treatment for the former in some respects, expanding the list of products reserved for exclusive production in small units to 800-odd (end of 1970s); widening the definition to make 'small-scale trading and service establishments' eligible for government concessions like purchase preference in procurement; expansion of the scope of fiscal concessions (second half of the 1980s) (Mohan 2002); and establishment of a financial institution exclusively catering to small-scale units, namely the Small Industries Development Bank of India (SIDBI) in 1990. Garg et al. (1996) provide a long list of fiscal concessions including excise concessions, income tax reductions, investment subsidy, subsidy on loans, and transport subsidy. However, there are no estimates of revenue forgone by these measures nor can they be easily estimated due to their complex nature and lack of reliable data both on the number of eligible units and their characteristics to which fiscal concessions were related. However, even their elaborate listing brings out the rising political influence of this segment in the 1980s.

DISTURBANCE OF EARLIER DISTRIBUTIONAL COALITION

What implications did these major changes in polity have for the distributional coalition of the earlier slow-growth phase? Unlike the numerically small economic interest groups from the modern segment of the economy with their internal nexuses and transmission mechanisms operating mostly outside the budget during the dirigiste slow-growth phase 1951–81 (Chapter 4), the new economic interest groups of farmers and small traders/industrialists who barged into the distributional coalition in the 1980s to stake claims were from the informal segment of the economy, numerically large in magnitude, and resorted to mass politics making heavy demands on the exchequer. The pressures on the exchequer were also rising from two other sources. One, demands from the earlier powerful economic interest groups had grown as they expanded in size. Two, hesitant liberalization in the 1980s led to a gradual shrinkage of unproductive rental income generation which provided a major extra-budgetary source to meet the demands of the powerful interest groups in the earlier period. The resulting pressures on the fisc could not be met even from a stepped-up growth (to be discussed in the next section) and disturbed the earlier distributional equilibrium. This was reflected in the fiscal crisis of 1991 (that opened the window for the 1991 reforms to be discussed in the next chapter). In fact, the plea for liberalizing reforms was made in order to raise the growth rate and accommodate the rising demands for an orderly transition to a new distributional equilibrium (Dhar 1990 and 2003).

Our attribution of the rising fiscal deficit of the central government in the 1980s to the rising political clout and pressures of farmers and small industrialists/traders is admittedly inferential and aggregative rather than direct and specific. In our view, this could not be helped given the mostly non-transparent channels through which pressures were conceded using a variety of discretionary budgetary and non-budgetary devices.

A PARADIGM SHIFT: ECONOMIC PERFORMANCE IN THE 1980s

Interestingly, despite major changes in polity, the decade of the 1980s marked the emergence of the Indian economy out of a three-decade-long low-growth phase but with the undercurrent of fiscal and external payments crises which made the stepped-up 5.7 per cent average growth rate of GDP unsustainable. What explains the step-up in growth? A plausible explanation lies in some rethinking about the earlier policies with regard to effectiveness and the impact of two major international events in the 1970s that hastened the process of strategy reassessment and its translation into certain hesitant policy actions that received a helping hand from nature.

Since the mid-1960s, perceptive observers had come to realize the problems with the earlier autarkic and dirigiste industrialization strategy. An eminent academician and the then deputy chairman of the Planning Commission had pointed out that inefficiencies in the public sector, inability of the government to control activities in the private sector, and lack of competition were the primary factors underlying what he described as '*an extremely high cost economy*' (Gadgil 1968, 1973: 258). He advocated partial domestic liberalization but, possibly because of the then raging controversy over the 6 June 1966 devaluation, did not suggest relaxation of controls on external trade. Bhagwati and Desai (1970) and Bhagwati and Srinivasan (1976) argued a well-documented case for domestic as well as external liberalization. India's present economist Prime Minister recently admitted that he had, way back in 1972 on taking over as Chief Economic Adviser to the Ministry of Finance, suggested liberalization of controls on the private sector.[6]

Two major changes in the international economy prompted rethinking about the ideology of economic nationalism and the resulting policy of insulation from the world economy. The first was the breakdown of the Bretton Woods system of fixed exchange rates in 1972 when the US government decided to delink the US dollar from gold. This was the beginning of the floating exchange rate regime that was marked by violent fluctuations in currency rates of major trading nations. The second change consisted of two steep hikes in the price of oil by the Organisation of Petroleum Exporting Countries (OPEC) cartel first in 1973 and again in 1979 that raised the cost of universal energy input in all the oil-importing countries. With chronic foreign exchange shortages and almost total dependence on oil imports to meet the growing energy needs, both the events forced Indian's reluctant entry into the world economy. While fluctuating exchange rates and steep hikes in energy costs destabilized the growth process in many other developing countries, paradoxically they proved a blessing in disguise rather than a disaster for the Indian policymakers. The floating exchange rate regime provided a means of devaluing the Indian rupee without announcing it. This proved convenient to Indian policymakers in the background of the politically explosive nature of the 1966 devaluation.[7] The Indian policymakers linked the overvalued rupee to the British pound sterling that was depreciating with respect to the US dollar. When India's oil-import bill was rising because of the first oil shock, this covert devaluation helped boost general Indian exports besides locational proximity facilitating penetration of Indian exports into the petro-dollar-rich Middle Eastern markets. The Middle East also opened up the job market for Indian migrant labour with middle-level skills whose remittances kept adding to the foreign exchange reserves since the late 1970s. As a consequence, after the second oil price hike in 1979, the Government of India did not resort to stringent import controls as it did after the 1973 price hike. In fact, accumulating foreign exchange reserves from rising remittances in the 1980s possibly opened up a window for the hesitant trade liberalization that was undertaken in the 1980s. Like other oil-importing countries, India also experienced external payments imbalances but they were overcome with soft loans first from OPEC and then from the international multilateral agencies (Mitra and Tendulkar 1994). Thus the two major upheavals in the international economy in the 1970s that proved disastrous for other developing countries in fact provided elbowroom to Indian policymakers and helped *favourably incline them* towards rethinking the earlier ideology of economic nationalism.

Turning now to the 1980s, during the final tenure of Mrs Gandhi as prime minister from 1980 that tragically ended in her assassination in 1984, she made some departures from the earlier radical stance and towards hesitant liberalization of the discretionary control regime. The first inkling is available in the intentions reflected in the Industrial Policy Statement (IPS) of July 1980. Although the IPS traced its origins to the earlier Industrial Policy Resolution of 1956 (Chapter 3), there was no reference to the Nehruvian socialist pattern of society among its eight socio-economic objectives. The top two objectives were optimum utilization of installed capacity and maximum production and achieving higher productivity in that order, thus bringing upfront the urgency of growth. The second major departure in the IPS related to the public sector: 'Noting *the erosion of people's faith in the public sector*, it is decided to launch a drive to revive the efficiency of public sector undertakings through a time-bound programme of corrective action on a unit by unit basis' (emphasis added).

The statement of intentions in the IPS was followed by the appointment of three official committees to re-examine the earlier discretionary control regime. These were headed by competent civil servants who had first-hand experience of the implementation of the earlier policies and who had been aware of their competition-restricting and growth-constricting consequences. The policy areas covered by these committees included controls on domestic investment, on imports and on capital issues (M. Narasimham committee), import and export policies (Abid Hussain committee), and public sector enterprises (Arjun Sengupta committee). The first two committees recommended cautious and hesitant liberalization of mostly prima facie counterproductive direct discretionary controls on investment, capital market, imports, and exports while the third suggested limited autonomy for public-sector undertakings. All the committees submitted their reports by December 1984 when Mrs Gandhi's son, Rajiv Gandhi with a massive majority of 415 seats in the lower house of 543 members, took over as Prime Minister after the assassination of his mother. Rajiv Gandhi belonged to the post-Independence generation that did not carry the baggage of socialism and was eager to usher a modernized India into the twenty-first century. Acting on the recommendations of the official committees that had submitted their reports earlier, he introduced reasonably wide-ranging de facto domestic investment liberalization but went about very cautiously on the external trade front.

On the domestic investment front, while the comprehensive formal system of industrial licensing under the Industries (Development and Regulation) Act 1951 remained intact, a large number of exempted industries were notified under specified provisions of the Act from time to time. These comprised complete de-licensing of certain industries, 'broad banding' of some others to establish capacity in related industries, permission to expand capacity up to 25 per cent of the maximum production in the preceding three years without seeking fresh licence, and industries with minimum efficient scale. There was also considerable relaxation of restrictions on large industrial houses falling under the Monopolies and Restrictive Trade Practices (MRTP) Act. In external trade, rules for importation of technology were considerably liberalized in view of the technology backlog caused by an earlier autarkic policy, and quantitative controls on (mostly non-competing) imports were replaced by tariffs to bring privately earned import premia into government revenues (see Desai 1999 and Panagariya 2004 for details). These measures reflected a more positive attitude towards harnessing the role of the markets and private business for development in welcome contrast to the earlier adversarial approach.

Similarly, there was some recognition of the fact that the lower profitability and losses of commercial PSEs could no longer be camouflaged under 'public interest' and were admitted to be due to poor management, absence of or limited professional and expert knowledge, inappropriate pricing policies, and bureaucratic and political interference (Rudolph and Rudolph 1987: 34). In order to improve their financial performance, central PSEs were given limited autonomy through the instrument of memorandum of understanding (MoU). A white paper on long-term fiscal policy was placed before parliament. Partial deregulation of the financial sector added to financial deepening. The price and distribution controls that had led to persistent shortages and corruption were also removed in the case of cement and aluminium. This led to the expansion of production and alleviation of shortages.

All these measures reduced the glaring degree of incompatibility (discussed in Chapter 3) that existed during the slow-growth phase between the regulatory regime of command and controls and the existing institutional environment of functioning markets and productive profit-seeking private ownership of means of production. They relaxed the supply constraints on existing capacity utilization and capacity creation in areas where shortages persisted. By themselves, they were not sufficient to step up the growth rate of aggregate GDP in the absence of stimulus from domestic demand. In what was then a very closed economy with import tariffs reaching their peak average levels in the 1980s, domestic demand stimulus to induce supply response might have been provided by an above average agricultural growth combined with an expansionary fiscal stance that led to fiscal crisis at the end of the decade. The fact that the demand stimulus came from the domestic market can be seen in the tiny share of exports in the sales of the domestic corporates and a very limited opening of the economy that did not dent much the higher profitability of selling in the domestic markets relative to external markets. In fact, trade to GDP ratio *declined* from 13.1 per cent in the first half to 12.4 per cent in the second half of the 1980s. The domestic market expansion was triggered by a healthy average annual growth rate of 4.4 per cent in agriculture and allied activities and rising consolidated fiscal deficits of the central and the state governments from 6.3 per cent of GDP in 1981–2 to 9.4 per cent in 1990–1. As a consequence there was a step-up in the average aggregate growth rate of GDP from 3 per cent in the 1970s to 5.7 per cent in the 1980s comprising 7 per cent growth in manufacturing and 6.7 per cent in services. This certainly heralded the emergence of the Indian economy from a thirty-year-long low-growth equilibrium. What is more important is that the stepped-up growth in the 1980s came from less wasteful utilization of resources, which can be seen from a reduced magnitude of ICOR (Table 4.1). However, it was unsustainable because of the still widespread persistence of distorted prices despite relaxation of some controls and, more important for distributional equilibrium, the undercurrent of fiscal and external payments imbalances to which we turn in the next chapter.

NOTES

1. These groups have been termed as 'demand groups' by Rudolph and Rudolph (1987) and their emergence 'mass politics' by Varshney (1999).
2. The political urgency was triggered by the US Administration's attempt to extract crude political leverage by holding back emergency PL480 food aid to force Indian to support the then raging Vietnam War (see Chaudhry et al. 2004. India opposed the Vietnam War as part of Nehru's Non-Alignment Foreign Policy). This was perceived by all the political parties as an attack on India's sovereignty a fact that reflected the pervasive influence of the legacy of economic nationalism.
3. The index of returns over operational costs computed by Varshney (1995: 162–3) shows a dip in the second half of the 1970s for wheat in Punjab, a flip-flop behaviour for wheat in Uttar Pradesh, and a continuous rise for paddy in Punjab after a dip in 1974–5.

4. See Varshney (1995: 101–5) for details.
5. The members of the parliament with agriculture/ horticulture as reported occupation increased from 22.5 per cent (99 out of 499 seats in the first election in 1952) to one-third (168 out of 521) in 1971, 39.3 per cent (206 out of 544) in 1980, and 44.1 per cent (230 out of 529) in 1989.
6. Interview published in the *Indian Express*, 23 May 2004, p. 7.
7. See Bhagwati and Srinivasan (1976: ch. 10); Bhagwati et al. (1972); and Sundaram (1972a and b).

6

The 1991 Reforms: Context and Timing

THE FISCAL CRISIS OF THE 1980s

To recapitulate briefly, we argued (Chapters 4 and 5) that there existed a possible low-growth, low fiscal, and external payments deficit distributional equilibrium during the first three decades of planning indeed with distorted prices caused by growth-constricting and competition-limiting direct discretionary controls on international trade, domestic investment, and markets. In the 1980s, numerically large groups of farmers and small traders and industrialists started asserting their rising political clout by making claims on the government revenues through parliamentary as well as extra-parliamentary channels (like mass demonstrations) while the demands of the earlier distributional coalition continued to rise in magnitude as reflected in the indiscriminate expansion of public-sector entities at all levels of government. Underpricing of the public as well as non-public goods and services they produced provided a major non-transparent mechanism of transfer for meeting the growing claims. Several ministries and departments were also directly engaged in producing and supplying non-public goods and services whose uncovered cost added to the government's revenue expenditure.

While the combined effect of the claims made by the political pressure groups that were accommodated through budgetary devices would get reflected in the overall gross fiscal deficits (which can be documented), three caveats are important here. One is the problem of attribution. It is not possible to pinpoint the claims of individual groups except by drawing on specific studies relating to them, which often use concepts and data that cannot be made directly comparable to the budgetary classification. Second, the deficit being the difference between the two magnitudes is the result also of complex and often non-transparent accounting adjustments across budgetary heads of expenditure. Finally, public expenditures would also include legitimate expenses of governance, which are not easy to segregate nor their cost-effectiveness easy to assess.

Hesitant and gradual de facto relaxation of discretionary controls in the 1980s started slowly eroding the scope for directly unproductive profit-seeking incomes that provided an important source of transfer to the powerful interest groups not only without impinging on the budget but even adding to the revenues in the slow-growth period. With its constitutionally stronger financial position, the central budget became the battleground of distributional coalition consisting of a criss-cross of vertical mobilizations of numerically large groups of farmers and small traders/industrialists in the 1980s, which added their demands on the fisc to the continued claims of numerically small but over time growing economic interest groups of the slow-growth period. This started getting reflected in the fiscal position of the central government. After averaging less than 4 per cent of GDP till the 1970s, the gross fiscal deficits of the central government started an upward climb from 5.77 per cent in 1980–1 to reach a peak of 8.47 per cent in 1986–7 and stayed higher than 7 per cent in the remaining years, ending up at 7.85 per cent in 1990–1. The revenue account remained increasingly in deficit after 1979–80, ending up at the then highest level of 3.26 per cent of GDP in 1990–1 (Figure 6.1).

Fiscal deficit being the difference between revenue and capital expenditure and current receipts plus non-debt sources of capital receipts, important components on the revenue and expenditure side are presented in Figure 6.2, which shows a rising trend of current revenue expenditure (topmost graph) and a downward trend in capital expenditure since the mid-1980s despite a slower but rising trends in both revenue and (total debt and non-debt) capital receipts. The pressure on current revenue expenditure at the cost of expenditure on capital account since the mid-1980s is obvious.

FIGURE 6.1
Deficits of the Central Government 1970–1 to 1990–1

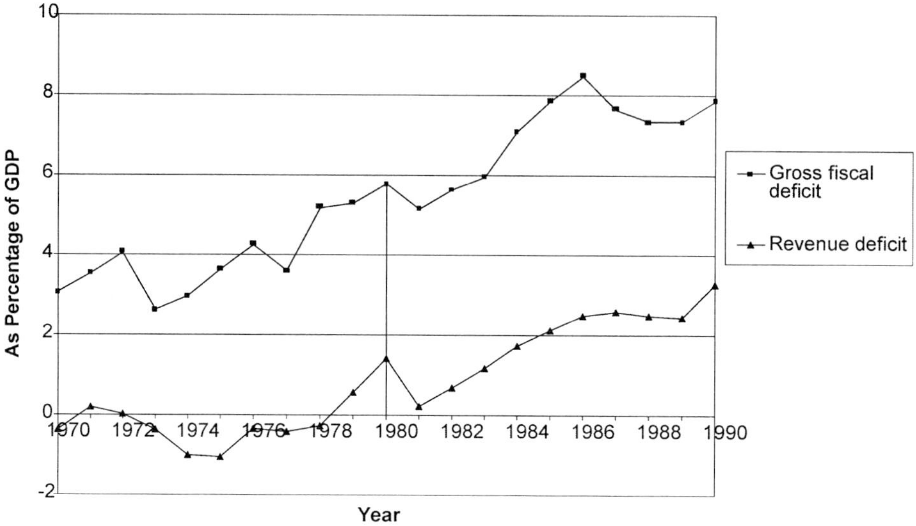

Source: RBI (2002–3), *Handbook of Statistics on the Indian Economy*, Table 221.

FIGURE 6.2
Expenditure and Receipts of the Central Government 1970–1 to 1990–1

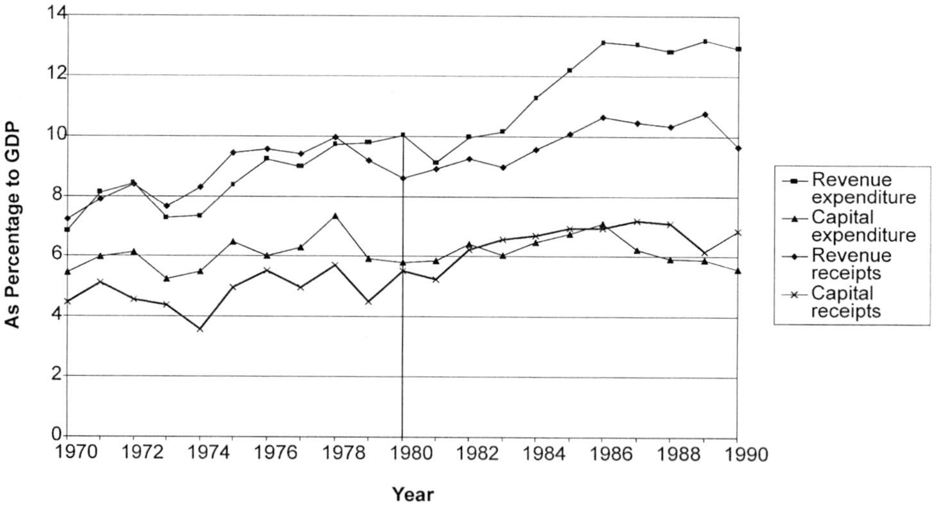

Source: RBI (2002–3), *Handbook of Statistics on the Indian Economy*, Table 221.

Major components of the current expenditure are shown in Figure 6.3. A steep rise in the interest payments in the 1980s was the combined result of a rise in the weighted average interest rate on central government securities (from 7.03 per cent in 1980–1 to 11.41 per cent in 1990–1 [RBI 2003: Table 114]) and a much steeper rise

FIGURE 6.3
Major Components of Expenditure of the Central Government 1970–1 to 1990–1

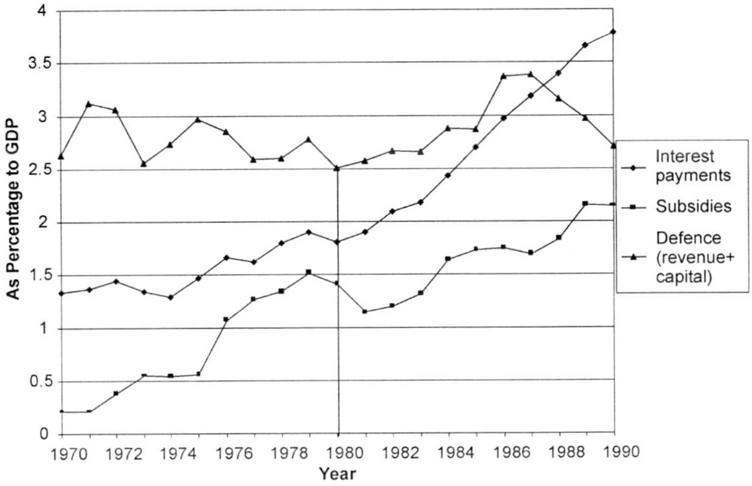

Source: RBI, (2002–3), *Handbook of Statistics on the Indian Economy*, Table 221.

in the volume of borrowings with the domestic liabilities of the centre rising from 33.7 per cent of GDP in 1980–1 to 49.8 per cent in 1990–1 (RBI 2003: Table 224). A significant rise in explicit budgetary subsidies is also apparent. Food and fertilizer subsidies showed continuous upward climb in the 1980s with fertilizer subsidies (that benefit all categories of [surplus-producing as well as deficit] farmers) becoming increasingly more important than food subsidies in the 1980s (Figure 6.4). They came to occupy an increasingly dominant combined share in the central subsidy bill . Their share exceeded 70 per cent from 1983–4 to 1988–9 and stayed between 55 and 65 per

FIGURE 6.4
Composition of Total Central Government Subsidies (%)

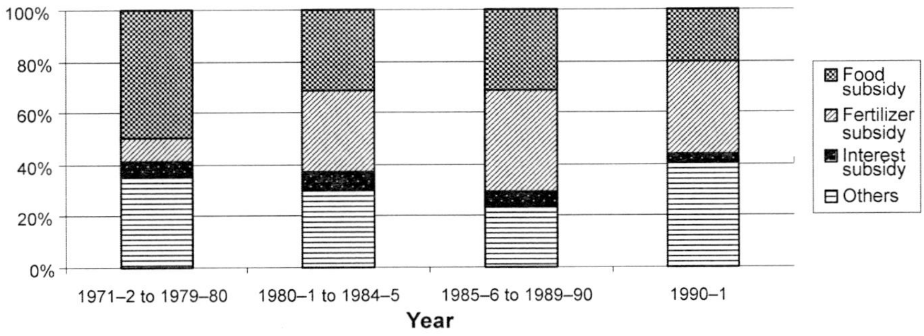

Sources: Srivastava and Sen (1997). *Government Subsidies in India*. National Institute of Public Finance and Policy, Annexure I, for 1971–2 to 1996–7.

cent in the remaining years of the 1980s (Srivastava and Sen 1997: Annexure 3, p. 139).

THE EXTERNAL PAYMENTS CRISIS OF THE 1980s

We now turn to a discussion of the external payments crisis that erupted in India towards the end of the 1980s. We noted in the last chapter, that India benefited on balance from the oil price hikes of the 1970s. Despite the second oil price hike in 1979–80 and the consequent recession in world trade, India's current account deficit did not show any significant deterioration in the first half of the 1980s with merchandise trade deficit improving from 4.3 per cent of GDP in 1980–1 to 2.7 per cent in 1984–5. With invisibles buoyed by rising remittances remaining in surplus though falling, the current account deficit fluctuated around 1.5 per cent of GDP (RBI 2003: Table 225 and Figure 6.5). It is since 1985–6 that serious imbalances emerged (Figure 6.5) with progressive deterioration of deficits on merchandise account and rapid erosion of surpluses on invisible account resulting from the end of the economic boom in the Gulf countries and its consequent effect on remittances from the Gulf

FIGURE 6.5
India's Trade Balance, Invisible Balance, and Current Account Balance 1980–1 to 1990–1

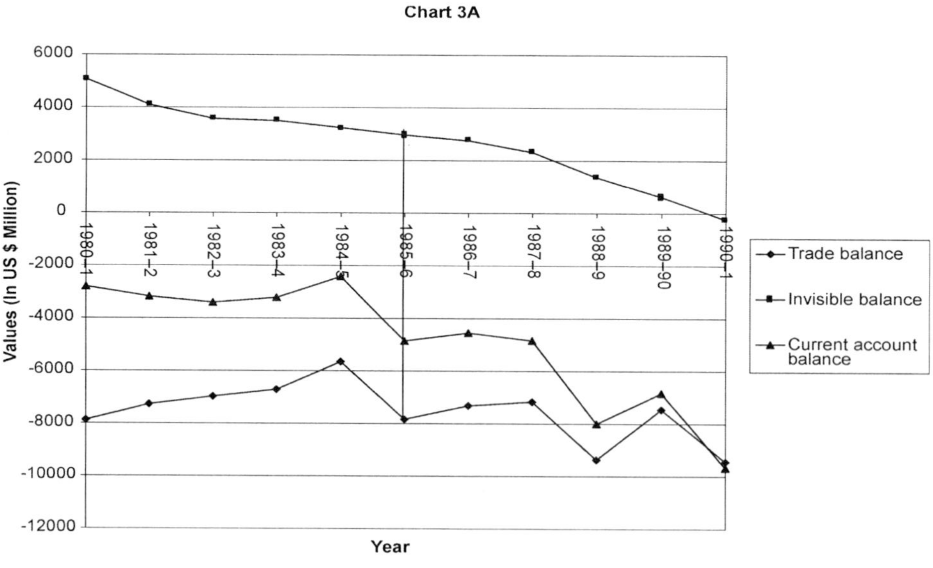

Source: RBI (2002–3), *Handbook of Statistics on the Indian Economy*, Table 135.

FIGURE 6.6
India's Merchandise Exports, Imports, and Trade Balance in US Dollars 1980–1 to 1990–1

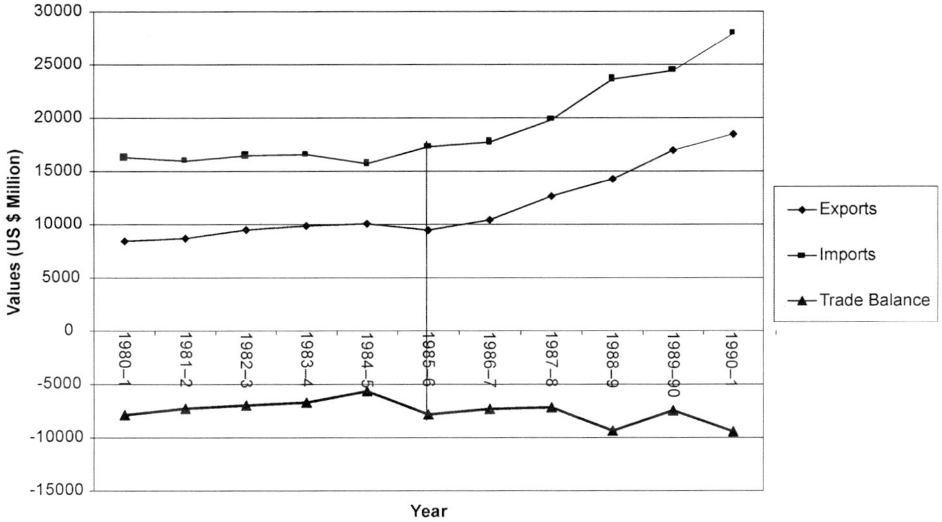

Source: RBI (2002–3), *Handbook of Statistics on the Indian Economy*, Table 135.

immigrants. This happened despite rapid expansion of merchandise exports (Figure 6.6) after 1986–7 with the next three years recording 24.1 per cent, 15.6 per cent, and 18.9 per cent growth rates in US dollar terms. Three factors contributed to the export performance. From the stagnation caused by the oil price hikes in the 1970s, the recovery in the volume of non-energy world exports after 1986 helped Indian exports. Second, the index of nominal effective exchange rate (NEER)[1] started depreciating rapidly after 1985–6. Given a higher rate of inflation in India than that in trading partners, real effective exchange rate (REER) followed a less rapid downward drift (Figure 6.7) but the real exchange rate depreciation improved the international competitiveness of Indian exports. Three, the scope and level of export incentives were enhanced in the 1980s to offset the reduced profitability of exporters with import tariffs rising. However, Figure 6.6 shows rapid growth in imports as well. This is indicative of the excess demand pressures emanating from the rising fiscal deficits, which we noted earlier in this section. It is clear that capital inflows were unable to finance the current account deficits and foreign exchange reserves had to be drawn down continuously after 1985–6 (Figure 6.8). Traditionally, India's current account deficits have mostly been financed by concessional external aid.

FIGURE 6.7
Indices of REER and NEER of the Indian Rupee: Export-based Weights 1980–1 to 1990–1
(36-Country Bilateral Weights)

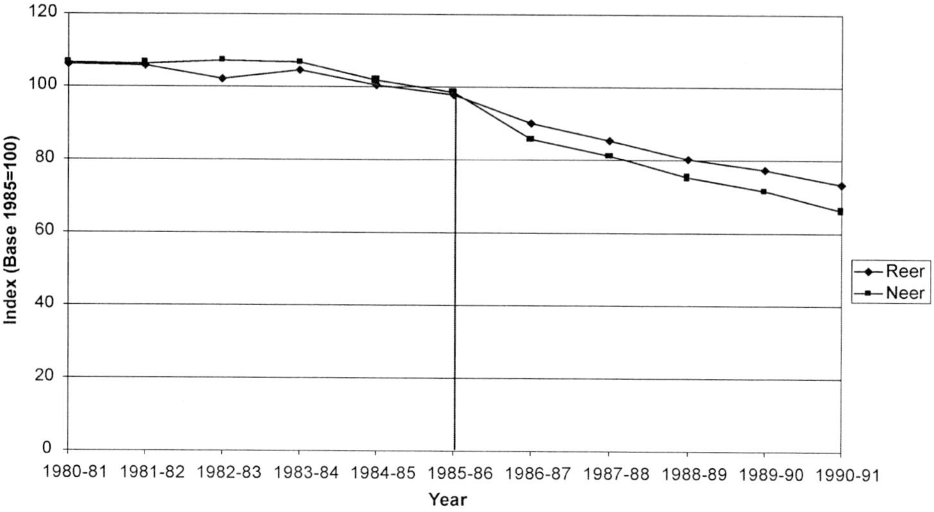

Note: REER: Real Effective Exchange Rate, NEER: Nominal Effective Exchange Rate
Source: RBI (2002–3), *Handbook of Statistics on the Indian Economy*, Table 142.

FIGURE 6.8
India's Current Account, Total Capital Inflows, and Changes in Foreign Exchange Reserves in US Dollars 1980–1 to 1990–1

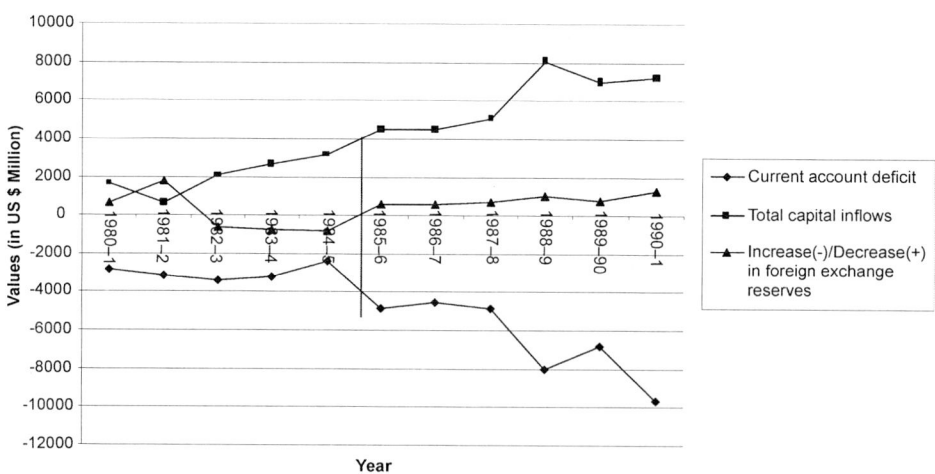

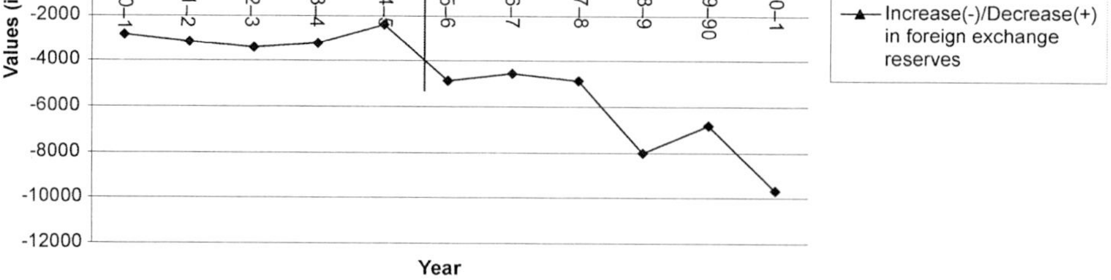

Source: RBI 2002–3, *Handbook of Statistics on the Indian Economy*, Table 135.

Figure 6.9 provides a picture of the major financing components of current account deficit with three new sources which contributed to the external payments crisis. In this figure, the residual component

FIGURE 6.9
Financing of Current Account Deficits 1980–1 to 1990–1

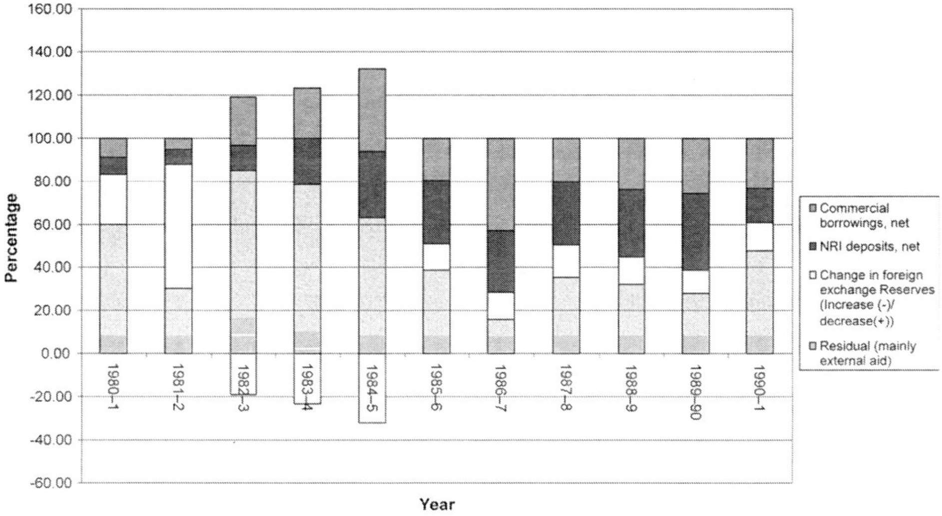

Source: RBI 2002–3, *Handbook of Statistics on the Indian Economy*, Table 135.

is mostly external aid which can be seen to be important in the first five years of the 1980s and whose relative share has been consistently lower since 1985–6. This was due to the drying up of external aid following the disruption caused by the energy price hikes in the developed countries. The government, therefore, had to look for alternative sources, one of which was the drawing down of foreign exchange reserves as noted in Figure 6.8. This was treated as a source of last resort in a foreign-exchange-constrained economy after exhausting other avenues of financing. In fact, the remittances from the Gulf migrants had made possible additions to the foreign exchange reserves from 1982–3 to 1984–5 (Figure 6.9). The two new sources that the government tapped were commercial borrowings in the international capital market and attracting deposits from non-resident Indians (NRI) by offering them more attractive terms. The last two sources, it may be noted, are not only more demanding and expensive in terms of debt-servicing obligations than external aid but are also volatile, being more vulnerable to expectations about foreign exchange risks. Even these two proved inadequate to bridge the widening current account deficit and resort had to be taken additionally to the most volatile, expensive, and demanding short-term debts whose rollover is subject to the confidence of foreign lenders in the solvency and policy of the government. The rising cost of more expensive new sources of financing started telling on the debt-service payments (as per cent of current foreign exchange receipts from merchandise exports and invisibles), which averaged as low as 13 per cent in the first half of the decade, shot up to 27.6 per cent in the next five years, and ended up at the highest level of 31.6 per cent[2] in 1990–1.

The rising current account deficits, steep rise in debt-servicing obligations, and depletion of foreign exchange reserves despite a rise in total external debt from US$ 20 billion in 1980–1 (12 per cent of GDP) to US$ 70 billion in 1990–1 (24 per cent of GDP) (World Bank 1992: 2) with a rising share of non-concessional loans led to a continuing decline in the import cover offered by the year-ending stock of foreign exchange reserves from 4.5 months in 1985–6 to the lowest level of 1.9 months[3] at the end of 1989–90. The export growth also slowed down to 9.2 per cent (in US dollar terms) in 1990–1 (from 18.9 per cent in 1989–90) as a result of breakdown of bilateral trade with the USSR and a slowdown in the Organization of Economic Cooperation and Development (OECD) countries. This constellation had been putting pressure on the foreign exchange rate that had been depreciating since 1985–6 (Figure 6.7). This pressure got further intensified by two exogenous shocks. The first came from the polity. Rajiv Gandhi who was elected in 1984 with an unprecedented majority of 415 seats out of 542 in the Lok Sabha, was defeated in the next general elections in 1989 where his party managed barely 197 seats out of 529. The immediate post-election period was marked by political instability with two non-Congress governments falling in quick succession necessitating a mid-term election in May 1991. This generated uncertainty in the minds of foreign lenders. It was further exacerbated by an external shock, namely a quantum jump in the price of imported petroleum, oil, and lubricants (POL) following the invasion of Kuwait by Iraq in August 1990 doubling the oil import bill from US$ 3.0 billion in 1988–9 to US$ 6.0 billion in 1990–1, or from a quarter of export earnings to one-third. The outflow of Gulf migrants leading to a reduction in remittances pushed the invisibles account into a deficit in 1990–1 for the first time in the decade. These exogenous events added to the already mounting pressures since 1985–6 on the exchange rate fuelling expectations about imminent devaluation, and resulted in the heavy pre-redemption withdrawals of NRI deposits (by paying penal interest rates) and drying up of commercial borrowings. In the face of capital outflow, the government resorted increasingly to short-term borrowings, which shot up from 5.3 per cent of foreign exchange reserves at the end of 1988–9 to 23.1 per cent at the end of 1989–90, and to as high as 146.5 per cent of foreign exchange reserves at the end of 1990–1.[4] This is when the international rating agencies in the US and Japan downgraded India's bonds so that rollover of short-term commercial debts became impossible and the unprecedented default on international debt loomed large. This unprecedented event shook the polity although, as noted earlier, a more serious undercurrent of growing fiscal deficits had already been leading up to a crisis.

Before turning to the response to the twin-crises next, we may mention at this point the findings of a very interesting study by Cerra and Saxena (2002) who analysed the causes of the 1991 currency crisis employing error correction econometric models and using quarterly data from 1979 to 1999. They postulated a time-varying long-term equilibrium rate of exchange,[5] which was made a function of certain economic fundamentals[6] suggested by various theoretical models. They found (p. 418) that the econometrically estimated long-term equilibrium path of real effective exchange rate (REER) on the basis of economic fundamentals was consistently below the actual path of REER (from the third quarter of 1985 to the first quarter of 1993) from the RBI data implying that the REER remained overvalued despite its downward drift in the annual data noted in Figure 6.7 as the moving equilibrium REER itself kept sliding downward. Our interpretation of this result is that the external payments crisis would have occurred even in the absence of exogenous shocks, which merely hastened its arrival and offered a window of opportunity as the external payments crisis shook the polity much more than the brewing fiscal crisis.

THE CONTEXT OF REFORMS: THE CRITICAL ROLE OF THE EXTERNAL PAYMENTS CRISIS

Twin crises of fiscal deficits and defaults on foreign debt provided the context of the 1991 reforms as the absence of reforms on both the fronts would have made the higher growth of the 1980s unsustainable and the emergence of a viable new distributional equilibrium impossible. We dealt with the fiscal crisis in detail because of its origin in the changing political economy, which also contributed to the external payments crisis whose origins were partly economic and partly exogenous. However, it was the external payments crisis and not the fiscal crisis, and the unprecedented spectre of default on foreign loans that shook the polity. Why? The possible reason lies in the deep-rooted and still widespread hold of the doctrine of economic nationalism (Chapters 1 and 3) and associated solvency in external payments as a matter of national pride and prestige. During the Bretton Woods regime of fixed exchange rates, devaluation of the Indian rupee by Indira Gandhi's government on 6 June 1966 (when the Indian currency was indeed overvalued) became embroiled in political controversy, with the measure being seen as having been taken under US pressure, and became inextricably linked to the loss of national prestige and sovereignty. It was criticized politically and in the press as a blow to India's sovereignty on the basis of its alleged demerits (Bhagwati and Srinivasan 1976: ch.10; Bhagwati et al. 1972; and Sundaram 1972a and b). The brewing fiscal crisis in the 1980s did not have the same emotional urgency in the Indian political psychology so long as it did not result in very high rates of inflation as on the past two occasions following severe agricultural droughts. Similarly, in the face of dwindling foreign exchange reserves in 1990 (following the Gulf War in August), the then short-lived central government (second since 1989) headed by Chandra Shekhar had to undertake emergency measures to avoid default on external debt. There were adverse political and press reactions to these measures that included borrowing of US$ 1.8 billion from the International Monetary Fund (IMF) under the Contingent Compensatory Finance Facility (CCFF) on 23 January 1991 and US$ 400 million from the Bank of England by shipping India's gold stocks in the spring of 1991, and sales of US$ 200 million of gold at the same time. The Finance Minister of the successor minority government (with outside support) that assumed power in June 1991 vowed in his budget speech to bring back the gold shipped to the Bank of England.

Along with the unprecedented external crisis, the polity was also shaken by the equally unprecedented political instability with two general elections and three central governments in a brief span of eighteen months between November 1989 and May 1991. After facing the electorates twice in a matter of one and a half years and violent changes in the electoral fortunes of different parties over this brief time-span, no elected member of parliament relished the thought of facing the electorate again before completing the five-year term. Needless to add, the political instability, by itself, was inimical to reforms and would not have resulted in reforms in the absence of the external payments crisis. The crisis-gripped atmosphere generated by their joint occurrence not only helped the minority government (with outside support) that assumed power in June 1991 survive and successfully complete its five-year term but also enabled the politically lightweight reforming minority within the government to undertake wide-ranging fiscal and structural reforms.

THE TIMING OF REFORMS: WHY 1991 AND NOT EARLIER?

The Congress government of Prime Minister P.V. Narasimha Rao came to power in the wake of the external payments crisis in June 1991 after the tragic assassination earlier of Rajiv Gandhi at an election rally. The Congress was the largest single party, forty-one members short of majority in the lower house of parliament. It was supported from outside by five regional parties. Rao was the second Prime Minister of the Congress Party not belonging to the Nehru–Gandhi family and he lacked a charismatic personality. He appointed Dr Manmohan Singh, a professionally trained economist with over two decades of experience in economic administration at various top-level positions in policymaking in the central government, as his finance minister. He was not a Member of Parliament or of the Congress Party or any other political party. His sole qualification in the context of the external payments crisis was that he commanded considerable respect and credibility in multilateral and international financial institutions. Prime Minister Rao was convinced that without assistance from the international bodies, the country would not be able to overcome the external payment crisis.

We noted earlier that the preceding short-lived Chandra Shekhar government had withdrawn the first tranche from the IMF's CCFF on 23 January 1991. The following budget presented in normal course on the last day of February every year was to meet the qualification criteria, namely to disinflate the economy, lower fiscal deficit, and improve balance of payments.[7] The government fell before the budget, parliament was dissolved, and mid-term elections ensued in May 1991. The second tranche of the CCFF was due in July before which the IMF expected corrective measures. These were presented in the (delayed) budget of Manmohan Singh in June 1991. The proposed (mutually negotiated) corrective measures included a strong dose of fiscal contraction and structural reforms involving, among others, an increase in prices of petroleum products,[8] a rise in tax–GDP ratio by 0.5 per cent, disinvestments up to 20 per cent equity in some PSEs to yield 0.4 per cent of GDP, a sharp cut in the central subsidy bill (abolition of sugar and export subsidies and a cut in fertilizer subsidy), a reduction in defence expenditure by 0.5 per cent of GDP, and a cut of 0.3 per cent in budgetary support to PSEs. The macroeconomic stabilization of aggregate demand through fiscal contraction was combined with industrial, financial, and trade policy changes which 'over the *last ten months* liberalized what was one of the most closed and regulated (*market*) economies in the world' (World Bank 1992: i, emphasis added).

It may be noted that many of the elements of structural reforms undertaken by the minority government of Narasimha Rao are found in milder form in Rajiv Gandhi's efforts in the same direction in the second half of the 1980s that failed despite unprecedented majority in the parliament.

This raises interesting questions about the timing of reforms. Why did they take place in 1991 even though the structural distortions had been apparent and noted by perceptive observers since the mid-1960s and even though India's Asian neighbours—not just from East and South East Asia but also from South Asia—had undertaken liberalization measures much earlier? (Tendulkar and Sen 2003; World Bank 2004). A partial answer to this question is available in Chapter 3 where it was noted that under Mrs Gandhi's regime from 1966 to 1977, populist radicalization became a substitute for reforms. But this still leaves unanswered the reasons for the absence of demonstration effect from the Asian neighbours. Two interrelated factors might have operated. Both have to do with the autarkic development strategy. The first is a cultural factor, noted earlier, namely the long-established and well-entrenched suspicion of markets in a society where a high moral stance was preferred to a pragmatic one (despite practice to the contrary), self-interest was wrongly identified with narrow selfishness, and profit-making from productive activities with speculative profiteering and greed so that capitalism was regarded as an *immoral* rather than ethically neutral amoral economic system. The second factor was the tendency among policymakers and intellectuals to treat the Indian case as unique in an effort to find 'Indian' solutions to 'Indian' problems rather learning from other economies which were deemed to be 'too small' to hold any lessons for a 'large' economy like India.

However, the phenomenon of populist radicalization under Mrs Gandhi still leaves unanswered another important question about timing. How is it that the minority government of the Congress Party with outside support managed to push wide-ranging reforms with just 211 seats out of 511 in 1991 when Rajiv Gandhi's government of the same party with an overwhelming majority of 415 seats in a house of 543 could not during 1984–9. This despite Rajiv Gandhi's open criticism of the earlier autarkic strategy and his express desire to take the modernized technology-driven India into the twenty-first century?

Rajiv Gandhi failed because (i) his attempts to scale down subsidies on kerosene, foodgrains, fertilizers, and diesel provided opportunities for vertical mass mobilizations against his government even though the upward climb of the subsidy bill continued due to later rollback; and (ii) corruption charges against his government. Both these factors made him vulnerable to attack from radical anti-reform ideologues. We suggest that two international and two domestic contingent events further contributed to the timing of reforms in 1991.

Internationally, two major events undermined the basic premises of the earlier social consensus regarding the development strategy. The first was the collapse of the erstwhile USSR (that provided not only a political alliance in the Cold War period but also an implicit economic role model of planned rapid economic development over the previous half century) and the East European socialist regimes, and their bumpy rides towards a market-oriented economic system seriously undermined India's long-established faith in the efficacy of economic planning.[9]

More important, the spectacular success of the so-called 'socialist market economy' of China with the aggressive opening up since 1978 and its associated achievements in poverty reduction raised serious doubts about the efficacy of persistent inward orientation and the underlying ideology of economic nationalism. Both these external events put the radical ideologues on the defensive and toned down the clamour of 'pro-rich' bias in liberalization that haunted Rajiv Gandhi's efforts in the 1980s.

Domestically, we pinpoint two factors: First, the hesitant liberalization efforts in the 1980s, helped by healthy agricultural growth, managed to bring about a doubling of the per capita GDP growth in comparison with the previous three decades along with a reduction in absolute poverty that had fluctuated without trend during the earlier slow-growth phase (Ahluwalia 1978; Tendulkar and Jain 1995; Tendulkar 1997). Although the twin crises of fiscal deficit and external payments made this growth unsustainable, the growth performance strengthened the hands of the pro-liberalization minority in the bureaucracy and in government that has been instrumental in the systemic liberalization in the 1990s. This minority was also helped by pressures from the IMF and the World Bank. Without the bailout package from these multilateral financial institutions, the spectre of default on foreign loans that shook the polity could not have been avoided. The polity, therefore, reluctantly went along with the liberalizing reforms.

Second, as mentioned in the previous section, the two parliamentary elections in quick succession (November 1989 and May 1991) and fluctuating electoral fortunes with hung parliaments and two unstable governments created a tremendous sense of insecurity among the elected representatives who were more interested in continuing for the full term of five years than in destabilizing the minority government. While making strident criticisms of the reform efforts in parliamentary debates, no opposition party issued a whip at the time of voting on critical resolutions, which could have defeated the minority government, so that members either abstained or absented themselves at the time of voting. Varshney (1999: 246 in support of a different hypothesis) provides an interesting discussion of the voting pattern, changing coalitions, and quotes from parliamentary debates in passing the first three central budgets of the minority government that could have defeated the government. In our view, the outcome described by Varshney could also have emerged from the polity shaken by the external payments crisis and the insecurity of elected members.

It was the nationally crisis-gripped atmosphere that made it possible to undertake a very sharp fiscal contraction equivalent to a reduction of 2.3 percentage points of GDP in gross fiscal deficit between the crisis year of 1990–1 and 1991–2. It consisted of a 0.63 point decline in revenue expenditure, 0.45 point rise in revenue receipts, and a sharp 1.3 point decline in capital expenditure. Within revenue expenditure, the subsidy reduction was 0.55 points, which was higher than overall average reduction in revenue expenditure (RBI 2003: Table 221). There was an expected sharp dip in aggregate real GDP growth from 5.6 per cent in 1990–1 to 1.3 per cent in the next year of fiscal contraction. The low growth rate was composed of a sharp decline of 3.7 per cent in manufacturing GDP (and a bigger dip of 2.3 per cent in its factory segment) and a 1.6 per cent reduction in GDP originating in agriculture and allied activities.[10] There was a reduced but positive growth in other major sectors, which offset the negative growth in manufacturing and agriculture. Only in GDP originating in public administration and defence, which was not affected by fiscal contraction, was the growth rate *higher* in 1991–2 than in 1990–1. Hence, barring the bureaucrats in government, all other economic interest groups (public-sector professionals, large industrialists, agriculturists, and small trader/ industrialists) accepted without protest the adverse effects of fiscal contraction and its expected adverse impact on growth to meet the national crisis.[11] The same argument applies to the early structural reform initiatives that were undertaken by the reforming minority in the Rao government and in bureaucracy. The number of ministers in the Rao cabinet, who were reformers by conviction, was only two and they had no political base. Others reluctantly accepted them as necessary evils for overcoming the external payments crisis and hence did not express their hostility openly.

The crisis, which could have resulted in a disaster, was turned into an opportunity. The opposition parties, indeed, were strident in their criticism of reforms (which were described as 'abject surrender to the IMF') but, as mentioned earlier, did not allow the minority government supported from outside to fall while passing the three successive budgets of Manmohan Singh as reported in Varshney (1999). The reforms were undertaken 'by stealth' as described by Jenkins (1999). Manmohan Singh in his first budget speech on 24 July 1991 paid tribute to the legacy of Nehru and Mrs Gandhi while (at a different point in his speech) admitting that 'overcentralisation and excessive burearucratisation of economic processes have proved to be counterproductive. We need to expand the scope and the area for the operation of market forces. A *reformed price system can be a superior instrument of resource allocation than quantitative controls*' (para 20, emphasis added). Departing from the convention of confining the budget speech to only budgetary matters of revenue, expenditure, and budget deficit, he unfurled systemic reforms in industrial, trade, foreign investment, capital market, and public-sector policies without admitting or mentioning the sharp break with the past and major shift in development strategy. In the next budget speech on 29 February 1992, he also (re)defined 'the vision of a self-reliant economy', as one 'which can meet all its import requirements through exports, without undue dependence on artificial external props such as foreign aid' (para 15)[12] and argued for private foreign investment, observing 'we must not remain permanent captives of the East India Company, as if nothing has changed in the past 300 years' (para 22). Even though the departures from past policies and strategy were obvious, they were not openly admitted to be so. Clearly, the Congress Party with its past history of socialist rhetoric could not afford to do so. More importantly, given the aversion of democratic regimes to sharp changes in status quo, which is further reinforced by the diversities in Indian society, a non-confrontational approach appeared to be a superior strategy. But the flip side was that in the absence of any open discussion of the political costs and benefits, the situation produced only a handful of reformers by conviction (some of whom had been so even prior to the crisis)[13] and mostly reformers by convenience.

NOTES

1. Since the mid-1970s, the exchange rate of a rupee had been linked to an (unspecified) basket of currencies.
2. The figures are based on the time series of debt-service obligations for the 1980s from the *World Debt Tables*, 1989–90 and 1990–1 of the World Bank. The

Economic Survey started providing this information only from 1990–1. A comparison with the figures available from the Reserve Bank of India (*Bulletin*, September 1991 for 1988–9 to 1990–1, and October 1993 from 1988–9 to 1993–4, and *Annual Report* 1994–5 from 1988–9 to 1991–2) suggests that the debt-service obligations in the *World Debt Tables* exclude those on non-civilian external debt but include accrued interest on NRI deposits. They are, therefore, underestimates for the second half of the 1980s when non-civilian defence imports are reported to have taken place.

3. The import cover of foreign exchange reserves dwindled further to as low as two weeks and reserve levels to $ 1 billion by end June 1991, when the minority government took over after the mid-term elections in May 1991.
4. The figure for 1990–1 is from the Economic Survey while the earlier figures are based on the World Bank's World Debt Tables where short-term debt is listed from 1985 to 1990.
5. Notice that in the dynamic context over time, equilibrium exchange rate does not remain constant but varies according to changing fundamentals not only of the Indian economy but also of India's trading partners in the global economy. Hence it is postulated as time varying in character.
6. Economic fundamentals are determinants of sustainability of economic growth of an economy. They are usually taken to be reflected in certain key interrelated indicators associated with economic growth such as current external account balance and fiscal balance in relation to GDP or, alternatively, rate of inflation, interest rate, and foreign exchange rate.
7. We draw on Desai (1999) in the following discussion.
8. The domestic prices of (mostly) imported petroleum products were artificially maintained lower than international prices by forcing the government-owned oil companies to bear the implicit subsidy.
9. Even before their collapse, the leading centrally planned economies had started exploring market-oriented options in various forms in trying to overcome persistent shortages. See Brus and Laski (1989).
10. Aggregate GDP growth rates at constant 1993–4 prices are given in RBI (2003: Table 211). The sectoral growth rates were worked out from the *National Accounts Statistics* of the Central Statistical Organisation.
11. We may mention that the efforts of Mrs Gandhi to reduce the fiscal deficit by 1.4 percentage points of GDP from 1972–3 to 1973–4 (RBI 2003: Table 221) to rein in very high inflationary pressures in the wake of drought were met with hostile social and political protests.
12. We may recall from n. 3 of Chapter 3, Nehru's emphasis on 'national self-sufficiency' to appreciate the 'redefinition' four decades later.
13. In a recent television interview before the 2004 general elections, Dr Manmohan Singh revealed that as far back as in 1972 he had suggested economic liberalization in a paper he had submitted to the then Prime Minister Mrs Indira Gandhi. See *Indian Express*, Pune, 23 May 2004, op ed., p. 7.

7

Continuing Reforms in the Era of Coalition Politics

The 1991 reforms were initiated as part of the mutually negotiated conditionalities associated with the bailout packages from the IMF and the World Bank in the wake of the external payments crisis. However, by 1993–4, the formal pressure had eased as the IMF loan with conditionalities was paid back with improvement in private capital inflows and accumulation of foreign exchange reserves. The ratio of short-term debt to foreign exchange reserves dropped to 18.6 per cent in 1993–4 from its disastrous 146.5 per cent level in the crisis year, and the import cover of foreign exchange reserves improved to a healthy 8.6 months from 2.5 months. However, the Rao government continued reforms well beyond the conditionalities. While the pace of reforms has varied over the last fifteen years, the direction of the systemic reform process towards liberalization and globalization has remained unchanged and withstood several prima facie formidable hurdles. The first has been the emergence of coalition governments at the centre for prolonged duration over one decade for the first time in Indian politics. This form of government is usually deemed inimical to stability and hence to the reform process. The second factor has been the political instability created by two mid-term polls in quick succession in 1998 and 1999. Finally, there have been major differences in the professed economic ideologies of as many as six different governments at the centre since 1991. The latest coalition government of the Congress-led United Progressive Alliance (UPA), formed in May 2004 and headed by Prime Minister Manmohan Singh (the architect of the 1991 reforms), reiterated its commitment to the reform process that has been opposed in the past by its present supporters from outside, the Left Front. What explains the more than decade-and-a-half long *staying power* of the reform process? Or, alternatively, how do we understand the eagerness of the major political parties to claim credit and own the reform process that started 'by stealth' without admitting the paradigmatic shift in 1991 and which was criticized as being imposed by the IMF and the World Bank not long ago? It is a challenging question of political economy.

Our suggested explanation has three critical interlinked ingredients in the context of a continuing environment of coalition politics at the centre. The first is the emergence of regional parties in national politics with neutral economic ideology. Their critical role for the stability of coalition governments and their participation in government out of opportunistic motives has brought upfront the need to step up economic growth that reforms try to push. The second factor has been the reluctant acceptance of the inescapable reality of coalition politics on the part of the major contending national political parties, the Bharatiya Janata Party (BJP) and the Congress, and the consequent pragmatic adjustments in their social and economic agendas, which helped the reform process. The third ingredient relates to the experience of gradual learning by (politically) adjusting and reforming over the last decade and a half and the growing and widespread acceptance of the need for a very rapid economic growth that can be served by the market-oriented reforms.

REGIONAL PARTIES IN NATIONAL POLITICS

The emergence of the regional parties can be traced to the de-institutionalization of the Congress Party in the wake of radicalization of politics in the 1970s and the institutionalization of the vertical mobilizations of the 1980s along local or sectional issues. The process of regionalization was consolidated in the turbulent terms-of-trade politics of the 1980s and gathered momentum in the 1990s. The progressively growing numerical importance of regional parties[1] as a group in the central parliament can be seen in Table 7.1. Many of the regional parties are personalistic and centred on one charismatic leader and founded on the appeal to pride and identity of the regional, ethnic, or social group, from which follows their ideological flexibility with respect to political alignments and (frequent) realignments (Palshikar 2003). It has coincided with the diminished numerical strength of the national parties in the central parliament. Table 7.2 shows the decline in the number of seats of the national parties in the lower house of parliament from 88 per cent in 1991 to 67 per cent in the recent 2004 elections. In the state legislative assemblies, too, *no* national party has a major presence in any of the major states (Arora 2003: 90–1).

Table 7.1: Number of Regional Parties and Their Seats in the Lower House of Parliament

Year	1977	1980	1984	1989	1991	1996	1998	1999	2004
No. of regional parties	23	23	23	23	49	49	49	49	
No. of Lok sabha seats	51	36	76	89	56	137	161	188	171*
Per cent share in total	9.4	6.8	14.0	16.8	11.0	25.2	29.7	34.6	31.3

Note: *includes 15 seats for registered unrecognized parties like the Telangana Rashtra Samiti. www.eci.gov.in

After losing heavily as a result of proliferation in number between 1989 and 1991, the regional parties progressively consolidated their position with pre-poll alliances with various national-level political groupings[2] so as to avoid the splitting of votes from their overlapping support bases with their partners.[3] They tasted power for the first time on the basis of their numerical strength in the two short-lived post-poll coalition governments (1996–8) of the (non-BJP, non-Congress) United Front (UF) with the outside support of the Congress. Appendix Table D5 clearly brings out the seamless movement in the political alignments of the regional parties from one national-level formation to another from poll to poll till date. In the emerging coalition politics, they have come to play a critical role for the stability of the governments at the centre disproportionate to their numerical strength in the Lok Sabha.[4] Some of the regional parties have managed to wrest important ministries that were lucrative for patronage distribution or consolidation of political power. A few have used them to promote their regional interests.

EMERGENCE OF COALITION POLITICS AT THE CENTRE

Coalition governments have not been uncommon in the states since 1967 although most of them have proved unstable. At the centre, the anti-Congress Janata Party coalition government came to power for the first time in 1977 but proved short-lived. Another experiment after the 1989 election that also ended prematurely in the face of political instability was followed by the minority government of P.V. Narasimha Rao in 1991 that lasted five years. But the elections since 1996 have been resulting in hung parliaments and coalition governments. While the Congress Party continued its downhill slide in the 1990s and the national Left parties found themselves reduced to regional presence in the face of vertical mobilizations of the 1980s, the Hindu Nationalist BJP emerged as the major contender for power. The BJP rose to national prominence in the volatile political atmosphere in the late 1980s by invoking the emotional religious issue of the Rama temple in Ayodhya (in Uttar Pradesh) in the north Indian Hindi heartland.[5] This raised its tally in the Lok Sabha from 85 seats in 1989 to 119 in 1991 (Table 7.2) on the basis of upper caste votes and cutting into the voter base of the Congress Party in the Hindi heartland states of Uttar Pradesh, Madhya Pradesh, and Rajasthan.

Table 7.2: Lok Sabha (Lower House of the Parliament) Seats of National Parties 1977–2004

Political Party	1977	1980	1984	1989	1991	1996	1998	1999	2004
Total No. of Seats*	542	529	542	529	511	543	543	543	541
Indian National Congress (INC)	154	353	415	197	227	140	141	114	145
Bharatiya Janata Party (BJP)	Part of JP		2	85	119	161	182	182	138
Janata Party (JP)/ Janata Dal (JD)	298	31	10	143	56	46	6	21**	—
Communist Party Marxist (CPM)	22	36	22	33	35	32	32	33	43
Communist Party of India (CPI)	7	11	6	12	13	12	9	4	10
Bahujana Samaj Party (BSP)	–	–	–	–	–	–	–	–	19
Nationalist Congress Party (NCP)	–	–	–	–	–	–	–	–	9
Total of national parties (seats)	481	431	455	470	450	391	370	354	364
Total of national parties (%)	88.8	81.5	84.0	88.9	88.1	72.0	68.1	65.2	67.53

Notes: * No. of Lok Sabha seats had become 543 from the earlier 542. Number less than that indicates the number of seats for which elections were held. ** JD(U) includes Samata and Lokshakti; Definition of national and state parties is given in the Appendix D2. Following the definition, the composition of national parties kept changing over time.

Source: Balveer Arora (2003). 'Federalization of India's Party System', in Ajay K. Mehra, D.D. Khanna, and Gert. W. Kneck (eds), *Political Parties and Party Systems*. Sage Publications, New Delhi, ch. 3, pp. 83–99. Table 3.3, p.87 and www.eci.gov.in

The BJP was the first national party to enter into the game of pre-poll alliances and coalition politics with a view to extending its narrow upper caste voter base with the help of regional alliance partners and in the process preventing the splitting of votes and capturing power at the centre. The strategy reflects the ex ante realization of its inability to expand its support base on its own. The party first tried this strategy on a limited scale to gain significantly in strength from 119 in 1991 to 161 in 1996 (Table 7.2). Encouraged by the success, it tried this strategy on a bigger scale in the mid-term poll of 1998 to form a government at the centre and again after another mid-term poll in 1999 to form the government that completed its full term in 2004. In the bargain, it had to put some of its key social issues like Hindu nationalism (Hindutva) on the backburner as they were not acceptable to the alliance partners, and invited the ire of its more communal and extremist extended family members like the Vishwa Hindu Parishad (VHP) and the Rashtriya Swayamsevak Sangh (RSS).[6]

The Congress Party was late in coming to terms with its downhill slide in central parliamentary politics and in recognizing the reality of coalition politics. It tried its hand at pre-poll alliance making for the first time on a limited scale in 1999 after watching the success of the BJP but openly rejected a coalition government mode till the recent 2004 election.[7] Table 7.3, which gives the percentage of seats and votes of the Congress, the BJP and other broad political formations in the last four general elections, gives an indication of what might have contributed to this late realization. The BJP managed to *maintain* 33.5 per cent of the seats *despite a decline* in its share of votes from 25.6 per cent in 1998 to 23.8 per cent in 1999. Between the same two mid-term polls, the Congress Party *reduced* its share of seats in the Lok Sabha from 26 per cent to 21 per cent *despite a rise* in its vote share from 25.8 per cent to 28.3 per cent! The Congress Party neutralized the BJP's advantage in the 2004 elections by entering into the pre-poll alliance game. The strategy succeeded in bringing the Congress-led UPA government to power in May 2004.

The game of pre-poll alliance making is not without its costs, however. The seat adjustment with alliance partner(s) often involves displeasing a long-time committed local worker in the constituency by either partner and thereby causing intra-party heart burning and dissidence. It requires intricate calculations of assessing ex ante the chances of increasing the number of seats by preventing vote-splitting and sometimes extending support base with the help of the alliance partner(s) against the cost of containing internal dissidence and the consequent erosion of support base. Stability of the alliance partners could also make for the repetitive inter-temporal cooperative game in which at each move, players learn from experience and plan the next move. It is too early to comment on this aspect given the turnover among the alliance partners in the coalition governments so far. The BJP had the first-mover advantage and has so far successfully played the game of coalition politics. This success came for the BJP at the cost of losing some credibility in its more militant Hindu nationalist sister organizations as it had to rein in its Hindu nationalist religious agenda in order to accommodate its regional alliance partners[8] who have not been sympathetic to it.

Our analysis indicates that in the foreseeable future, with the increasing hold of regional parties and the corresponding decline of the major national parties, coalition governments at the centre are going to be the order of the day. Whether two stable coalitions emerge or not is still an open question.

Table 7.3: Seats and Votes (%) Won by Categories of Parties in the Lower House of Parliament in the 1996, 1998, 1999, and 2004 Elections

Parties	Election Year							
	1996		1998		1999		2004	
	Seats	Votes	Seats	Votes	Seats	Votes	Seats	Votes
Congress	25.8	28.8	26.0	25.8	21.0	28.3	26.90	26.69
BJP	29.6	20.3	33.5	25.6	33.5	23.8	25.60	22.16
Sub-total	55.4	49.1	59.5	51.4	54.5	52.1	52.50	48.85
Multi-state parties*	18.8	20.0	11.8	16.6	13.3	15.0	15.03	14.22
State parties and independents	25.8	30.9	28.7	32.0	32.2	32.9	32.47	36.92
Sub-total	44.6	50.9	40.5	48.6	45.5	47.9	47.50	51.14

Notes: *Classified as National Parties. These are:
CPM, CPI, Samata, Janata Dal, AIIC (Tiwari) and Janata Party (1996)
CPM, CPI, Samata, Janata Dal, and Bahujana Samaj Party (1998)
CPM, CPI, Samata, Janata Dal (United) and Bahujana Samaj Party (1999)
CPM, CPI, Bahujana Samaj Party and Nationalist Congress Party (2004)
The definition of national and state parties is given in the Appendix D2.
Source: Balveer Arora (2003). 'Federalization of India's Party System', in Ajay K. Mehra, D.D. Khanna, and Gert. W. Kneck (eds), *Political Parties and Party Systems*. Sage Publications, New Delhi, ch. 3, pp. 83–99. Table 3.4. p. 88; www.eci.gov.in

CONVERGENCE IN ECONOMIC ACTIONS: CONVICTION OR PRAGMATISM?

The third reason for the staying power of the reform process relates to the convergence in the economic actions of different governments, which maintained the market-oriented and globalizing direction of reforms despite professing different economic ideologies. This is not to say that the same parties, while in opposition, did not stridently criticize the policies of the ruling coalitions. However, the parliamentary debates and party manifestos of the major national contending parties have focused on differences in detail rather than wholesale opposition to the basic direction of reforms.[9] The minority government (1991–6) that initiated systemic reforms belonged to the Congress Party that had professed socialist ideology in all its previous governments except possibly that headed by Rajiv Gandhi. The BJP in the early 1990s supported internal liberalization but opposed external liberalization of the minority Congress government.[10] However, the BJP-led coalition (1998–2004) pushed external liberalization and announced measures for attracting large private foreign investment. The Communists and ex-democratic socialists had opposed the internal liberalization as well as dismantling of the public sector commercial enterprises as 'abject surrender to the IMF' in 1991. However, the post-poll coalition United Front governments (1996–8) in which one faction of the Communist parties and ex-socialists participated while another faction supported from outside pushed stock market and financial-sector liberalization and private investment in infrastructure, announced intentions of attracting private foreign investment of US$ 10 billion every year, and appointed the first Disinvestment Commission for the central PSEs. The current Congress-led UPA government supported by the Left Front from outside has been continuing with the market orientation of reforms despite opposition from the Left parties. What explains the directional convergence in actions despite different ideological positions of the central governments since 1991?

Our explanation for this directional convergence of economic actions combines the increasing importance of a large number of mostly ideologically neutral regional parties for the stability of the central government and their growing claims on the centre's resources, the reluctant acceptance of coalition politics by the major national contenders, that is the Congress and the BJP, and the realization of the inescapable need for rapid economic growth to meet the growing demands of newer (regional) and old interest groups without which the moving fiscal distributional equilibrium would be infeasible or unstable in either of which case all political actors perceive themselves to be collectively losing out. Thus convergence in their economic actions towards maintaining the liberalizing and globalizing direction can most plausibly be explained in terms of this collectively felt urgent need to step up the tempo of growth.

Both the major political parties—the Congress and the BJP—have accepted the imperative need for a rapid double-digit growth in their 2004 election manifestos and the associated need for attracting private foreign investment to supplement domestic savings and to upgrade the technological base towards international competitiveness. The redefinition of self-reliance (Chapter 6) indicates a major change in the earlier autarkic position of the Congress Party. The change in the autarkic (Swadeshi) stance of BJP can be seen in its vision document for the 2004 parliamentary election, which re-interprets Swadeshi to mean domination of the 'Made in India brand' in the world markets in a wide range of products by the for creating large-scale prosperity and employment at home 'by making them compete not only on cost but also on quality and technology'. Hindu nationalism is thus smartly recast for pragmatic reasons into increasing India's economic muscle in order to enhance its national strength and become 'a Great Power'.[11] Not to be left behind in competitive politics, the Congress also resurrected the reforms that it had disowned since 1996 and claimed credit for initiating them in 1991!

Although reformulations of the established ideologies on the part of the two national contenders reflect welcome pragmatism to tailor them to the reform process, it would be too hasty to take the convergence of economic actions to indicate the conversion of 'reformers by convenience' into 'reformers by conviction'. Reformers by conviction have remained a small minority in all the six central governments besides being political lightweights. There is still an undercurrent of hostility to reforms among the majority of influential politicians, reflecting the pervasive influence of economic nationalism and socialism. As mentioned in the preceding paragraph, the Congress

Party had disowned reforms till competitive politics induced it to claim credit for them as a reaction to the BJP's vision document of 2004. It is interesting to recall that after the debacle in the 1999 general elections, the Congress President Mrs Sonia Gandhi had appointed the so-called 'Introspection Committee' headed by A.K Anthony with Mani Shankar Aiyar as convener. Pinpointing the decisions on liberalization from 1991–6 as one of the reasons for the defeat in 1999, *the committee emphasized the need to go back to its pro-poor roots and Nehruvian socialism.* Dr Manmohan Singh, who had initiated the 1991 reforms, was criticized by Arjun Singh and Aiyar (currently his ministerial colleagues in the central cabinet) in the Congress Working Committee meeting in the second week of December 1999.[12] The BJP discovered the merits of reforms only after practising them for five years of leading the central coalition government and felt the need for reformulations of its Hindu nationalism only for the latest 2004 elections to get re-elected by downplaying its traditional militant Hindu religious agenda, which restricted its support base. For this purpose, the highest ever GDP growth rate of 8 per cent in 2003–4 and reforms came in handy. Influential ideologues in different national parties have still not reconciled to the liberalizing and globalizing direction of reforms but go along with them passively citing the changed world economy or expediency of coalition politics as the excuse for having to 'make the best of a bad bargain'.[13] This latent opposition to reforms is not erupting into the open due to the slow process of collective 'learning by reforming' that seems to be going on given the politically perceived indispensability of rapid economic growth to sort out distributional conflicts in a peaceful and orderly fashion.[14] This is where the gradualism that is typical of democratic politics characterized the reform process in India and successfully minimized the pains of stabilization and structural adjustment, making way for their wider acceptance for opportunistic reasons of political survival on the basis of economic performance. This has also been reinforced by the neutrality of regional parties with respect to economic ideology.

We may mention the possible factors that facilitated the process of collective learning by reforming. The significant step-up in the GDP growth rate that was associated with the hesitant liberalization of the 1980s strengthened the hands of the reforming minority in the Congress government in 1991. The crisis-ridden atmosphere that helped tide over the pains of sharp fiscal contraction in 1991–2 was reinforced by a remarkable rebound from the sharp stabilization-induced dip in the growth rate to 1.3 per cent in 1991–2. Good agricultural harvests, and improved world economy, and the inherent resilience of the economy helped the corporate investment boom following the liberalization of controls on private (domestic and foreign) investment, boost the GDP growth rate to 5.1 per cent in 1992–3, 5.9 per cent in 1993–4, and an unprecedented 7 per cent plus continuously over the next three years averaging 7.5 per cent. This was the fastest recovery in international experience (Acharya 2001). This helped convince the sceptics among intellectuals and politicians that reforms worked, not just in other reforming countries, as international agencies had been pointing out, *but in India too*. Many critics of the hesitant liberalization process of the 1980s were converted to the view that sustained liberalization worked better when their early apprehensions about the large-scale unemployment and social unrest that was expected to emerge from structural adjustment were belied. Between 1993–4 and 1999–2000, the GDP growth rate averaged a healthy 6.5 per cent annually. Over the same period, the results of the large-scale sample surveys of consumer expenditure indicated a decline in absolute poverty in the 1990s.[15] (Deaton 2003; Deaton and Drèze 2002; Sundaram and Tendulkar 2003a). These experiences might have contributed to developing an intellectual consensus that liberalization and opening up resulted in rapid growth, which in turn led to a reduction in poverty and muted the pro-rich criticism (that haunted the hesitant liberalization of the 1980s) by the left intellectuals although many were yet to be convinced. The intellectual consensus came in handy for the minority reformers in coalition governments in making the political case for reforms and appears to have gradually percolated into the political consciousness as a pragmatic necessity. This was reflected in the election manifestos of the Congress and the BJP for the recently held 2004 general election as discussed earlier in this section.

This process of collective learning and reforming has received unexpected reinforcement from regionalization and coalition politics of the 1990s which in normal course would be taken to be inimical to reforms. The regional parties whose support is critical for stable government at the centre are neutralizing the political heavyweights in the national parties who are not yet convinced about the reforms but accept them as a matter of expediency or a necessary evil in coalition politics. Most of the alliance partners provide opportunistic support to reforms to serve their narrow regional/sectional objectives, that is their support to reforms is conditional on their specific constituency or group gaining or at least not losing in the bargaining process.[16] The changing composition of alliance partners in different governments at the centre has enabled the pursuit of different reform initiatives by offsetting the diehard ideologues in the major national parties. In view of the increasing importance of the regional parties in national politics and given the revealed preferences of the voters,[17] 'national politics' is getting redefined and restructured in relation to the local and the regional, and the structure of the representative system is being gradually adapted to the needs of federal polity and the multi-ethnic, multicultural, and multi-regional diversities of Indian society. The mass politics of the 1980s under single-party majority government is being increasingly replaced in the 1990s by organized politics through regional parties. It is clear that given their critical role in the stability of the central government, the latter has to accommodate the growing demands of diverse regional identities and interest groups, which is not possible without stepping up the rate of economic growth. At the same time, their representation in the central government enables harnessing support of diverse interest groups and regional and ethnic formations so that 'today's coalition governments are able to take major policy initiatives of a kind the governments enjoying comfortable majority would not have dared' (Sheth 2005: 36).

The instrumental role of rapid economic growth in poverty reduction is convenient as political rhetoric in a country where no party can derive social legitimacy without invoking some variety of socialism or the other. However, the real political convenience of rapid growth lies in its ability to meet the growing claims made by newer and old interest groups. The growing recognition of the imperative need for rapid growth on the part of most political parties across a wide spectrum in the context of the emerging coalition politics augurs well for the continuation of the reform process oriented towards markets and opening up. The reform process is basically treated as an open-ended one without any pre-specified outcome except broad directional consistency. Given the changing composition of regional coalition partners and ideological predilections or pragmatic adjustments of the main contending parties, there would inevitably be 'two-step forward, one-step backward, some steps sidewards' movements. Support for or opposition to specific initiatives may emerge from opportunistic grounds of favourable/adverse influence on the immediate constituency or as a result of a complex trade-off between the social and economic components of the party agenda. As long as the instrumental role of rapid growth for sorting out distributional conflicts in an orderly fashion is recognized by all the political parties in the coalition game, in our view, the reform process is bound to continue.

NOTES

1. The quantum jump in the number of regional parties from twenty-three in 1989 to forty-nine in 1991 reflects the attempt by several non-political mass movements of the 1980s to organize themselves as formally registered political parties with identities distinct from established national parties.
2. See Appendix Table D5.
3. The regional parties have further increased their vote shares in the recent 2004 general election (see the last column in Table 7.3) at the cost of the two national parties although their numerical strength is somewhat reduced.
4. Appendix Tables D6 and D4 show the number of ministerial berths that different regional parties managed to secure in the last twenty-one-party National Democratic Alliance (NDA) government in 1999 and in the just-formed United Progressive Alliance (UPA) government.
5. Ayodhya was the birthplace of the Hindu god Rama. The original Hindu temple was claimed to have been demolished by the Muslim king Babar to build a *masjid* there.
6. For more details that are not relevant here, interested readers may access their web site www.rss.org.
7. The decision to form pre-poll alliance was taken as late as in January 2004 for the elections in April. See the interview with Jairam Ramesh of the Congress Party's Economic Cell in the *Indian Express*, 25 May 2004.
8. L.K. Advani, Deputy Prime Minister of the NDA government, was quoted as saying 'When a party is in opposition it can be dogmatic about ideology. When in power, it has to modify the dogma to run a government and to keep the people with it' in 'Voices', *India Today*, 17 May 2004, p. 13. L.K. Advani has since been elected leader of the opposition in the lower house of parliament.
9. The extreme case of a wide disconnect between precept and practice is that the Left Communist Parties currently supporting the Congress-led coalition from

outside at the centre while ruling in the eastern state of West Bengal. Their government in West Bengal has been following privatization of state PSEs while their elected members in the central parliament have been vociferous in their opposition to the measures in the same direction proposed by the ruling Congress-led coalition government. For specific instances in recent times, see *India Today*, 25 October 2004, pp. 41–2.

10. For quotations from parliamentary debates and BJP manifesto, see Lakha (2002).
11. Bharatiya Janata Party; *Vision Document—2004*, Press Release, 31 March 2004.
12. *Indian Express*, Pune, 24 May 2004, p. 4, reported by Uday Kumar A.R. from Thiruvananthapuram.
13. The classic case in this context is that of the former defence minister George Fernandes in the BJP-led NDA coalition government and convener of the NDA of twenty-two parties to thrash out differences. He was one-time socialist and heads one of the factions of the Janata Dal and a confirmed MNC basher (having driven out Coke and IBM from India as industries minister during 1977–80). In a recent interview (*The Times of India*, Mumbai, 4 March 2004, p. 2), he was reminded about his past and asked to comment on the reforms that the NDA pushed. 'Sure I fought the reforms of 1991', he said 'but the BJP (his major coalition partner in NDA) also campaigned against it. *Now the world has changed.* Both of us are *saddled with policies* we fought against. *We have to pursue these policies* but with modifications *to minimize the damage* from trade and MNCs.' His solution: 'I want to make Indian companies to become multinationals and spread all over the world'. He admitted the urgent need to '*do something*' about solving India's economic problems and lamented in the end, 'Meanwhile, *you try to make the best of a bad bargain*' (emphasis added).
14. This poses the a tantalizing question of whether the post-reform distributional equilibrium has emerged since the earlier one during the dirigiste phase was disturbed by the entry of numerically large groups of farmers and small industrialists/traders into the distributional coalition in the 1980s. It is too early to answer this in the affirmative. For brevity, we merely list the reasons underlying our judgment. (1) Coalition politics at the centre that has been in operation since 1996 is yet to stabilize in the multi-party political culture. Only the last BJP-led coalition out of the five so far has successfully completed one full electoral term. (For a different view, see Sheth 2005.) (2) The BJP, possibly because it never tasted power earlier, successfully managed the internal contradictions of coalition politics by making compromises. The other national contender, the Congress Party that is currently leading UPA coalition, has long been used to enjoying power in single-party governments since 1947, and is yet to prove its skills at managing intra-coalition conflicts. (3) It appears that while managing the distributional claims with a little over 6 per cent GDP growth annually since 1992–3, the fiscal and revenue deficits in relation to GDP were back to or exceeded the crisis levels of 1990–1 at the beginning of the twenty-first century, but without the accompanying external payments crisis and inflationary pressures. It is not clear if another fiscal crisis is brewing. (4) The fiscal deterioration has been associated with a slowdown in average growth since 1997–8 with adverse consequences for the ability of the growth process to meet the distributional claims. Because of the foregoing features associated with the polity and economy, it is too early to claim the successful

emergence of a stable distributional equilibrium despite unmistakable convergence in economic actions and the widely accepted imperative need for rapid growth in this connection. We may add by way of postscript that the economy has clocked 7.5 per cent plus growth of real GDP in the three years since 2003–4 but its sustainability need to be watched.

15. We may note in passing that the results of Sundaram and Tendulkar (2003) and Deaton (2003) were presented in a widely attended seminar organized jointly by the Indian Planning Commission and the World Bank in January 2002.
16. In the 2004 National Election Survey, voters were asked about the ordering of their collective loyalties. As high as 67 per cent of the voters gave precedence to their *region* over *nation*, only 21 per cent gave precedence to the *nation* over *region*, with the remaining 12 per cent had no opinion. On another question, performance of the central government mattered to only 23 per cent of the voters in the *parliamentary* election (quoted in Sheth 2005).
17. Refer to n. 16.

8

The Political Economy of Reforms: Some Individual Initiatives

In the previous chapters, we have attempted an explanation of the intermittent but unambiguously persistent liberalizing and globalizing *macro-level direction* of the economy during the post-1991 *reform process* as a whole that has been evolving in the political and economic domains in the environment of coalition politics at the Centre in India's low-income democracy. Our explanation revolved around the opportunistic support for the reform process as an unavoidably indispensable instrument for ensuring rapid growth, which is collectively perceived to be necessary to accommodate the competing claims of a growing number of new and old, economic and regional interest groups in a complex, repetitive game of coalition politics. In this perspective, reform process is the result of *interaction* amongst individual reform initiatives which have been undertaken—sometimes haltingly, sometimes decisively—in the direction of liberalizing the restrictions on private enterprise and markets and opening up of the economy to international trade and investment. When the interaction is mutually reinforcing, the sum total is clearly greater than the sum of individual ingredients. The individual reform initiatives seek to bring about a *micro-level structural adjustment* of the economy in the growth-promoting direction. In this penultimate chapter, we examine the political economy of selected individual reform measures to provide a flavour of the interplay of specific domestic and international economic interest groups in influencing their time path of reforms.

INDIVIDUAL INITIATIVES

How do we choose among the wide range of reform initiatives which have been mentioned in the beginning? For this purpose, it would be useful to classify the reform measures into three broad groups, keeping specifically in mind the environment of coalition politics:

(i) Measures that are carried out by an agency other than the central government. Financial sector and exchange rate reforms carried out by the Reserve Bank of India (Central Bank of India) belong to this category. These measures are usually not subject to political pulls and pressures and can be carried out mostly in an unobtrusive manner.
(ii) Measures that lie within the discretionary powers of the government. These need to be discussed and debated in the parliament but require only parliamentary approval without formal voting or legislative amendments. Policy statements and budgetary measures belong to this category. In this case the interest groups try to influence the policy formulation level itself, failing which, at the implementation stage, to swing the discretionary elements in their favour at best or to minimize damage at worst.
(iii) Measures that require legislative amendments. This is by far the toughest and the most time-consuming category especially under coalition politics because formally legislated rules of the game are sought to be changed. These measures are subject to usually accepted parliamentary procedural delays and eventual passage depends on the explicit political consensus as reflected in parliamentary voting in the face of changing alignments in coalition politics.

Given the known constraints of a developing country democracy operating in an environment of social, regional, and economic diversities, the progress of reforms can be fastest in category (i), slow and halting in category (ii), and extremely difficult in category (iii).

In view of the focus of this study on the political economy and institutional issues in understanding the reform process, we discuss two reform initiatives [(1) and (2) below)] in category (ii), one [(3) below] which overlaps between (ii) and (iii), and the last one [(4) below] belonging to category (iii). The idea is to provide the flavour of the India-specific reform process to illustrate the interplay of underlying contradictory pulls and pressures operating on the reforming leadership.

We start by listing the measures:

(1) Liberalization of domestic and foreign private investment;
(2) Liberalization of international trade in goods and services;
(3) Partial or complete privatization of commercial public-sector enterprises;
(4) Organized labour market reforms.

We state upfront why we have deliberately omitted two 'large' and widely discussed reform measures from the above list. The first relates to the political economy of fiscal management of the central budget where diverse social and economic interest groups interact in a complex and non-transparent fashion. The fiscal adjustment continued till 1996–7, after which the fiscal and revenue deficits have been on the rise but without any apparent crisis till 2002–3. Despite inability to curb unproductive expenditures, real GDP growth exceeding 8 per cent since 2003–4 has helped a reversal of this trend. In our view, political economy and institutional questions in this context cannot be appropriately posed without deeper *economic* analysis of this fiscal behaviour which is beyond our expertise. The second major reform measure that we have excluded from the discussion is the political economy of power-sector reforms where the picture is complicated due to the deep involvement of diverse state governments. We have confined the present study to the reform process of the central government only.

DOMESTIC AND FOREIGN PRIVATE INVESTMENT LIBERALIZATION

We mentioned in Chapter 3 what Desai (1999) called the caste system in modern industry for according policy priorities. The highest caste or the most favoured were public-sector enterprises. The next in policy preference came the modern small-scale industries that received protective and promotional concessions in an attempt to reconcile the Gandhian ideal of decentralization and dispersed industrialization with the Nehruvian socialism aiming at 'commanding heights' of large public sector. The third in the hierarchy were those industries that required government permission under the Industry (Development and Regulation) Act (IDRA) 1951 for undertaking domestic *private* investment above a certain pre-specified floor level. The fourth were domestic large capitalists represented by large interrelated business houses which are subject to additional conditions while undertaking investment. These were laid down under the Monopolies and Restrictive Trade Practices (MRTP) Act 1968. The most discriminated against were the subsidiaries of foreign companies which were subjected to stiffer condition under the Foreign Exchange Regulation Act[1] (FERA) 1974. The mandatory government permissions required under the IDRA, MRTP Act, and FERA constituted the major discretionary negative instrument[2] of case-by-case disposal which were used to prevent private domestic investment (above a certain floor level) or foreign investment from taking place in specefied industries by not according the mandatory permission. As we have mentioned in Chapter 3, there were still areas of private investment which were left out of the ambit of these legislations possibly for reasons of high administrative costs or in areas of social priority where public sector efforts were needed to be supplemented by private investment. The caste system operated under the doubtful premise that the omnipotent and omniscient government rather than the functioning markets knew what was the 'best' investment allocation for the society. Acting as a strong deterrent to privately productive activities, the regulatory environment managed to create a chronic shortage economy and stifle large-scale private investment in areas where shortages had been endemic. The Industrial Policy Statement dated 24 July 1991, which was issued during the crisis-ridden atmosphere of imminent external payments default, abolished at one stroke all mandatory sanctions under the IDRA except for a small negative list of eighteen industries justified for reasons of security, environment, and balance of payments.[3] The statement also opened up for the private investment industries earlier reserved for the public sector, did away with pre-entry scrutiny of investment decisions regarding expansion, merger, new capacity and diversification of large industrial houses under the MRTP Act, and very cautiously liberalized private foreign investment. As far as large-scale domestic investors were concerned, this was a sweeping change as emerged from an illustrative exercise reported by the World Bank (1992). The exercise subjected 9227 approvals under the IDRA granted between 1988 and 1991 to the new policy to find that only 421 (or hardly 5 per cent) would have required mandatory approval. The comparison did not take account of the number of rejected applications that could have been automatically permitted under the new policy in which *positive instruments* constituted a general rule. The measures were in line with domestic [but not the external] liberalization advocated by the main opposition party, namely the Bharatiya Janata Party. They consisted mainly of removal of the entry barriers operating under the earlier caste system in industrial policy and sought to introduce potential competition driven by market signals for efficiency improvements. The losers from these measures were two groups: rent-receiving bureaucrats who could grant investment licenses in industries with chronic shortages and those large industrialists who perceived these sanctions as a protective cover to deter competitors or used them to pre-empt capacity by obtaining permission only with a view to blocking the entry of potential competitors. The gainers were those industrialists who were constrained in a situation of persistent shortages, excess demands, and small scale of operation. They were also helped by the complementary financial-sector reforms which progressively expanded the available options for financing of additional investment. Several industrialists also took advantage of the removal of the MRTP Act restrictions and restructured themselves through acquisitions, mergers, hiving off non-core activities, and strategic alliances. Real GDP originating in the registered manufacturing sector posted an average 10.9 per cent annual growth over the five-year period from 1992–3 and 1996–7, with aggregate GDP growth averaging an unprecedented 6.7 per cent annually over the same period. It appears ex post that the potential gainers from the measures must have far outweighed the losers.

However, what explains the widespread support to these measures at the time of announcement? It may be recalled that Rajiv Gandhi's government had also undertaken hesitant liberalization in the same direction in the 1980s: delicensing more than forty-odd industries in two instalments, permitting diversification in related areas without licence in a number of industries, announcing minimum efficient scale for a number of others, allowing limited expansion subject to certain conditions for a few others, and finally, raising the asset limit for sanctions under the MRTP Act (Panagaria 2004). This resulted in a healthy 7.9 per cent annual average growth in GDP in registered manufacturing in the second half of the 1980s. Buoyed by this experience, the industrialists' support for liberalization at the time of announcement appeared rational.

Why did the bureaucracy that was losing out not stall the measures? More than 3000 approvals per year between 1988 and 1991 in the World Bank (1992) exercise mentioned earlier reflected *de facto* a very liberal approach in granting investment licenses, which may have reduced the rent-seeking possibilities earlier in the 1980s. The crisis-ridden atmosphere might also have had its share.

While investment at the upper end of investment was liberalized by freeing it from mandatory government sanctions of various kinds under IDRA, the policy statement did not permit large-scale investment into products reserved for exclusive production in small-scale units. This reflected the hold of small-scale industrialists and traders who formed the support base of the Hindu nationalist BJP and who had emerged as a dispersed yet politically well-connected group in the 1980s (Chapter 5). Imports had been freed for most of the reserved items with the removal of quantitative restrictions (QRs) on most intermediate and capital goods in 1991 and rapidly declining import tariff rates since then as part of trade liberalization. (This has been discussed later in the chapter.) The number of reserved products was as high as 836 as late as in 1997. This created an anomaly that importers could compete with SSI but not the domestic large industrial units. The policymakers were not unaware of this anomaly, but they were unable or unwilling to act because of the political influence of the potential losers. The number of reserved items started to decline very slowly with 15, 9, and 15 products being taken out of the reserved list in April 1997, February 1999, and June 2001 respectively. The process has picked up since 2002 and as of May 2006, as many as 499 more products had been de-reserved (www.smallindustryindia.com). Nevertheless, as many as 286 products still remain on the reserved list. This has been preventing a rise in the scale of operation in many exportable labour-intensive industries and adversely affecting the competitiveness of domestic industry.

In contrast to the wide-ranging and sweeping nature of liberalization of private *domestic* investment at the higher-end of scale of investment, that of private *foreign* investment has been extremely cautious despite the then Finance Minister Dr Manmohan Singh's appeal in February 1992 'not to remain permanent captives of the (colonial) East India Company' (Chapter 6) and despite the fact that Indian policymakers have been eager to attract private foreign investment primarily for two reasons. One, as a source for supplementing domestic resources when the traditional source of foreign aid had been drying up. Second, as a non-debt source of financing the current account deficit during the post-reform period. The need for seeking non-debt capital inflows was basically a reaction to the experience of the previous decade. In the face of widening current account deficit in the second half of the 1980s despite double-digit growth in exports, and drying up of concessional foreign assistance, Indian policymakers resorted to more expensive and demanding commercial borrowings and deposits by non-resident Indians (NRIs) at higher than LIBOR rates as financing sources. As discussed in Chapter 6, this was one of the major factors leading to the external payments crisis of June 1991.

The IMF package under the compensatory contingency financing facility in the wake of the external payments crisis suggested to the government to explore non-debt sources of financing current account deficit. This included capital-gain-seeking private foreign portfolio investment (FPI), risk-sharing private foreign direct (equity) investment (FDI), and permitting domestic firms to raise resources abroad through Global and American Depository Receipts (GDRs and ADRs).

In the crisis year 1990–1, as high as 83 per cent of the total capital inflows amounting to US$ 7.1 billion were debt-creating inflows of all kinds (including 15.2 per cent short-term credits) to finance the current account deficit of 3.2 per cent of GDP, which was the highest in the previous two decades that included the years of energy price hikes in the 1970s. The percentage shares of non-debt-creating capital inflows averaged 57.8 per cent over the fourteen-year period from 1992–3 to 2005–6 during which India received nearly US$ 172 billion of capital inflows of all kinds out of which US$ 72.5 billion (42 per cent) came only in the last three years 2003–4 to 2005–6 (Table 8.1; RBI 2003; Table 1.76).

Cumulatively, India attracted US$ 48 billion net foreign private non-debt capital inflow[4] (Table 8.1) between 1992–3 and 2002–3, which was divided almost equally between relatively stable and risk-sharing FDI and relatively volatile and capital-gains-seeking FPI. It is also interesting to note that India managed to attract *higher* amounts of FPI than FDI during the immediate post-reform investment boom between 1993–4 and 1996–7 (Table 8.1). Of the cumulative FDI of US$ 24.2 billion, as high as 62 per cent was accounted by the SIA/FIPB discretionary route and the remaining 38 per cent through the liberalized 'automatic' route, which too was not without its prior conditionalities in regard to sectoral list and sectoral caps. This gives a good idea of the still largely *discretionary* nature of FDI policy till 2002–3. Some major changes in the last three years till 2005–6 are striking. One, private foreign investment flows of all kinds[5] have been US$ 46.3 billion over just the three year period (US$ 15.4 billion annually) in comparison with US$ 54.0 billion (or average annual US$ 4.9 billion) over the previous eleven years. A massive contribution of US$ 29.5 billion (or nearly 64 per cent of total flows) came from the capital-gains-seeking FPI compared to its cumulative level of just US$ 24.2 billion in the preceding eleven years. The share of FDI (amounting to US$ 11.0 billion) in total non-debt flows came down to less than 25 per cent from 50 per cent in the preceding eleven-year period. Even in absolute terms, the volume of FPI more than quadrupled from US$ 2.2 billion in the previous eleven years to US$ 9.7 billion in the last three years in comparison with just 45 per cent increase in the average annual FDI from US$ 2.2 billion to just US$ 3.7 billion over the same two periods. While India managed to attract a much larger volume of capital-gains-seeking FPI than risk-sharing FDI in the last three years, a welcome feature of FDI in the last three years has been a reduction in the share of discretionary (SIA/FIPB) route in FDI to 28 per cent from as high as 62 per cent

Table 8.1: Foreign Investment Inflows by Different Categories 1992–3 to 2002–3

(In Million US Dollars)

	1992–3	1993–4	1994–5	1995–6	1996–7	1997–8	1998–9	1999–2000	2000–1	2001–2	2002–3	Cumulative 1992–3 to 2002–3
A. Direct investment	315	586	1314	2144	2821	3557	2462	2155	2339	3904	2574	24,171
a. RBI automatic route	42	89	171	169	135	202	179	171	454	767	739	3118
b. SIA/FIPB route	222	280	701	1249	1922	2754	1821	1410	1456	2221	919	14,955
c. NRI (40% and 100%)	51	217	442	715	639	241	62	84	67	35	–	2553
d. Acquisition of shares	–	–	–	11	125	360	400	490	362	881	916	
B. Portfolio investment	244	3567	3824	2748	3312	1828	-61	3026	2760	2021	979	24,248
a. FIIs	1	1665	1503	2009	1926	979	-390	2135	1847	1505	377	13,557
b. GDRs/ADRs	240	1520	2082	683	1366	645	270	768	831	477	600	9482
c. Offshore funds and others	3	382	239	56	20	204	59	123	82	39	2	1209
Total A+B	559	4153	5138	4892	6133	5385	2401	5181	5099	5925	3553	48,419
Share of SIA/FIPB in FDI	70.5	47.8	53.3	58.3	68.1	77.4	74	65.4	62.2	56.9	35.7	61.9
Share of FDI in total	56.4	14.1	25.6	43.8	46	66.1	102.5	41.6	45.9	65.9	72.4	49.9
C. Other investment flows	n.a.	n.a.	n.a.	n.a.	n.a.	n.a.	n.a.	n.a.	1629	2036	1960	
a. Re-invested earnings	n.a.	n.a.	n.a.	n.a.	n.a.	n.a.	n.a.	n.a.	1350	1646	1498	
b. Other capital	n.a.	n.a.	n.a.	n.a.	n.a.	n.a.	n.a.	n.a.	279	390	462	
Total A+B+C	559	4153	5138	4892	6133	5385	2401	5181	6728	7961	5513	54,044

Notes: (1) Acquisition of shares in direct investment relates to the acquisition of shares of Indian companies by non-residents under section 29 of FERA and section 5 of the Foreign Exchange Management Act. (2) FII portfolio investment represents fresh inflow/outflow of funds by FIIs. (3) GDR/ADR figures represent GDR amounts raised abroad by Indian corporate. (4) The table excludes equity capital of unincorporated bodies given in RBI (2002–3). *Annual Report*, Table 6.9, (pg. 111) for the years: 2000–1 ($ 61 million), 2001–2 ($191 million) and 2002–3 ($ 126 million). These figures are not available for the earlier years. The RBI table also mentions that the coverage of FDI has been widened since 2000–1 to approach international best practices. The additional items covered are given under C in Table 8.1 here. A definitionally consistent time series from 1992–3 to 2002–3 is given by total A+B in the table. (5) Abbreviations: (i) SIA: Secretariat for Industrial Approval; (ii) FIPB: Foreign Investment Promotion Board; (iii) GDR: Global Depository Receipts, ADR: American Depository Receipts.

Source: *Economic Survey 2002–3*, p. 119; RBI (2002–3). *Annual Report* p. 111.

in the previous eleven years. Within the FDI under automatic route in the recent past, RBI approvals became relatively the largest component with a share of 37 per cent and the remaining 35 per cent was accounted by acquisition of equity shares.[6] For the possible external and domestic factors underlying the recent spurt, a reference may be made to the Box 1.20 in RBI (2006: 97).

Srinivasan and Tendulkar (2003: Tables 2.9 to 2.13) provide international comparison of long-term private (debt and non-debt) resource flows of various types to developing countries between 1990 and 2000 and the share that China and India managed to attract from each type of long-term capital flows. Internationally, of the total (debt and non-debt) net capital flows, FDI occupied a dominant share and showed a dramatic rise from US$ 47 billion in 1992 to US$ 172.5 billion in 1997 and stagnated around the peak following the East Asian currency meltdown. FPI, however, fluctuated from year to year and was on a much smaller scale than FDI. How did India perform in comparison with China? Figures 8.1 and 8.2 provide the absolute magnitudes of FDI and FPI attracted by India and China from 1990 to 2000. In relative terms, a large share (24 to 34 per cent) of the dominant FDI component went to China in the 1990s. India's share in FDI reached a peak of just 2 per cent in 1995 and again in 1997.[7] India's share of the more fluctuating FPI was interestingly *higher* than its share in FDI, but even in this component barring four out of nine years from 1990 to 2000, China's share has been higher.

How did China manage to attract a much higher share of FDI than India? Why did India not seek higher share of relatively more stable FDI and opt for more volatile FPI instead? In our view, the long-time presence since pre-Independence days of an influential class of private capitalists in India and their virtual absence in China seems to provide a major part of the explanation. Private industry, large and small, which received protection from a stringent import controls regime for forty years till 1990–1 did not want FDI in competing areas but advocated it mostly through the joint-venture route (which was non-competing and beneficial for domestic capitalists) and in areas like physical infrastructure (which remained constrained by the fiscal situation) where it would be complementary. However, given the still high tariff and non-tariff barriers in India, FDI was clearly

FIGURE 8.1
Foreign Direct Investment Flows to India and China

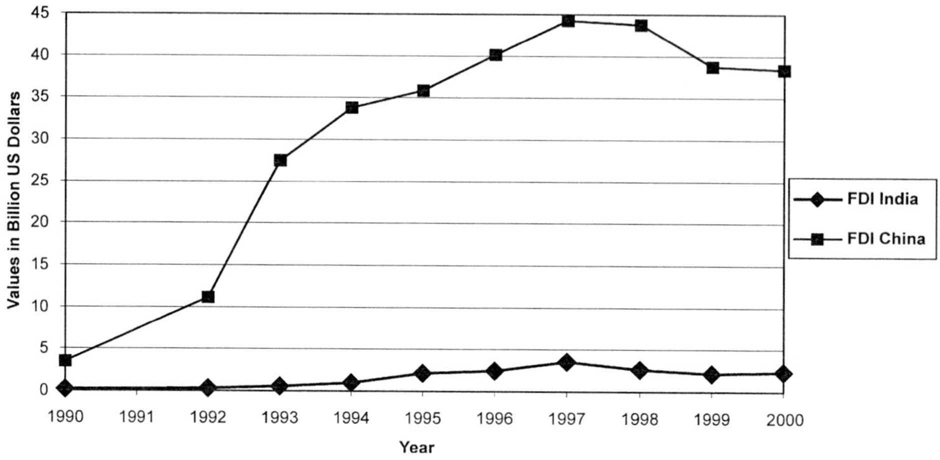

FIGURE 8.2
Portfolio Investment Flows to India and China

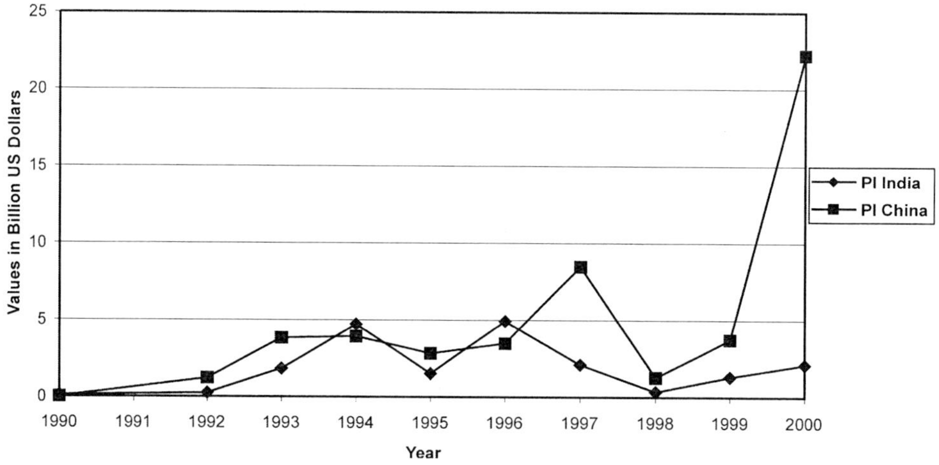

Source: World Bank. *Global Development Finance 2002, Analysis and Summary Tables.*

more lucrative in competing areas by jumping over the tariff wall in order to exploit the Indian market characterized by chronic shortages and pent-up demand.[8] FPI was also attractive because of higher capital gains in a protected market. Balancing the pressure from domestic industry to confine FDI to non-competing activities and that from the IMF to seek non-debt sources of revenue, the government seems to have struck a compromise by relaxing restrictions on capital-gains-seeking FPI, which helped domestic corporates raise funds from the capital market, while FDI is still being kept under mostly case-by-case licensing restrictions and conditionalities. Over time, however, as tariff levels were being progressively lowered, the Foreign Investment Promotion Board (FIPB) has been liberal in granting licences, thereby introducing competition for domestic industry. This interplay of counteracting pressures exerted by domestic industrialists and international financial institutions provides, in our view, a plausible explanation why India's share in the total FPI to developing countries has been higher than its share in FDI and also why China has managed to attract a much higher share of FDI than India despite the virtual absence of a well-established legal and judicial system in China. This is not to deny that there are other factors at work as well, such as more severe physical infrastructural bottlenecks, greater bureaucratic hurdles, and a less flexible organized labour market in India than in China.

An important additional dimension of restrictive policy of FDI in India deserves a brief discussion. Bulk of the FDI under discretionary SIA/FIPB route during the post-reform investment boom (1995–6 and 1997–8) came mostly through joint ventures in which domestic industry wanted to piggyback on the earlier banned importables of foreign well-known branded products by producing them at home. Both the foreign and domestic investors apparently overestimated the size of the market by mistaking the immediate surge in *pent-up demand* for the earlier banned importables as *normal demand*.[9] Some branded products did not click with the Indian consumers, while in some others the chemistry of joint venture did not work out. This caused dissatisfaction among the foreign investors who wanted to establish wholly-owned subsidiaries in activities in direct competition with those of the domestic joint venture partner. This is when the domestic Indian corporates lobbied with the central governments to protect the Indian joint venture partners. The result was the Press Note Number 18 in the 1998 series dated 14 December 1998. Under this Press Note, foreign investors already in joint venture were required to: (i) get government permission for establishing wholly-owned subsidiary in the *same or allied fields*[10] even in areas listed under the automatic route; (ii) provide detailed circumstances of the necessity of such new venture; and (iii) prove that such new venture would not jeopardize the interests of the Indian joint venture partner. The sanction in practice was made conditional on obtaining a no-objection certificate from the existing Indian partner, which provided a convenient instrument for blocking the FDI in competing areas.

This discriminatory tactic managed to drive away FDI. Foreign investors had been seeking the removal of stringent conditionalities in their meetings with the Indian leaders and officials. Their protests were heeded only recently when the current Prime Minister, Dr Manmohan Singh, announced after more than a year-long deliberations, what he described as 'doing away with the respective provisions of Press Note 18' on 12 January 2005 at the Partnership Summit 2005 held at Kolkata. In effect, however, the Press Notes 1 and 3 (2005 series) dated 15 March 2005 giving effect to the announcement indicated that only rigour of the conditions in Press Note 18 has been somewhat diluted in the sense that exemption from mandatory prior approval can be granted for new venture in the (non-competing) 'allied' field or in the same field in case the Indian venture is sick or defunct and the onus of proving in the existing joint venture that interests of the Indian partners are not 'in jeopardy' (to quote the Press Note) has been put *equally on both the foreign and the Indian partner*. In other words, even though the ambit of the automatic route has been made wider over time, the discretionary approach in this context reflects the continued hold of the protectionist ideology of economic nationalism. However, discretion in practice can work in the direction of protectionism or liberalization. According to the information made available to us, there appears to be welcome change in practice. Between 1 January 2005 and 10 October 2006 (the last meeting of the FIPB till date), out of the total of 79 applications considered under Press Note 1 of 2005, as many as 78 were given an approving nod.[11] This suggests a healthy change in the direction of raising international competitiveness of the Indian industry as well as for attracting FDI. In practice, however, India also has to compete with other developing countries which follow much more liberal policies in respect of FDI. We also hasten to add that approval of FDI is only the first hurdle for actual investment to materialize.

LIBERALIZATION OF INTERNATIONAL TRADE IN GOODS AND SERVICES

In our earlier discussion, there have been frequent references to the fact that prior to 1991, Indian industry in particular and the entire economy in general was being insulated from international competition through a complex variety of tariff and non-tariff barriers till 1991. Trade liberalization involved loosening or removing these tariff and non-tariff barriers. We begin by providing some quantitative indicators for the year 1987 with regard to trade restrictions.

Starting with international comparisions with South Asian neighbours, the World Bank (2004) noted that in the year 1987, 80.7 per cent of the harmonized six-digit tariff lines were subject to quantitative restrictions (QRs) on imports in India compared to 25.4 per cent in Pakistan, 56 per cent in Bangladesh, and 13.9 per cent in Sri Lanka. Similarly, for the same year, the (simple) average of the ad valorem tariff rates over all six-digit tariff lines was 98.8 per cent in India, 68.9 per cent in Pakistan, 81.8 per cent in Bangladesh, and 27.3 per cent in Sri Lanka. A comprehensive picture of the customs tariff structure for 1987–8 is given by Ahluwalia (1994) for different sectors and product groups. For manufactured goods as a group—that accounted for more than four-fifths of imports and a higher share of customs duties—simple average of protective (P) nominal tariff rates was 119.2 per cent and the corresponding simple average of total (T) tariff rates (inclusive of all other duties) was higher at 146.6 per cent. In other words, a domestically produced average import-competing commodity could make profit so long as its cost fell short of 2.4 times that of an average imported commodity! The corresponding trade-weighted average rates were somewhat lower at 85.6 per cent (P) and 102.2 per cent (T) respectively. The collected import duties were nearly two-thirds the c.i.f.[12] value of imports. India was thus clearly one of the most heavily protected countries in the world. Progressive integration with the world economy has indeed been an integral part of the unstated shift in the development strategy since 1991. Given the very high degree of protection [noted above] enjoyed by the Indian producers for more than three decades and their strong political clout, the process of trade liberalization appeared to be prima facie very difficult. Politically, the ruling Congress Party had been the architect and practitioner of autarkic industrialization strategy initiated in the 1950s (Chapter 3). This was also ideologically consistent with the Left political parties. The Hindu nationalist Bharatiya Janata Party supported the internal but opposed the external liberalization. Apart from ideological objections, trade liberalization measures also had significant revenue repercussions for the fiscally strapped government.

However, significant and progressive external trade liberalization has taken place since 1991, starting with the removal of QRs on most capital and intermediate goods, a drastic reduction in an absurdly high level of basic peak tariff rate from 350 per cent in 1991 to 15 per cent in 2006, and, over time, a reduction in the average level as well as dispersion of nominal tariff rates. The process continued apace during Narashimha Rao's regime when the simple average of the total [basic plus other] nominal tariff rates on all commoditers declined to less than one-third of its initial level of 128.0 per cent in 1991–2 to 39.5 per cent in 1996–7 while the standard deviation of nominal rates declined from 41.0 per cent to 18.7 per cent over the same period. There was, however, some reversal in later years (see Figures 8.3 and 8.4, Tables 8.2 and 8.3).

Note that the reversal is only partial and in terms of a rise in the average level of tariffs but *not* in dispersion. In other words, the degree of distortions introduced in relative prices by *differential* tariff rates has progressively declind over time, thereby improving the associated allocative efficiency.

Tariff or import duty rates constitute transparent entry barriers to potential import competition. Non-tariff barriers in the form of a variety of QRs are non-transparent entry restrictions on imports, which were often combined with tariff barriers. As noted above, progress on this front was initially swift with one-shot removal of QRs on as many as 6161 tariff lines out of the total of 10,000-odd lines[13] covering most capital and intermediate goods in 1991 in the crisis-gripped atmosphere. Further advance has been very tardy as most of the remaining QRs applied to what the policymakers had regarded as 'non-essential' consumer goods. Apart from their perverse incentive impact (Chapter 4), their persistence also reflected the political clout of the domestic producer lobby that was averse to import competition. Rapid reduction in QRs on consumer goods took place under the pressures from the World Trade Organization in response to complaints filed in this connection by the United States and the European Union. They were very reluctantly removed in three big instalments between 1999 and 2001, with tariff lines on restricted import list reduced from 2314 as on 1 April 1998 to 1183

FIGURE 8.3
Average Import Duty Rates in India (Basic)—Consumer Goods

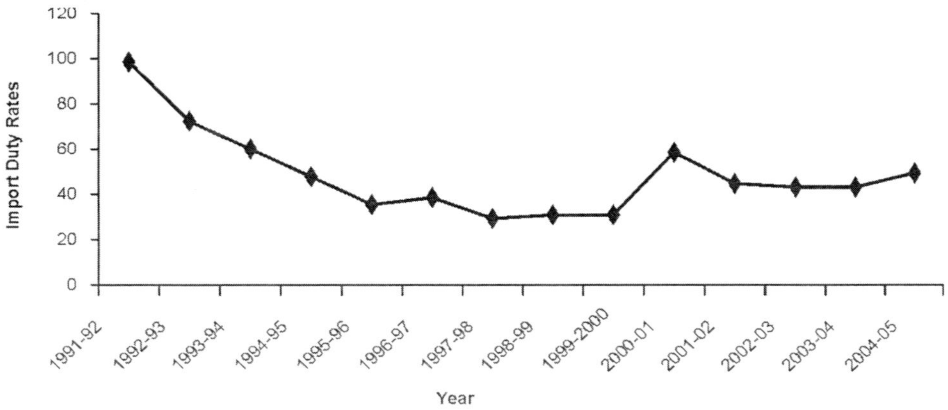

Source: Mathur and Sachdeva (2005: Table 1A, p. 536.)

FIGURE 8.4
Average Import Duty Rates in India (Basic)—All Commodities

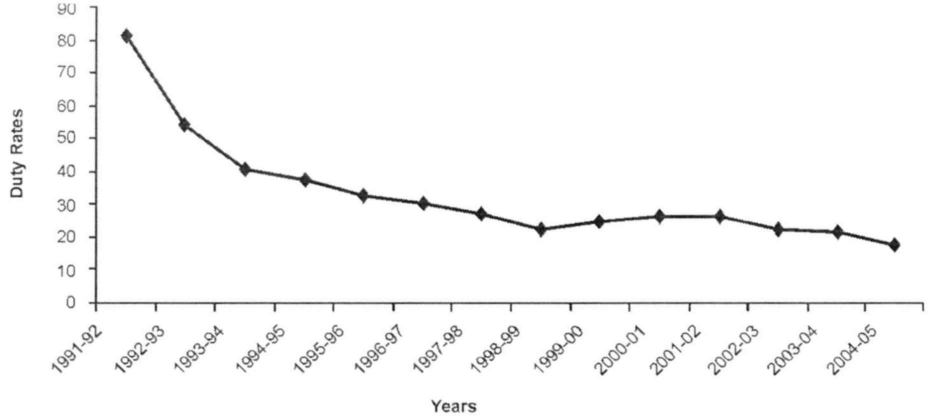

Source: Mathur and Sachdeva (2005: Table 1A, p. 536.)

in 1999, 968 in 2000 and further to 479 in 2001 (GOI-MOF 2002a, Box 6.3, 142). This was, however, combined with other forms of GATT and WTO-compatible non-tariff barriers with increasing resort to anti-dumping and safeguard duties. Safeguard duties are countervailing duties (CVD) in the Indian jargon, which are *excluded* in total nominal duty rates in Table 8.2. Notice that while simple

Table 8.2: Simple Average of Total Nominal Import Duty Rates and their Dispersion: 1991–2 to 2004–5

Commodity Group	1991–2	1992–3	1993–4	1994–5	1995–6	1996–7	1997–8	1998–9	1999–2000	2000–1	2001–2	2002–3	2003–4	2004–5
Agriculture	108.0	49.0	40.0	32.0	25.2	28.7	26.3	29.5	29.4	40.0	39.3	37.4	37.1	32.9
	(47.0)	(50.0)	(40.0)	(28.0)	(22.1)	(20.8)	(17.0)	(18.7)	(16.9)	(16.8)	(17.8)	(21.6)	(21.7)	(21.1)
Mining	108.0	99.0	72.0	47.0	30.0	25.4	24.8	29.6	26.6	26.8	24.6	24.1	23.4	12.5
	(19.0)	(23.0)	(26.0)	(25.0)	(15.7)	(11.7)	(11.6)	(12.2)	(12.3)	(12.6)	(11.5)	(10.9)	(10.3)	(5.7)
Consumer	141.0	108.0	85.0	67.0	45.5	45.6	40.1	45.4	42.7	45.1	41.7	36.9	33.5	25.9
goods	(36.0)	(47.0)	(41.0)	(37.0)	(26.8)	(27.1)	(20.6)	(20.6)	(19.1)	(16.9)	(17.2)	(16.0)	(19.1)	(16.7)
Intermed. goods	132.0	118.0	91.0	71.0	43.8	39.8	35.3	39.9	41.0	39.8	36.5	32.9	29.9	21.3
	(42.0)	(28.0)	(26.0)	(23.0)	(12.2)	(12.8)	(10.0)	(11.0)	(9.7)	(9.3)	(8.8)	(8.0)	(7.1)	(7.0)
Capital goods	105.0	97.0	69.0	55.0	33.2	34.6	30.3	34.7	34.6	34.6	32.5	31.2	29.8	20.4
	(33.0)	(33.0)	(32.0)	(28.0)	(12.4)	(11.8)	(9.4)	(10.1)	(8.0)	(7.8)	(12.3)	(11.6)	(11.5)	(11.4)
All commodities	128.0	107.0	82.0	64.4	41.0	39.5	34.9	39.6	39.3	39.9	37.1	33.7	31.1	22.8
	(41.0)	(40.0)	(35.0)	(30.0)	(19.0)	(18.7)	(14.5)	(15.2)	(13.7)	(12.7)	(13.3)	(12.6)	(12.1)	(12.4)

Notes: Total import duty rate includes basic rate, surcharge, special additional duty, education cess and excludes countervailing duty. Rates are in percentages and standard deviation of rates is given in brackets.
Source: Mathur and Sachdeva (2005), Table 1B, p. 537.

Table 8.3: Weighted Average of Total Nominal Tariff Rates

(Rates in Per Cent)

Commodity Group	1991–2	1992–3	1993–4	1994–5	1995–6	1996–7	1997–8	1998–9	1999–2000	2000–1	2001–2	2002–3	2003–4	2004–5
Agriculture	47.0	22.8	19.8	16.8	16.7	25.2	25.3	22.8	24.4	30.0	26.2	30.3	32.1	29.2
Mining	56.9	32.6	33.4	30.3	31.1	25.7	23.8	19.9	21.4	15.3	15.2	10.7	14.7	5.2
Consumer goods	97.8	83.2	68.7	55.9	36.1	40.6	33.8	40.1	37.4	66.2	50.7	48.4	49.1	50.4
Intermed. goods	69.5	62.6	47.6	38.4	34.8	34.7	33.4	31.8	33.1	37.1	36.1	32.1	29.0	19.6
Capital goods	94.8	85.2	58.4	45.5	29.1	29.3	25.9	29.4	31.0	30.7	27.8	25.4	25.5	18.1
All	81.4	60.6	46.8	43.2	32.9	32.2	30.2	30.3	31.4	30.7	29.6	25.7	26.1	18.0

Notes: Total import duty rate includes basic rate, surcharge, special additional duty, education cess and excludes countervailing duty. Weights used are the level of imports of the year except: for 1991–2 to 1994–5, imports of 1992–3 have been used as weights; for 1996–7, Imports of 1995–6 have been used as weights; for 1999–2000, imports of 1997–8 have been used as weights; for 2004–5, imports of 2003–4 have been used as the weights.
Source: Mathur and Sachdeva (2005), Table 1B, p. 537.

average of total nominal duty rates on consumer goods went up only slightly between 1999–2000 and 2001–2 before coming down in later years (Table 8.2), import weighted average duty rate on consumer goods rose sharply from 37.1 per cent in 1999–2000 to 66.2 per cent in 2001–2 before coming down to and levelling around 50 per cent till 2004–5. While this is still considerably lower than the initial duty rate of 97.8 per cent on consumer goods in 1991–2, it is obvious that consumer goods producers in India continue to be heavily protected.[14]

Despite significant reductions in both tariff and non-tariff barriers since 1991, World Bank (2004), in its international comparison, concluded that the Indian tariff rates on manufactured products in 2002 were the second highest among 105 developing countries and non-tariff barriers the highest among South Asian countries. An interesting comparative table from that study reveals that the simple average of total protective duties was 35 per cent in India, 21.2 per cent in Bangladesh, 18.2 per cent in Pakistan, 16.2 per cent in Nepal, and 10.5 per cent in Sri Lanka. This is despite the repeated promises of several Finance Ministers in successive governments since 1991 to bring down tariff levels to match those in the East Asian countries.

Although India was in 1987, and continues to remain (in international comparative perspective) till date, one of the most heavily protected economies in the world, especially in respect of consumer goods and to a much less extent in other commodities, Tables 8.2 and 8.3 clearly bring out a significant decline in the average tariff level as well as in the non-tariff barriers compared to the pre-1991 period. There has also been an equally remarkable reduction in the dispersion of tariff rates (Table 8.2) from 41 in 1991–2 to 12.4 in 2004–5 and hence in the associated distortions in allocation. This was reinforced by the sweeping liberalization of domestic investment and much more cautious one of private foreign investment (discussed earlier in the chapter) and considerable financial liberalization providing *additional and cheaper* avenues for raising funds. The economy has doubtlessly experienced significant improvements in efficiency gains resulting from increased domestic and external competition and restructuring over the last decade-and-a-half. Remarkably, the weighted average tariff level on capital goods came down from 94.8 per cent in 1991–2 to 18.1 per cent in 2004–5 and that on intermediate goods from 69.5 per cent to 19.6 per cent over the same period (Table 8.3). Not only have domestic capital goods producers become more competitive, easier access to foreign technology has also brought about technological upgradation. Consequently, the economic structure has become much more cost and quality competitive and much less distorted than what it was prior to 1991. It is indeed true that after the initial exuberance in the post-reform investment boom that resulted in excess capacity and structural adjustment arising from increased competition, the economy experienced a slowdown in real GDP growth (and a steeper decline in growth rate in factory manufacturing) during 1997–8 and 2002–3 but it clocked unprecedented average 8 per cent real GDP growth between 2003–4 and 2005–6.

Who were the losers and gainers from this adjustment process of opening up domestic industry to foreign competition? We may start by noting that tariff *reductions* lie entirely within the discretion of the central government by issuing notification and reporting the change in the gazette. While passing the budget, the parliament approves the *ceiling* rates of excise and customs, which cannot be exceeded through executive discretion. However, any rate can be fixed *below* the ceiling level by notification. Producer groups interested in protection exert pressure for raising the ceiling rates of tariff announced in the budget. Users and consumers of importable products (the latter being dispersed and unorganized), on the other hand, exert opposite pressures for discretionary reduction or exemption. In a regime of declining average tariff level and dispersion, users and consumers of importable products have been the gainers and would support the trend. The major losers have been the producers of import-competing products. Like governments of all the industrialized countries, the Indian government has also been much more favourably disposed towards protecting the interests of producers than those of consumers and users. This has been reinforced by the long-time influence of the ideology of economic nationalism under which, as noted already, self-reliance had been identified with self-sufficiency irrespective of costs. Equally important has been the concern regarding potential job losses from import competition.

How did the government manage to overcome the pressures from the producer lobby against the fairly steep import tariff reduction between 1991–2 and 1996–7? At least three objective factors must have helped. The first relates to the 1980s. Starting from high levels in the 1970s, the tariff rates peaked in 1988 (under persistent shortages of foreign exchange), averaging between 130 and 140 per cent (World Bank 2004). There was, therefore, a considerable element of tariff redundancy[15] as a consequence. Second, about an 85 per cent rupee exchange rate depreciation in real terms took place between end 1985 and end 1990 during pre-reform period. This was followed by external payment crisis-induced 16.4 per cent devaluation in real terms between June and December 1991 (RBI 2003a: Table 190, p. 363). Both the factors contributed significantly towards softening the competitive as well as revenue impact of almost complete abolition of QRs on capital and intermediate products as well as subsequent tariff reductions. The necessity for exchange rate correction in the overvalued exchange rate despite significant depreciation in the 1980s was noted by Cerra and Saxena (2002). It was also part of the Contingent Compensatory Finance Facility (CCFF) package with the International Monetary Fund (IMF) in order to abolish export subsidies at one go. Finally, as discussed in Chapter 3, the high transaction costs associated with complex, comprehensive and often internally inconsistent foreign exchange and import control regime might also have overweighed the protective cover offered by high tariff rates and QRs.

Since the mid-1990s, there has been partial rollback of tariff reduction. Can the partial reversal in tariff rate reduction since 1997–8 be attributed to the ideological preference of the BJP for domestic Indian industry and a consequent opposition to external liberalization? Objective circumstances do not support this attribution on various grounds. One, the environment of a slowdown in industrial growth since 1997–8 was hardly congenial to further tariff reduction. Second, the BJP-led coalition government carried out the nuclear tests in 1998, following which there were international sanctions against India. It was in that situation that the uniform Special Additional Duty in two instalments of 5 per cent each was introduced in the budgets. Another exogenous event working in the same direction was the East Asian currency meltdown in 1997 when the Indian currency experienced revaluation in real terms. Finally, steep increases in the weighted average tariff rates on consumer goods in 2000–1 and 2001–2 are attributable to the forced removal of most

QRs on consumer goods after losing the dispute with the United States in the WTO, replacing QRs with mostly peak rates of tariff. However, the uniform nature of special additional import duty did not increase the distortions as the dispersion of the tariff rates came down progressively.

The downward slide of the peak rates of import tariff has continued during the United Progressive Alliance (UPA) regime since May 2004, reaching 15 per cent in the 2005–6 budget. However, the peak rate applies only to the *basic* rate of duty. Inclusive of auxiliary and countervailing rates and surcharges, the average tariff rate in India continues to be the highest in the Asian region. The progress in reducing the number of exemptions has also been very slow. Consequently, Indian industry still enjoys its most protected status in the Asian comparative perspective. As late as 29 November 2005, the Prime Minister, Dr Manmohan Singh, felt it necessary to reiterate that 'Our tariff levels are coming down and we are committed to bringing them down to ASEAN levels' when he addressed the India Economic Summit organized jointly by the World Economic Forum and the Confederation of Indian Industry in New Delhi. This is not to deny the major change that has come about as result of increased international competition resulting from significant reductions in trade barriers. Dr Singh who was also the Finance Minister between 1991–6, recalled at the same function the initial concerns among the Indian industrialists about 'increased competition', about 'exposure to global market forces' and 'about the impact on our industry and on our country', and described the radical change during the reform period thus: 'The Indian economy has become more open, more globally integrated, and more competitive (than in 1991). The seekers of protection then line up now seeking greater openness. Truly, times have changed; mindsets have changed; attitudes have changed; aspirations have changed; our hopes for the future have also changed.'

PRIVATIZATION OF COMMERCIAL PUBLIC-SECTOR ENTERPRISES

There is no uniformity in the usage of the term 'privatization' in the Indian debates. The entry of private-sector units in the construction of physical infrastructural facilities (such as roads, telecommunications, electric power generation) has usually been described as privatization. In recent times, the same phenomenon is being termed as public–private partnership. Any sale of government-owned equity in the legally autonomous but fully government-owned commercial entities to private individuals or entities is usually covered under the term 'disinvestments' in government policy discussions. A sale of even minority equity stake in such entities is, however, decried as privatization by the Left political parties. Privatization in all these senses has been an integral part of the post-1991 liberalizing reform process even though the progress has been tardy.

Because of the still dominant hold of the ideology of socialism and because these entities serve powerful sectional interests (Chapter 4), there has been tremendous resistance to this process. In the popular mindset too, the socialist instrument of public sector has been (wrongly) identified with the socialist goal. The compulsions for undertaking privatization have their origins in the constellation of fiscal crunch with adverse impact on public investment in infrastructure and the increasing bite of infrastructural bottlenecks in the face of a step-up in GDP growth arising from liberalization and globalization. The downward slide in the central government's capital expenditure in the 1980s has already been noted (Chapter 6). This slide continued in the 1990s because of the inability to contain the upward climb of current revenue expenditures (Figure 6.2). In the first half of the 1990s, it was prompted by the fiscal adjustment negotiated with the IMF whereas in the second half, it was part of the efforts to contain rising fiscal and revenue deficits (Figure 6.1). However, the surge in private economic activities in the 1990s has been pushing the existing infrastructural facilities to the limit despite some improvements over time in their operational efficiency. In these circumstances, the continued slide in public capital expenditures has been forcing the pace of privatization of infrastructural facilities and services (the traditional domain of departmentally run public sector entities) indeed at uneven speed in different sectors in the face of the varying intensity of infrastructural constraints restricting the pace of growth.

It is privatization in the second sense of partial or total sale of government-owned equity in legal entities distinct from government, or what we term commercial public sector enterprises (PSEs) that we are dealing with here. They are 'commercial' in the sense that they engage in economic activities that involve production of 'non-public' goods and services.[16] They are non-departmental enterprises legally distinct from government and hence formally expected to be autonomous. However, in the intervention-addicted Indian political and bureaucratic culture, most of them, if not all, had been operating as non-transparent instruments in the hands of politicians, bureaucrats, and organized trade unions to pursue their narrow ends at public expense. They have been offshoots of the indiscriminate expansion of public-sector activities during the radicalization of Indian politics after the mid-1960s. This expansion went well beyond the provision of public goods[17] into the production of private goods and services of all kinds, and well beyond the administrative, organizational, and managerial capabilities of the government. We have already noted how the PSEs have been used as a convenient instrument for organized-sector employment 'generation' with absorption of labour well beyond the limits dictated by considerations of commercial viability and other (mis)uses of these entities (Chapters 3 and 4). The losers from the privatization [that is, by reducing public ownership to less than 51 per cent and passing management control to commercially oriented private hands] of PSEs are clearly politicians and bureaucrats who occupy strategic positions in government decision-making and overstaffed public-sector employees (including white-collar professionals) who had been more favourably placed in terms of job security than those in the expanding private enterprises, and who apprehend large retrenchment/lay-offs (in view of the well-known and well-recognized redundancy) besides losing their long-enjoyed aristocratic status in the otherwise unskilled less-educated workforce.

On objective economic and analytical grounds, the case for privatization of commercial PSEs has been strong in the Indian context. To elaborate, most of the commercial PSEs, being producers of *private* goods and services, do not serve any objectively worthwhile *public purpose* to be justifiably government-owned. Clearly, it is not the business of the government to run a five-star hotel and the like that can be supplied more efficiently by private players in competitive markets. This is especially true when in an administratively and managerially overstretched situation the government is unable to perform what is its legitimate core business, namely, provision of adequate and satisfactory social services like primary and secondary education and basic health services and other infrasturctural facilities that are not privately profitable in competitive markets and which the government is expected to undertake in a *fiduciary* capacity on behalf of the society. Second, strictly commercial considerations of maintaining economic viability in a market environment take a backseat in commercial PSEs because of the availability of government support from budgetary and extra-budgetary means. Third, the incentives facing the managers of these enterprises bear little resemblance to those in a competitive commercial enterprise. Legally and constitutionally (by virtue of their being government owned), they are accountable to parliamentary committees and subject to usually procedure-driven public audit by the Comptroller and Auditor General of India in addition to commercial audit under the Indian Companies Act. Like other government servants in public administration, they are subject to investigation by the Central Bureau of Investigation and the Central Vigilance Commission in cases involving loss to a PSE when the loss may have been not necessarily due to malafide intentions in breach of fiduciary position occupied by public servants, but part of the honest commercial risk inherent in the activities carried out by that PSE like, for example, state trading. This environment leads to procedure-oriented and a risk-averse managerial behaviour [like other government administration] that is inherently inimical to commercial operation. Even in exceptional cases of well-run PSEs, the rate of return on employed capital is usually low because managers have little freedom in adjusting their prices or output according to market conditions. The recent saga of the inability of the government-owned oil companies to adjust their domestic prices in the face of rising international prices of mostly imported crude oil provide a pertinent illustration of this point. The freedom of commercial PSEs to undertake investment even with internally generated resources requires permission from the administrative ministry if it exceeds certain pre-specified ceiling. Notice that all our foregoing discussion is purely on objective grounds and without bringing in the Indian context. These grounds become much stronger in the Indian context of intervention-addicted political and bureaucratic culture. This context becomes critical in the most touted argument of no disinvestment in profit-making PSEs operating in competitive markets. The simple point is that in the environment of changing coalition governments, profit-making status of a PSU is dependent not only on the market conditions and management but is also subject to getting non-interventionist ministers and bureaucrats in future about which there is no guarantee whatsoever!

In the pre-1991 period, most PSEs operated under a local monopoly situation or in areas exclusively reserved for the public sector. The Industrial Policy Statement of July 1991 opened up most of these areas to private entry. Such a decision has placed the existing PSEs in a disadvantageous position of having to compete with private units not having the burden of redundant workers. More importantly, private units have been freed from licence-permit restrictions but commercial PSEs remain shackled by the need to obtain administrative clearances from a procedure-driven bureaucracy in the parent ministry and are being financially squeezed by the fast-vanishing budgetary support besides having to compete with private entrants.

Given the arguments presented above on objective and analytical grounds, the Indian political and bureaucratic context and the post-1991 adverse conditions faced by PSEs, rapid privatization is imperative not only for efficiency gains but, even more importantly, given the overload on the government, for refocusing public activities on more legitimate core functions of basic governance, including adequate supply of public goods and services like basic health and primary education. It would also generate revenues for the fiscally strapped government for increased government spending on social services and investment in infrastructural facilities. Lamenting 'UPA's painfully incremental sale of PSE equity', one leading daily newspaper editorially observed, '...it would be equally perspective distorting not to remind ourselves just how much India loses by not having a radical disinvestments policy.'[18]

However sensible on rational grounds, privatization has proved to be one of the most difficult components of economic reforms. The obvious reason is that the losers, namely ministers and bureaucrats in the parent ministries and the well-organized PSE employees, are not only politically influential but also strategically placed in government to stall the process. More importantly, they are able to glorify their selfish interests by invoking Nehruvian socialism whose hold is weaker but still reasonably powerful to oppose disinvestments by bringing in emotive considerations like (unspecified and untested) strategic importance, sale of 'national' assets to private profiteers, sale of family silver, and creation of private monopoly, which also sway public opinion.[19] They are also able to garner support from Fabian socialists and radical intellectuals who continue to be naively committed to socialist instruments despite the collapse of the USSR and the remarkable strides made by the so-called socialist market economy of China.

Politically, ideological positions of the major national parties have influenced the course of disinvestments. The process of disinvestments started on the wrong foot in 1991. It was insisted upon by IMF as part of the CCFF conditionalities (Desai 1999: 28) and continues to be undertaken for an entirely wrong reason, namely, to generate capital account revenue for bridging the fiscal deficit,[20] which makes it convenient for maintaining unproductive current expenditure while keeping fiscal deficit within tolerable limits. It has been an ongoing battle between the administrative ministry unwilling to lose control over a PSE and the Ministry of Finance whose job it is to maintain some semblance of fiscal discipline. Whenever the conflict was resolved at cabinet level, the administrative ministry tried its best to delay the process by raising procedural hurdles. When these were crossed, workers organized nationwide demonstrations and managed to take the matter to the court to get judicial stay. Successful privatization could take place only after crossing these hurdles.

Table 8.4 provides the year-wise performance of disinvestments in terms of (i) the number of PSEs in which equity was sold; (ii) budgeted receipts; and (iii) actual receipts and broad description of modalities of disinvestments.

During the immediate post-reform period, the minority government was that of the Congress Party, which was haunted by the public-sector-dominated socialist pattern of society of the 1950s and had expanded public sector indiscriminately under populist radicalization of politics since the mid-1960s. Forced by the commitment to the IMF, it is no wonder that its approach was hesitant and half-hearted. The shares of disinvested PSEs were offloaded mostly on government-

FIGURE 8.5
Deficits of the Central Government 1980–2003

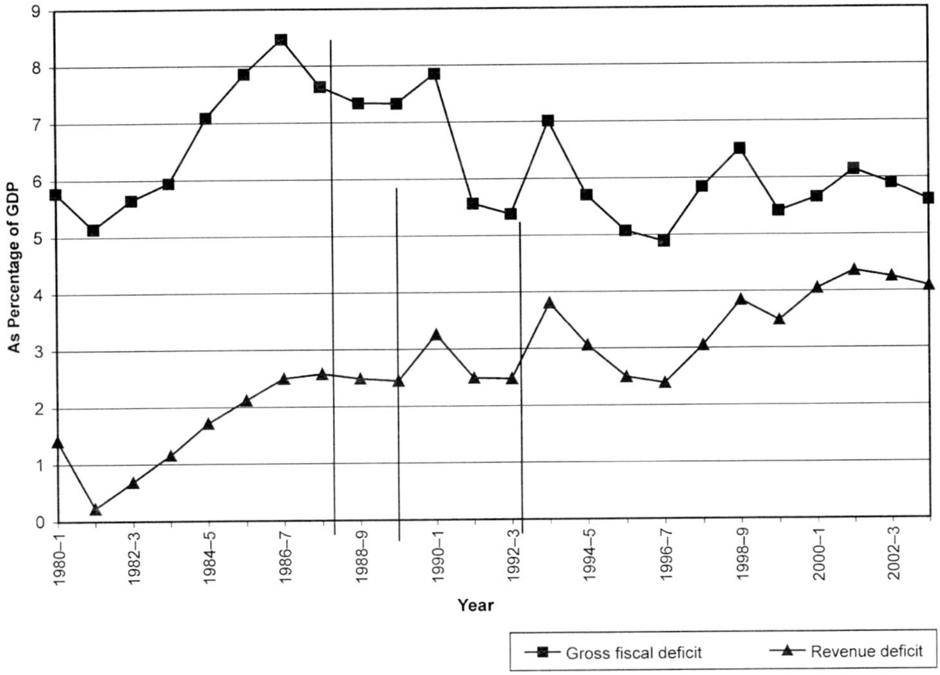

Source: RBI (2002–3), *Handbook of Statistics on the Indian Economy*, Table 221.

FIGURE 8.6
Expenditure and Receipts of the Central Government: 1980–2003

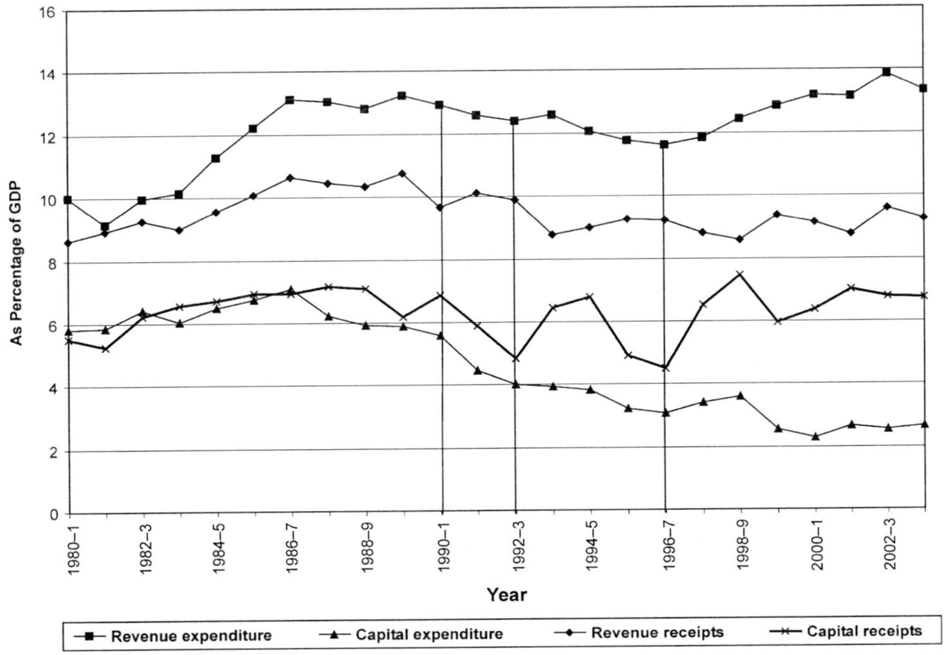

Source: RBI (2002–3), *Handbook of Statistics on the Indian Economy*, Table 221.

Table 8.4: Budgeted and Actual Receipts and Modalities of Disinvestment: 1991–2 to 2003–4

Year	No. of companies in which equity sold	Budgeted receipt for the year (Rs in billions)	Actual receipts (Rs in billions)	Modality
1991–2	47 (31 in one tranche and 16 in another)	25.00	30.38	Minority shares sold by auction method bundles of 'very good', 'good', and 'average' companies.
1992–3	36 (in 3 tranches)	25.00	19.13	Bundling of shares abandoned. Shares sold separately for each company by auction method.
1993–4	–	35.00	Nil	Equity of 7 companies sold by open auction but proceeds received in 1993–4.
1994–5	13	40.00	48.43	Sales through auction method in which NRIs and other persons legally permitted to buy, hold, or sell equity were allowed to participate.
1995–6	5	70.00	3.62	Equities of 4 companies auctioned and government piggybacked on the IDBI fixed price offering for the fifth company.
1996–7	1	50.00	3.80	GDR(VSNL) in international market.
1997–8	1	48.00	9.02	GDR(MTNL) in international market.
1998–9	5	50.00	53.71	GDR (VSNL)/ Domestic offerings with the participation of FIIs (CONCOR, GAIL). Cross purchase by 3 oil sector companies, i.e. GAIL, ONGC, and Indian Oil Corporation.
1999–2000	4	100.00	18.29	GDR–GAIL, VSNL domestic issue, BALCO restructuring, MFILs strategic sale and others.
2000–1	4	100.00	18.70	Strategic sale of BALCO, LJMC, KRL (CRL), CPCL(MRL)
2001–2	9	120.00	56.32 **	Strategic sale of CMC 51%, HTL 74%, VSNL 25%, IBP 33.58%, PPL 74%, and other modes: ITDC, HCI, STC, MMTC.
2002–3	5	120.00	33.48 **	Strategic sale of JESSOP 72%, HZL 26%, MFIL 26%, IPCL 25%, and other modes: HCI, Maruti.
2003–4	3	132.00	145.00 (P)	
2004–5***		N.A	27.65	IPO in NTPC, sale to employees of IPCL, and balance receipts of ONGC sale
2005–6***		NIL	15.68	Sale of shares of MTNL to public sector financial institution and public sector banks and sale to employees
Total	49*	915.00	483.21 **	

Notes: * Total number of companies in which disinvestment has taken place.

** Figures inclusive of amount expected to be realized, control premium, dividend/dividend tax and transfer of surplus cash reserves prior to disinvestment, etc.

*** Communication dated May 10, 2006 from Saurabh Chandra, Joint Secretary, Department of Disinvestment, Government of India.

Source: Disinvestment Commission Onsite. www.disinvest.gov.in.

owned public financial institutions as part of the stabilization process. Even then, the targets were modest and actual receipts were 52 per cent of the budgeted receipts.

The next two (short-lived) governments were left of the centre (post-poll) United Front (UF) coalition governments with outside support from the Congress Party and the Marxist Communist Party. The targets remained modest and the new modality of tapping Global Depository Receipts was tried for two telecom monopolies that had exploited their domestic monopoly position to build up good reserves. The performance, however, was very poor, with accrual of hardly 13 per cent of the budgeted receipts. The UF government also appointed the first Disinvestment Commission in 1997, to which fifty-eight PSEs were referred. The Disinvestment Commission had recommended strategic sale of twenty-nine PSEs, trade sale of five and closure/sale of assets in the case of four others, partial disinvestments in five, and no change in ownership/management in the case of the remaining twelve PSEs referred to it. It had also suggested the creation of an earmarked Disinvestment Fund out of the proceeds to be used for restructuring viable PSEs before disinvestment, funding voluntary retirement scheme to reduce redundancy, and financing social-sector investment with a view to enhancing social and political acceptability of the disinvestment process. Hardly any of its recommendations were implemented in the face of resistance from the administrative ministries and the Left parties supporting the coalition government. The UF Finance Minister, a reformer by conviction who was also in the earlier Congress government, clearly found himself helpless.

The next two National Democratic Alliance (NDA) coalition governments were led by the Hindu nationalist Bharatiya Janata Party (BJP), which did not have an ideological preference for the public sector. During its first stint lasting one year, it resorted to a new artificial device of cross-purchases from each other of government equity by three oil-sector companies that exceeded the budgeted target for the government in 1998–9 but at the cost of defeating the very purpose of disinvestment.

The approach till the second BJP-led NDA coalition government was to sell minority shares in the central PSEs to raise capital account revenue for bridging the fiscal deficit. During its second stint (1999–2004) the BJP-led NDA coalition government gave a big momentum to the disinvestment process. Finance Minister Yashwant Sinha in his first budget speech stated the general policy decision of the new government to reduce the government's stake in non-strategic PSEs to 26 per cent. He also doubled the budgeted targets of disinvestment. This government also set up the Department of Disinvestment on 10 December 1999 to deal with all matters in this connection and clarified what it regarded as strategic sectors. The department was later converted into the full-fledged Ministry of Disinvestment. The department undertook the first strategic sale of the government-owned bakery (Modern Food Industries Limited) with a transfer of management control to an Indian multinational—Hindustan Lever Limited. This was really the first-ever total privatization of a central PSE.[21] Fourteen more PSEs were disinvested through the strategic sale[22] route in the following three years from 2000–1 to 2002–3. The strategic sale route hit roadblock in 2003–4 when the Minister for Petroleum objected to the strategic sale of two oil PSEs, HPCL and BPCL, proposed by the Ministry of Disinvestment. After a prolonged battle within the NDA, a compromise was struck by agreeing to the modality of Initial Public Offer (IPO) of equity in the case of six PSEs. This yielded Rs 141 billion compared to the budgeted figure of Rs 132 billion.

The NDA coalition was defeated in the General Elections of 2004. The Congress-led UPA government announced its intentions in line with the Left parties' demands and along the path taken by the earlier Rao government (1991–6). The Left parties had called for the abolition of the Ministry of Disinvestment after the 2004 election and before formation of the UPA government. The UPA government promptly obliged as the Left parties decided to support the UPA coalition government from outside.

The National Common Minimum Programme (NCMP) of the UPA coalition government was released on 28 May 2004. In the context of the public sector, consistent with the Congress Party and the Left parties' traditional allegiance to socialist ideology, NCMP confirms commitment of the UPA government to 'a strong and effective public sector', and lays down the following vague but restrictive guidelines: (i) 'all privatizations (no definition offered) will be considered on a transparent and consultative and case-by-case (ad hoc) basis'; (ii) 'generally profit-making companies (no definition furnished) will not be privatized'; (iii) 'The UPA will retain existing "navaratna"[23] companies in the public sector'; (iv) 'while every effort will be made to modernize and restructure sick public sector companies and revive sick industry (meaning unclear), chronically loss-making companies will either be sold-off or closed' (words in bracket added by authors). In the old-style closed-economy mindset, the NCMP 'believes that privatization should increase competition, not decrease it. It will not support the emergence of any monopoly that only restricts competition'. It seems to be blindly equating 'large' units with monopoly power without asking the question whether their activity is already subject to international competition through imports or multinational corporations operating within the country. Nor are (vaguely defined) 'profit-making' or 'loss-making' PSEs being subjected to any objectively reasonable criteria for their remaining under public ownership. There is no assessment whatsoever about whether commercial PSEs serve any worthwhile social purpose to continue to be under public ownership.

It must be mentioned, however, that the Finance Minister has been making some honest but unsuccessful attempts at disinvestment in his efforts to maintain fiscal discipline. On 26 May 2005—one year after the UPA government assumed power—he announced the intention to disinvest 10 per cent of government-owned equity (the residual government-owned equity share exceeded 51 per cent *after* sale) in the navaratna company BHEL (Bharat Heavy Electricals Limited) with a view to creating National Disinvestment Fund to undertake social sector investments.[24] He argued that the minority equity sale met the NCMP commitment to keep navaratna companies under public sector and hence did not violate NCMP. However, calling the announcement to be the 'first serious breach of NCMP with serious repercussions',[25] the Communist Party of India (Marxist) successfully blocked the move because its external support was crucial for the stability of the coalition government. After vocal protests from the Left parties, the Minister of Heavy Industries and Public Enterprises announced that he had put on hold the decision regarding disinvestment in BHEL *and other proposals* (for disinvestment) in his ministry.[26] The Finance Minister also ruled out the strategic sale route of disinvestment while keeping open the offer of sale route[27] in thirteen profit-making PSEs identified by the earlier BJP-led NDA coalition government.[28] Ruling out the option of strategic sale route in disinvestments did not make any prima facie economic sense.

Another attempt was made in June 2006, this time for the sale of 10 per cent stake each in two non-navaratna profit-making companies—NALCO (National Aluminium Company) in Orissa and NLC (Nayveli Lignite Corporation) in Tamil Nadu. A 'visibly happy' Finance Minister was quoted as saying after the Cabinet Committee on Economic Affairs approved the decision, 'In a meeting on 21 November 2005 between the UPA and the Left, it was agreed that small portions of equity in profit-making non-navaratnas to raise funds for the National Investment Fund can be sold.'[29] While the Left disputed the assertion forthwith (see the same report), they did not threaten agitation as in the past. The roadblock came from another unexpected quarter—from the Finance Minister's own home state, Tamil Nadu. The workers at NLC declared indefinite strike on 6 July and refused to accept preferential allotment of shares as a compromise for agreeing to the sell off. Interestingly, two factors are noteworthy. First, the workers' union was affiliated not to the Left, but to the regional DMK Party ruling in the State, that is an ally in the UPA coalition at the Centre and has no ideological preference for the public sector. Second, the two DMK ministers in the Union Cabinet were party to the cabinet decision on disinvestments with the tacit approval of the DMK supremo, the Chief Minister of Tamil Nadu. However, the workers' resistance proved too strong for the Chief Minister and he threatened to withdraw support to the coalition government and the UPA government was forced to 'consign its disinvestment agenda to the backburner' on 6 July. A disappointed Finance Minister regretted that the purpose of disinvestments was 'misunderstood' and pleading for the consensus, said it was now up to the Prime Minister to take a decision on that issue. A cryptic statement from the Prime Minister's Office said, 'The Prime Minister has decided to keep *all disinvestments decisions and proposals* on hold, pending further review.'[30] This saga brings out the strength of the workers' union in a regional party[31] and also how the regional allies do not mind flouting the cabinet responsibility with impunity in the face of regional pressures.

As if this was not enough, the Comptroller and Auditor General (CAG) of India provided further setback to the disinvestment process.

Unmindful of the complications in the commercial decision-making process under uncertainty, the report of this procedure-driven accounting agency (submitted to the parliament on 24 August 2006) passed strictures against the disinvestment decisions involved in the strategic sales of nine PSEs under the earlier NDA government. Alleging far too conservative assumptions by global advisers aversely impacting their valuation, it reportedly offered a prima facie strange logic that *because* as many as forty-eight of the seventy initially interested applicants of Letters of Intent in becoming strategic partners had withdrawn from the bidding process, this indicated that competitive tension generated to the process was not encouraging enough to have maximized the value of the stake under disinvestments.[32] In the face of the NALCO and NLC fiasco, the CAG report is possibly responsible for putting *all the existing proposals on disinvestment* on hold. When asked about the disinvestment process, the Prime Minister, at the recent Press Conference with the Party Chief Sonia Gandhi at the end of the Congress Chief Ministers' Conference in Nainital, said, 'It is certainly true that because of certain differences among the partners of UPA, I had to put that process on hold. We will talk to our colleagues before we move forward in that direction.'[33]

It may be mentioned that even the informative factual discussion that had been a regular feature of the annual pre-budget *Economic Survey* of the Ministry of Finance has been conspicuous by its absence since 2004. A few PSEs are successfully coping with the increased competition even under the adverse circumstances. A large number of others have been getting increasingly in the red. Some others have been referred to the Board for Industrial and Financial Reconstruction (BIFR) for revival/liquidation. Budgetary support and revival are being rolled out from year to year depending on the political pressures and other budgetary compulsions. The talk of giving 'autonomy' to PSEs has been revived (again!) in the context of the report submitted by the ad hoc Arjun Sengupta Committee, which has reportedly[34] recommended, among others, (i) significant but graded rise in the cap on capital expenditure by PSEs without receiving the administrative ministry's sanction; (ii) daily affairs of PSEs and conduct of their CEOs to be kept out of discussions in parliament; (iii) accountability to the parliament only through annual reports;

and (iv) only one parliamentary panel to cover all aspects of a given PSE. These commendable recommendations still remain only on paper.[35] However, the ad hoc committee has made a very strange suggestion that any reduction in the government stake below 51 per cent in consistently profit-making PSEs should be done only with parliamentary consent. It is not clear why the executive should be deprived of the autonomy to reshuffle its portfolio of government equity in commercial PSEs so as to meet increasingly more pressing demands in the field of social sector and infrastructure. In our judgment, autonomy of the PSEs under the existing Indian political-bureaucratic intervention-addicted culture would remain a mirage to be pursued only with the outmoded Left ideological blinds. There has thus been an unfortunate backtracking on the policy of disinvestment that reflects the firm hold of the Nehruvian socialism. It is a pity since the pragmatist that Nehru was, he himself might have shed his 1950s' variety of socialism (that his avowed followers are currently clinging to) in the light of the past and the present experience of the Indian public sector and the newly emerging resurgent Indian economy driven by vibrant and dynamic private enterprise in the rapidly globalizing world.

ORGANIZED LABOUR MARKET REFORMS[36]

The term 'organized labour' usually describes the unionized segment of labour. This is not meaningful in the Indian context (as we argue here) where the term is broadly used to include those workers employed in non-agricultural sectors and having *regular and hired* employment with wages and salaries considerably above the average earnings per worker for the economy as a whole. We may add that well-above-average wages and salaries (i) can be regularly paid only if the corresponding economic activities are characterized by well-above-average productivity per worker in a sustained manner;[37] and (ii) may constitute in part returns to their relatively scarce educational and skill endowments. Because of their privileged service conditions in an environment of unlimited labour supplies, they are justifiably described as labour aristocracy. We argue herein that they owe this privileged status—not to the organized strength of trade unions—but to the benevolent activist labour legislation.

We start by noting that the Trade Union Act 1926 (amended finally in September 2001) permitted any seven workers in an establishment/enterprise to form a trade union and register it. Proliferation of trade unions was the inevitable result.[38] There was no provision for the procedure and criteria for union recognition for collective bargaining. It is no wonder, therefore, that the TU movement has remained weak and fragmented.

How did this segment come to occupy an aristocratic status despite the trade unions being weak and fragmented? Three factors contributed. One, the public-sector dominated autarkic industrialization strategy resulted in an import- and capital-using inefficient high cost industrial structure that limited organized labour absorption. Two, government activism in the labour market sought to put in place complex and comprehensive labour legislation to strengthen the trade unions, improve wage outcomes, and ensure job security. This legislation, meant originally for protecting workers against exploitation by employers, ended up raising the transaction costs of hiring and maintaining regular wage workers and imposing restrictions on labour allocation by employers. Three, despite their fragmented character, the trade unions formed opportunistic coalitions to exploit their critical location in public-sector monopolies in organized services like banking and insurance. Consequently, organized trade unionism is more prevalent among white-collar professionals mostly in the organized public sector services than among blue-collar workers in manufacturing.

The first two factors mentioned have also been responsible for another stylized fact. The proportionate share of this segment in total workforce has shown a *significant decline* over the last forty years.[39] In other words, the organized–unorganized duality of the Indian labour market has been accentuated over the period when the objective of economic development was to *raise* the share of this segment characterized by well-above-average productivity per worker and hence above-average wages and salaries. The accentuation of the organized–unorganized duality is the result of the autarkic public-sector-dominated industrialization strategy and the discretionary control regime associated with it as much as of activist labour legislation. The outcome has been clearly socially inequitable because it kept the overwhelming proportion of unorganized labour outside the higher-than-average productivity segment. The change in the development strategy during the post-1991 reform period sought to tackle a part of the first factor responsible for the social inequity by introducing both domestic and external competition and a significant reduction, if not total abolition, of discretionary controls. As we noted earlier in the chapter, the public sector has been on the retreat, albeit very slowly, as it still is shackled by a weaker but still very important omnipresent hold of the outdated Nehruvian socialism on public perceptions and a captive to the politically powerful interest groups.

It is the second factor of activist labour legislation that is associated with increased social inequity whose persistence forms the theme of discussion here.

Government activism sought to put in place complex and comprehensive regulations to strengthen the hands of the weak trade unions, improve wage outcome, and provide or enhance job security. There are about fifty labour-related statutes by the central government alone dealing with various aspects such as minimum wages, accident benefits, death of workers, maternity, conditions of employment including dismissal and disciplinary action, and industrial disputes. Labour being a subject on the concurrent list of the distribution of powers specified in the Indian Constitution, there are several additional state statutes covering different aspects or segments of labour. The labour laws are implemented both by the centre and/or state governments, which has added to the dimensions of complexities in respect of labour legislation. Zagha (1999), citing Gopal (1994), observes that while dealing with common issues in different contexts of employment conditions without reference to an internally consistent framework, India's labour laws introduced uncertainty and ambiguity about key legal concepts and definitions, thus creating the scope for conflicting interpretations. In this situation, the courts made legislation more encompassing by widening the scope of certain terms like 'industry', 'workman', 'wage', and 'employed person' beyond what was originally intended. In the event, litigations abound (with government as a party in most) and disputes take a long time to settle. The effective coverage of this extensive legislation has been confined mostly to large units, probably for reasons of administrative cost.

Clearly, the cleaning up of outdated statutes and amending others to bring them under a uniform framework of concepts and definitions to reduce uncertainty and ambiguity are major challenges for legal reforms. However, procedural simplifications for reducing the paperwork required under multiple laws applicable to the same units and for minimizing the corruption and harassment by inspectors can indeed be undertaken without legislation but have not so far been attempted.[40] Their urgency was emphasized by the present Prime Minister as late as in December 2005 in his address to the tripartite 40th Indian Labour Conference. No follow-up action is reported till date.

The most pervasive as well as possibly the most contentious pieces of legislation have been the Industrial Disputes Act (IDA) 1947, particularly Chapter V-B that was added in 1976, and the Contract Labour (Regulation and Abolition) Act (CLRA Act) 1970. Section 10 of the CLRA gives wide-ranging powers to the 'appropriate' government 'to prohibit employment of contract labour in any process, operation, or other work in any establishment'. Till 1976, lay off, retrenchment, and closure subject to the payment of prescribed compensation to the workers under the IDA did not require the permission of the government. Chapter V-B was added during the Emergency in 1976. This was the continuation of populist radicalization of Indian politics since the mid-1960s by Mrs Indira Gandhi. Under Chapter V-B, large industrial establishments, namely factories, plantations, and mines employing not less than 300 workers have to seek prior permission from the appropriate government to undertake lay off, retrenchment, or closure. These provisions in the two legislations (CLRA and IDA) restricted the freedom of employers to tailor employment in response to changes in market conditions for output. During her return to power (1980–4) after the brief Janata Party coalition government (1977–80), Mrs Gandhi made Chapter V-B of the IDA more restrictive by making it applicable to industrial establishments employing 100 or more workers.[41] This accentuated labour market inflexibility in the organized segment. This, however, was at odds with the 'pro-business' tilt in policy that Mrs Gandhi is said to have imparted during this period (Kohli 2006). These provisions remain on the statute books till today and have generated perverse incentives for costly and lengthy adjudications and lock-outs, and discouraged plant-level collective bargaining. The 'jobless growth' in the factory manufacturing segment in the 1980s, discussed in the following pages, was widely attributed to these legislative provisions.

Private employers have found various legal and extra-legal ways of getting around the legislative regulations. These included (i) adopting capital-intensive technologies to minimize employing permanent production process workers; (ii) outsourcing activities to unregulated and unregistered units; (iii) passing on excess labour costs to consumers/users in the form of mark-up pricing where product market structures permitted; (iv) moving units to areas with lax enforcement; and (v) splitting establishments into multiple smaller units to escape coming under the purview of the legislation.

However, the private sector accounts for hardly 30 per cent of the reported organized employment, the overwhelming share being employed by an overstretched and overextended public sector which has also been a monopoly or a dominant provider of several organized services that include banking, insurance, wholesale trade in foodgrains and fertilizers, railway transport, finance, and telecommunications.[42] The same is also true in some segments of mining, metals, and manufacturing. At the same time, the owner of these enterprises, namely the government, is also the architect and enforcer of overprotective labour legislation as also responsible for the smooth provision of the services produced by them. The trade unions, by forging alliances among the multiplicity of trade unions in each industry for pursuing common interest, have successfully managed to exploit the dual role of their employer to their own advantage.[43] It is this segment that is going to lose with privatization, which it has been opposing tooth and nail. The national trade unions belonging to the major national parties, including the Communist parties, have been shirking even the debate or discussion on labour market reforms including the amendment of the IDA on which there has been no political consensus in the two houses of parliament. This amendment has been on the agenda of all the union governments since 1991. The issue has been repeatedly discussed in the periodical Indian Labour Conferences, a tripartite forum of employers, workers, and government. The reforms have been recommended by various expert bodies, including the Indian Planning Commission and the Prime Minister's Economic Advisory Council. However, the central trade unions have been making all efforts to protect the existing organized employment in the declining and increasingly economically unviable public-sector units. In the process, they are forcing the resources already tied to non-viable enterprises to continue and pour more public money into these losing economic activities. They are thus preventing the reallocation of resources to more viable activities and generation of more productive future employment which could absorb some of those from the unorganized sector with much lower than average productivity. The central trade unions have thus become an obstacle to the advancement of social equity.

Is the overprotective legislation of the IDA really protecting existing employment? Tendulkar (2004) studied the course of manufacturing output and employment growth at two-digit industry level during the pre-reform decade (1980–1 to 1990–1) and post-reform period (1990–1 to 1997–8) based on relatively most reliable data source—the Annual Survey of Industries (ASI).[44] The pre-reform decade of the 1980s was marked by a step-up in the rate of output (real value added) growth to 7.1 per cent per annum compared to 4.65 per cent in 1970s. As already noted in Chapter 5, this was the period of Rajiv Gandhi's hesitant attempts at liberalization. However, in terms of manufacturing employment, this was a period of virtual stagnation prompting the description of it as the decade of 'jobless growth'. A comparison showed that seven out of eighteen two-digit industry groups suffered net job losses amounting to 518,000 which were not offset by net job gains in the remaining eleven industry groups, resulting in a net decline of 52,000 in the average number of factory workers between the first and the last trienniums of the decade. In other words, a major industrial restructuring did take place despite overprotective labour legislation being in place. During the post-reform period, there was again a significant industrial restructuring as a result of the stabilization and structural adjustment described earlier. As Acharya (2001) has observed, there was a rapid rebound of the economy leading to a post-reform investment boom and a factory manufacturing output growth of 9 per cent per annum. This was a period of more drastic industrial restructuring than the 1980s, without any change in protective labour legislation.

Two clear messages emerge from this comparison of the decade of jobless growth with the post-reform period. One, overprotective labour legislation could not prevent a major industrial restructuring and stagnation in factory employment during the decade of jobless growth, nor could it stop drastic restructuring during the post-reform period when a fair amount of labour reallocation took place in the corporate sector. In other words, it was ineffective in protecting existing employment. The argument of the trade unions and political parties against amending the legislation is that if it is not coming in the way of restructuring, there is no need to amend it. The second message is equally important, namely the more rapid industrial growth during the post-reform period promoted *net*[45] employment growth.

What has been happening is that despite formal overprotective labour legislation in place, there appears to have been labour market flexibility in practice in response to changing incentives generated by the hesitant liberalization of the 1980s and more wide-ranging liberalization of the post-reform period. This has been made possible, as discussed earlier, by private employers getting around the legislation in various legal and extra-legal ways. Even in the case of mandatory permission required by the Industrial Disputes Act, there has been a major change during the post-reform period. The state governments, with declining public investment, have been forced to attract private investment—both domestic and foreign—for productive employment generation and in the process have been giving permission for lay offs and retrenchment more liberally than earlier. In other words, confronted by *formal legislative rigidity*[46] in the organized labour market, the incentive structure generated by liberalization has induced *informalization* of labour market flexibility. Workers at plant level looking for jobs in a situation of overall unlimited labour supplies have accepted the need for 'hire and fire' which their elite leaders in the central trade unions and political parties still refuse to accept as necessary for the growth of productive jobs and hence the need for amending the protective legislation.

However, it is important to underline that informalization of labour market flexibility is not without costs. The various practices of private employers mentioned earlier or the lockouts to which they resort involve open or hidden transaction costs for employers besides their adopted devices often being at the cost of workers themselves. In other words, the formal legal interests of workers in terms of due compensation are not respected by these informal practices. Even more important is that public-sector employers, being part of the government that enforces labour legislation, cannot resort to these informal practices and have to bear the cost of inflexibility in terms of efficiency losses arising from resource misallocation. While Indian investors familiar with informalization are possibly not deterred, those who are not familiar would certainly feel daunted by the prospect of setting up a unit without flexibility of adjusting employment according to derived demand for labour. Among the latter group are potential private foreign direct investors whose investment successive central governments have been seeking. The net result is that organized labour market rigidities have been undercutting the efficiency gains of trade liberalization which has been unfairly attacked by opponents of globalization for being anti-labour.

The absence of political consensus on labour market legislative reforms cut across all the governments at the centre. The minority government headed by Narasimha Rao (1991–6) faced resistance to liberalizing reforms from within the Congress Party as well as from the opposition parties while dealing with the adjustment problems resulting from sharp fiscal contraction and progressive lowering of import tariffs. The UF governments (1996–8) as well as the BJP-led NDA governments (1998, 1999–2004) were caught in the phase of slowing down of industrial growth from 12.6 per cent (during 1993–4 and 1996–7) to average 3.7 per cent during the subsequent six years till 2002–3 (based on GDP in registered manufacturing at 1993–4 prices). There was also a corresponding rise in the man-days lost per declared strike as well as per declared lockout in 1998, 1999, and 2000 (Tendulkar 2004). This was hardly the environment for legislative change. However, valiant effort was made by the Finance Minister Yashwant Sinha in his budget (2001–2) speech to raise the Chapter V-B exemption limit under the IDA to establishments with less than 1000 from the current one of less than 100 workers but also raise the associated compensation to workers from 15 days' to 45 days' wages.[47] He faced stiff opposition not only in parliament but also from his cabinet colleagues.[48] After the parliamentary election in 2004, the NCMP released in May by the Congress-led UPA government explicitly ruled out any change in the existing labour laws, in particular the much-contested IDA. This reflected pressure from the Left Front led by the Communist parties, which support the UPA government from outside. The formal labour market rigidity, therefore, is destined to stay in the foreseeable future.

Interestingly, in the face of the inability of the legislature and executive to evolve consensus in this context, the third arm of the state, namely the judiciary, has been coming out with judgments in favour of employers and general public vis-à-vis employees. In one of the earliest post-reform judgments dated 13 September 1994, Justice Kuldeep Singh enunciated the principle of 'no work no pay' when the strike was illegal or unjustified. He observed, 'To be entitled to the wages for the strike period, the strike has to be both legal and justified. Whether the strike is legal or justified are questions of fact to be decided on the evidence on record' (*Syndicate Bank* vs. *Umesh Nayak*). In the context of a *bandh* (compulsory closure of all activities in a city) organized by the Left trade unions in collaboration with their supporting political parties, the Kerala High Court, in its judgment dated 28 July 1997, declared it illegal because

> a call for a bandh holds out a warning to the citizen that if he were to go out for his work or to open his shop he would be prevented …[and consequently] it entails restriction of the free movement of the citizen and his right to carry on his avocation.

A three-judge bench of the Supreme Court endorsed the Kerala High Court's reasoning on 17 November 1997 and observed, 'There cannot be any right to call or enforce a 'bandh' which interferes with the exercise of the fundamental freedom of other citizens, in addition to causing national loss in many ways'. Defying this judgment, the BJP and the Shiv Sena (SS) organized the Mumbai bandh on 30 July 2003 to protest against the bomb blasts at Ghatkopar, a suburb of Mumbai. In response to a public interest litigation (PIL) filed in the Mumbai High Court, a two-judge bench of Acting Chief Justice A.P. Shah and S.U. Kamdar imposed exemplary fine of Rs 20 lakh each on the BJP and SS and rejected the BJP–SS stand that the bandh was a spontaneous reaction while maintaining that (i) it was open to the parties to protest without calling a bandh; (ii) the bandh had violated the fundamental rights of the Mumbai citizens; and (iii) the parties were aware of the Supreme Court Order and Kerala High Court judgment holding bandhs illegal.[49] Before admitting their appeal against the Mumbai High Court judgment, the Supreme Court asked the BJP and SS to deposit the exemplary fines. The appeal was due for hearing on 17 July 2006 but stood adjourned till date.

Two judgments delivered by the two-judge bench of the Supreme Court, Justices M.B. Shah and A.R. Lakshmanan in August 2003 held that (i) government employees had no fundamental right to go on strike (dated 6 August) and (ii) employees of public sector undertakings (PSUs) were not government servants and were covered by the Company Law and BIFR guidelines so that 'if the company is sustaining losses and does not have the financial capacity to revise or enhance the pay scales, the employees cannot claim any legal right to ask for a direction to the Centre to meet the additional expenditure which may be incurred on account of revision of pay scales.'[50] The hands of the government as employer were further strengthened through a more recent Supreme Court judgement in the case of the PSU Awas Vikas Sansthan (AVS) of the Government of Rajasthan. With its far-reaching implications, it would be useful to dwell on it in a little detail.[51] The Rajasthan government decided to close down AVS as it was incurring heavy losses and directed that the affected employees numbering 650, including forty-five daily wagers, be employed in vacant posts in local bodies in a staggered fashion on compassionate grounds. The employees went to the High Court where a single-judge bench ordered the government to give them alternate employment. On appeal, a Division Bench of the High Court went further and ordered pay protection and ruled that the services of employees be counted for pension and certain other benefits. Allowing a batch of appeals against the High Court Order, the two-judge bench of Justices H.K. Sema and A.R. Lakshmanan of the Supreme Court agreed that abolition of posts either for streamlining the administration or for lack of funds was a matter of policy and was an inherent right of the employer. It set aside various orders of the Rajasthan High Court and made the government's right *unimpeachable* by ordering that lower courts should not direct re-employment of discharged persons. It endorsed the alternative staggered employment scheme as 'fair and benevolent'[52] but maintained that employees could not claim pay protection or make their past service count towards computation of their pension and gratuity. The Delhi edition of the *Times of India* cited earlier observed: 'While the government is finding it difficult to change the rigid labour laws, the Supreme Court is slowly moving towards relaxing them in line with contemporary practice [the informalization of labour market flexibility observed earlier] in *labour market*'. This marks the departure of the court's view of government as a 'benevolent employer' with special duties towards its employees. The same newspaper editorially remarked (1 April 2006) that the Supreme Court at one stroke 'unintentionally paved the way for both PSU and labour market reforms...if this happens, the private organized sector is also certain to demand its right to exercise exit option.' While all this sounds prima facie unfair to labour, the empirical evidence of the 1980s and 1990s discussed earlier clearly indicates that the existing labour laws protected neither labour nor honest employers besides preventing investment in large-scale labour-intensive (mostly exportable) industries, discouraging companies from hiring more labour, and forcing employers to resort to contract work and outsourcing and other devices that adversely impact the legal rights of labour.

To conclude, the legislative inflexibility of India's organized labour market and the resultant socially inequitous labour market duality appear certain to persist because of the staunch opposition of the central trade unions and the absence of consensus among political parties on the issue of labour market legislative reforms. Pragmatic informal arrangements have emerged that permit labour market flexibility at plant level but these are not without transaction costs, nor are they good enough to attract investment in labour-intensive exportable industries that require large scale of operation. In this environment, the judiciary through its pro-employer and pro-government judgments during the post-reform period has provided an enabling opportunity to carry out both labour market and public-sector reforms. It remains to be seen if the polity shows courage to seize this opportunity.

NOTES

1. This Act has since been repealed and replaced by the Foreign Exchange Management Act, 1999.
2. In economic policy terminology, a negative instrument is a measure which *prevents* a particular economic outcome. A positive instrument, in comparison, induces a

given economic outcome. The centralized investment planners in India in the earlier regime used negative instruments of these legislations as a general rule to 'govern' the allocation of large scale private instruments and positive instruments as exceptions. A liberalized regime, on the other hand, uses positive instruments as a rule and negative instruments as exceptions. In other words, investment planners mainly rely on centralized commands while liberalization relies on inducement mechanisms.

3. The industries under this category have been removed with improvement in the balance of payments.
4. These figures from the Ministry of Industrial Development differ from the balance-of-payments (BOP)-based figures from RBI (2003b). RBI (2003b) which gives both sets of figures mentions (p. 111) that BOP-based figures also include direct imports against foreign investment abroad as well as disinvestments.
5. We exclude, for comparability over time, US$ 839 million of equity capital of unincorporated bodies that was included as part of FDI only since 2000–1. See footnote (4) to Table 8.1.
6. RBI 2006, Table 1.75, p. 96.
7. RBI (2006: 97) reports further peak of 3.7 per cent in 2005 for FDI and 12–15 per cent for FPI in 2004 and 2005.
8. Pent-up demand, being a function of past stringent supply restrictions on importables, showed a tendency to get exhausted quickly as import tariffs were also being progressively lowered.
9. Normal demand for high-end importables, being a function of low per capita income, had a narrow base in India.
10. The 'same' field was clarified to be detailed 4-digit code of National Industrial Classification (NIC) 1987 whereas the 'allied' field was defined to be the broader 3-digit code of NIC 1987 in the Press note 10 (1999 series dated 12 April 1999).
11. A recent news report mentions that during June and 10 October 2006, as many as 23 cases approved by the FIPB pertained to Press Note 1 of 2005. See : Monica Gupta : 'Jeopardy to existing JVs to be defined clearly', the *Business Standard*, New Delhi, 21 October 2006. This may suggest a more liberal approach in an effort to attract more FDI. However, the reported information is insufficient to reach a definitive conclusion in the absence of the number of applications which have been *rejected* and the corresponding volumes of investment involved in approved and rejected applications under Press Note 1 of 2005
12. Inclusive of [c]ost, [i]nsurance, and [f]reight, that is, cost of imported commodity at port of entry into India.
13. As per Harmonized System of India Trade Classification.
14. The Indian critics opposed foreign direct investment (FDI) because unlike in Korea, Thailand, and China, it had been coming to India not for producing goods for tapping the third country export markets but for exploiting the domestic Indian market. Still heavy protection provides a plausible explanation why most of the FDI has been domestic market-seeking in character rather than third-country export-seeking.
15. Tariff redundancy is said to exist when the ruling domestic price is lower than cost of corresponding imported product at port of entry plus tariffs. This situation is also sometimes described as having 'water' in tariff.

16. Recall n. 17 in Chapter 3 on the concept of 'public' goods. We admit the legitimate role of government in the production of public goods.
17. See n. 17 in Chapter 3.
18. *Indian Express*, Pune, 23 June 2006, p. 8.
19. For a sample, see *Business Standard*, New Delhi, 2 June 2004, which carries the comments of Mr A.B. Bardhan, General Secretary of the Communist Party of India on disinvestment.
20. This was the first objective of disinvestments. The then Finance Minister, Dr Manmohan Singh, said in his 1991–2 budget speech: 'In order to raise resources, encourage wider public participation, and promote greater accountability, up to 20 per cent of government equity in selected public sector undertakings would be offered to mutual funds, investment institutions, and also to workers in these firms'. Quoted by G. Srinivasan in 'Disinvestment: will the Approach Pay Off?' *Business Line*, Delhi, 29 October 2004.
21. For a blow-by-blow account of the quick-changing fortunes of this deal, see Mayer (2002).
22. See n. 26 below for an explanation of this modality of disinvestments.
23. Navaratnas (nine jewels literally) comprise some currently profit-making large PSEs that include steel, oil and power transmission companies, and a few more have been added to the list since then.
24. *Times of India*, New Delhi, 27 May 2005, p. 1.
25. *Times of India*, New Delhi, 6 June 2005, p. 8, Times News Network report from Kolkata titled 'BHEL sell off, clear beach of CMP: Left'.
26. 'BHEL disinvestments put on hold' Agencies report from New Delhi, *Times of India*, New Delhi, 6 August 2005, p. 8.
27. Offer of sale of equity in the capital market and strategic sale are two alternative modalities of disinvestment. Strategic sale involves sale of large chunk of equity on pre-negotiated terms (including pricing of equity) to a strategic investor selected through open bidding process who simultaneously takes control over management. Strategic investor can be so chosen (by putting pre-qualifying conditions on the bidders) to have strengths in areas complementary to the business of the company so that the economic position of the company is strengthened after the sale. Proceeds from the offer of sale route depends on the conditions in the capital market and hence on the timing chosen. Realization from strategic sale route could be higher because the buyer is expected to pay a premium for acquiring management control. Even though government may retain major stake, strategic sale is associated with 'instant privatization' because of the transfer of management.
28. 'Divestment Programme at Crossroads', by C.R.L. Narasimhan, *Hindu*, 22 August 2005, from hindu@web1.hinduonet.com
29. 'Left 'bends' to Chidambaram's right', Times News Network report from New Delhi, *Times of India*, New Delhi, 23 June 2006, p. 17.
30. 'Hassled PM puts off disinvestment ', Times News Network report from New Delhi, *Times of India*, New Delhi, 7 July 2006, p. 11.
31. This workers' union had also successfully resisted disinvestment move in NLC earlier in 2002 during the National Democratic Alliance regime.
32. 'NDA sold PSEs cheap: CAG Report vindicates our stand, says CPM', *Times of India*, New Delhi, 25 August 2006, p. 11 quoting Times News Network from New Delhi. Also see the rebuttal of the CAG report by the then Minister of

Disinvestment, Arun Shourie in *Economic Times*, New Delhi, 26 August 2006 in the report by Political Bureau titled 'Shourie Rebuts CAG Charge on Divestment.'

33. 'We will talk to Partners before recommending disinvestments: PM', *Hindustan Times*, 24 September 2006, Press Trust of India report from Nainital.
34. *Indian Express*, New Delhi, Tuesday, 26 July 2005, p. 1 quoting ENS Economic Bureau entitled: 'In BHEL Season, PSUs Empowered'.
35. An unsuccessful attempt was made in March 2005 by the Prime Minister's office (PMO) through a circular of the Department of Public Enterprises (DPE) to take away the discretion of the administrative ministries in the appointment of Managing Director and other Independent Directors on the Board of PSEs. Under the protests from the administrative ministries, the PMO asked DPE to restore pre-April 2005 guideline. *Times of India*, New Delhi, 21 March 2006, p. 21, Press Trust of India report from New Delhi titled, 'Ministries have their way in appointment of PSE officials'.
36. This section draws on Tendulkar (2004).
37. Higher-than-average productivity may be due to much higher than average capital–labour ratio which is typical of autarkic, public-sector-dominated industrialization.
38. As many as 30,810 registered TUs were reported in 1977, their number doubling to 61,592 by 1998 according to the Annual Returns received under the TU Act 1920 and reported in the *Indian Labour Year Book*.
39. This statement is based on Tendulkar (2004) who discusses alternative data sources for approximating the organized segment. He shows the organized workforce to be predominantly urban and engaged in mostly non-agricultural activities. Even after making due allowance for possible underestimation in the existing official estimates of the organized workers, their share in total urban/ total non-agricultural/ urban non-agricultural workforce has gone down significantly between 1961 and 1999–2000.
40. See GOI-MOF (2004: Economic Survey 2003–4, Box 7.2, p. 149) for proposed changes in the two states of Gujarat and Karnataka and applicable only to Special Economic Zones established for exports.
41. The Communist Party (Marxist)-led Left Front government in West Bengal lowered the exemption limit further to establishments employing less than fifty workers.
42. In the latest Forbes 2000 list of Corporate Titans in the world released on 31 March 2006, seventeen out of thirty-three Indian companies in the list are owned by government. Six out of top ten Indian companies in the list are from the public sector. *Times of India*, New Delhi, Saturday, 1 April 2006, p. 15 quoting Times News Network.
43. The latest instance is the recent week-long strike (3–9 April 2006) by the employees of the state-owned State Bank of India (SBI). See Chapter 4.
44. The post-reform period is restricted by the availability of comparable data. The ASI switched to National Industrial Classification (NIC) 1998 since 1998–9 which is not comparable to the data for the earlier period based on NIC 1987.
45. Net after offsetting job gains against job losses in a given year resulting from industrial restructuring.
46. One major exception deserves mention. In order to attract private domestic and foreign investment in Maharashtra, the state government sought the permission of the centre to restore the pre-1982 exemption limit of 300 or more workers

under the IDA and relax the provisions of the CLRA in the state. The union government granted permission to amend the IDA and CLRA to enable employers not only to hire casual workers but also outsource services. *Times of India*, Mumbai, Friday, 21 December 2004, p. 1, quoting Times News Network.

47. S.S.A. Aiyar (*Times of India*, New Delhi, Sunday, 24 February 2002, p. 13) has correctly suggested supplementing this proposal by a formal contributory unemployment compensation fund to pay 100 per cent of basic wages for six months, falling to 75 per cent and 50 per cent in the next three six-month periods till a fresh job is found. Very few employers will have the liquidity to pay the proposed legal compensation.
48. *Times of India*, New Delhi, Saturday, 23 February 2002 labour reforms shamble on cabinet divide by Akshay Mukul, p. 1
49. *Times of India*, Saturday, 24 July 2004, p. 1 and 12, quoting Times News Service from Mumbai.
50. *Times of India*, New Delhi, Tuesday, 29 August 2003 p. 9, quoting Times News Network.
51. *Hindu*, New Delhi, Wednesday, 29 March 2006, p. 14 and *Times of India*, New Delhi, 29 March 2006, p. 1 and 11.
52. Reported in the *Times of India*, Hyderabad, 29 March 2006, p. 1.

9

Reforms in Perspective: General Issues for India

We explored the institutional and political issues in the context, timing and directional persistence in the post-1991 reform process at the macro level (Chapters 5–7) with the post-Independence development strategy in the background (Chapters 3 and 4). This was followed by an analysis of four individual reform initiatives to illustrate the interplay of interest groups in governing their time paths (Chapter 8). This final chapter seeks to take the discussion further by offering some reflections on certain general issues in the reform process in the light of experiences in India and other countries (Fanelli 2004).

LEARNING FROM OTHERS' EXPERIENCES: AN INTERPRETATION

It is useful to get one important question out of the way. The North–Baumol evolutionary framework (Chapter 2) that we have adopted in this study postulates that each country charts out its unique path-dependent evolutionary dynamics of economic change that is distinct from other countries. It shows that the same (formal or informal) rules of the game that succeeded in one country, when introduced in another country produced different outcomes. If this is so, what is the meaning of a given country 'learning' from the experiences of others? It cannot be taken to mean replicating or repeating the policies that other countries have followed.

One possible way in which 'learning' can be interpreted is in terms of what economists have known as demonstration effect. Translated in the current context, the lesson lies in starting to think how other countries, faced with more or less same or similar situation and constraints in the past, managed to overcome them and bring about a better economic performance and the resulting improvements in the living conditions of its population. Obvious though this may seem prima facie, the societal learning process is clearly a much more complex process as North (1994) pointed out. To rephrase his arguments in the present connection, we start by noting an obvious phenomenon about which there would be little disagreement. Given the phenomenal spread of audio-visual and other communication media, countries and their populations have been brought closer together as never before. Major events in the world polity and economy and remarkable progress of different communities and countries reach people in a given country very rapidly, and sink into their consciousness at uneven pace and depth. These events are interpreted in the light of their socio-cultural influences and past experiences, and slowly work towards convincing them about the need to change their own environment, that is, informal rules of the game operating in their immediate surroundings. Some among them— particularly intellectuals, opinion-makers, political leaders, and businessmen—may perceive opportunities for gaining social recognition, prestige, power, or wealth in the changing informal rules and hence turn entrepreneurs in the social and economic domain through their chosen medium and proactively work towards changing the existing rules of the game. This process would be resisted by beneficiaries of the existing rules of the game who become potential losers from change and who may derive active or passive support from those having inertia for change. The final outcome as well as the time taken to bring it about in this tug-of-war is uncertain. Societies clearly differ in their degrees of tolerance of major changes in status quo as well as time taken to arrive at social consensus about the change(s). One thing appears to be clear. Legislative and other changes in the formal rules of the game cannot become effective till their acceptance percolates to the level of informal rules of the game—surely a gradual path-dependent process. It is often taken for granted that changing formal rules of the game is relatively easier than those in the informal realm because it requires consensus in a somewhat restricted circle of elite politics. However, sometimes changes in the informal rules of the game may precede rather than follow those in the formal rules of the game, as our example of informalization of labour market flexibility in the face of formal legislative rigidity in India's organized labour market showed (Chapter 8). The blue collar workers at the plant and factory level seem to be learning faster and accepting the inescapable need for flexibility in hiring on the part of employers out of compulsion for earning their livelihood than their elite leadership in the trade unions and in their affiliating political parties. Some of the fiscally strapped state governments have also realized the need for informal flexibility in order to attract private investment for productive employment generation. It is this continuing interaction—sometimes mutually conflicting, sometimes mutually reinforcing—that is informed by societal learning process that lends gradualism to institutional change.

EXTERNAL INFLUENCES ON INDIAN REFORMS

As mentioned briefly in Chapter 6 in the context of timing of the Indian reform process, two major international events exerted a deep influence on Indian intellectuals and public which helped change their perceptions of the efficacy of the two ideological bases underlying in the earlier development strategy.

The first event was the collapse of the leading centrally-planned economy of the USSR and other East European socialist economies in the 1980s. It started a rethinking process among those who firmly believed in the socialist ideology whose appeal had been pervasive and powerful in India. To start with, the event undermined the naive faith that the Indian policy- and decision-makers had placed on the efficiacy of centralized planning that was regarded as a panacea for the social and economic ills afflicting the country. In addition, it also helped shake their belief in the expansion of the socialist instrument of public sector (that had been wrongly identified with and elevated to the socialist goal) as superior alternatives to large-scale capitalist enterprises.

The second was the spectacular economic growth posted by the so-called 'socialist' market economy[1] of China since the aggressive opening up in 1978 and its success in reducing income poverty in the process. It forced a serious rethinking of faith in the ideology of economic nationalism that had started getting slowly undermined earlier by the international events of the 1970s (Chapter 5). This process could as well have been initiated earlier by the similarly spectacular success stories of rapid growth in the East and South-East Asian economies in the 1960s and 1970s. However, they were (wrongly) brushed aside by the Indian intelligentsia as being irrelevant to India because of their being 'small' economies. While some murmurs about authoritarian regime in China persisted, the growth performance of the most populous economy in the world could not possibly be ignored as being irrelevant to India. China being a socialist country carried a strong demonstration effect for the Indian intellectuals' autarkic mindset in respect of the positive contribution of international markets in economic development. As we noted in Chapter 3, the influence of the ideologies of economic nationalism and socialism had delegitimized the potential contributions of the functioning markets for their being socially iniquitous and private capitalists for their alleged greed and unfair profiteering. Pervasive introspection and questioning of these conventional belief structures resulted from the two international experiences discussed above. Consequently, most, if not all, have reluctantly come round to recognizing the positive contributions that liberalized domestic markets, private capitalists, and opening up of the economy to international trade could make to economic development. As a result, the intensity of their open hostility to liberalization and globalization has been reduced and their stance has changed to passive, if not active, support to the reform agenda.

The multilateral institutions like the World Bank, IMF, earlier GATT, and now WTO have always had an uneasy relationship with the Indian policymakers. The roots may be traced to the unhappy episode of devaluation combined with selective liberalization on the recommendation of the World Bank (possibly an earlier incarnation of the later structural adjustment loans) in June 1966 by the then new Prime Minister, Mrs Indira Gandhi. The Indian currency being overvalued then under the (untested) assumption of export pessimism, the move appeared to be in the right direction from economic point of view. However, the episode happened to coincide with adverse circumstance of the political instability in the mid-1960s (Chapter 3) and inflationary pressures caused by the natural calamities of two back-to-back droughts of 1965 and 1966 in the heavily monsoon-dependent agricultural economy. It also got embroiled in political controversies when the World Bank reneged on the promised non-project aid of US$ 1 billion as part of the devaluation-cum-liberalization package. This further undercut whatever potentially beneficial consequences the move might have had. The World Bank reportedly took the step at the behest of the US President Johnson's administration which was displeased by India's stand against the then raging Vietnam war.[2] The episode generated open hostility to the World Bank and the US administration among the Indian intellectuals and politicians across the political spectrum.

The multilateral financial institutions were more discreet the second time around in 1980 when India approached IMF for a concessional loan to support balance-of-payments (BOP) in the wake of the second oil price hike that accentuated the current account imbalances. In this case too, IMF wanted it to be a stabilization-cum-structural adjustment loan while India agreed only to the BOP stabilization support. Despite discreetness, this episode too did not escape the political controversies over the IMF conditionalities, which were regarded as unacceptable encroachment on India's sovereignty by the intelligentsia, the press, and the opposition parties.[3] The criticisms also prompted the Government of India not to accept the third tranche of the loan in order to establish its political credentials as protector of India's supreme sovereignty.[4]

The third loan was in the context of the external payments crisis of 1990–1. The IMF loan package was originally negotiated by the short-lived government of Chandra Shekhar (Chapter 6) and re-negotiated further by the minority government of Narasimha Rao that succeeded in July 1991. This time around, the World Bank and IMF maintained a low profile operation to work out joint and mutually negotiated conditionalities, apparently taking into account the political sensitivities. In the crisis-gripped atmosphere, the package provided the much needed support to overcome the external payments crisis and enabled the politically amateur but professionally competent Finance Minister, with the political support of his Prime Minister, to combine stabilization with structural adjustment, that ushered post-1991 reforms.

REFORMIST LEADERS

The North–Baumol evolutionary institutional framework (Chapter 2) enables us to treat the reformist leaders as political entrepreneurs operating in the interface of politics and economics to bring about transaction-augmenting institutional change that helps raise the rate of economic growth. In most countries, economic reforms have been undertaken to overcome some serious economic or political crisis. In the past, to the best of our knowledge, economic reforms have been initiated and sustained without a helping hand of an apparent crisis on two prominent occasions. In both cases, the reformist leaders happened to be charismatic and politically domineering personalities with unwavering commitment to economic reforms. Coincidentally, both took place around the same time but in contrasting political environments. The first case was that of Deng Xiaoping who ushered what he called the 'socialist market economy'[5] in the world's most populous country, China, in the late 1970s following the demise of Mao Zedong. We have already noted the positive influence of China's spectacular growth on the mindset of Indian intellectuals, policymakers, and general public earlier in the chapter and also in Chapter 6. Deng's strategy was to use rapid growth as a means of legitimizing the Communist Party rule after the chaos and disorder of the Cultural Revolution.[6] The second case was that of Ms Margaret Thatcher who at around the same time carried out reforms in the world's longest living democracy—Great Britain. She forced a drastic change in not only the political agenda of the nation but also the political ideology of the left of the centre British Labour Party[7] in the opposition, which had been a committed votary of trade unions and the public sector. The Chinese case is often cited in support of the off-quoted theory that an authoritarian regime is necessary for systemic reforms and democracy an obstacle. It also gets support from the reformist political leadership provided by Deputy Prime Minister Goh Keng Swee of Singapore, Chiang Ching-Kue (who became Prime Minister in 1972 and President in 1978) of Taiwan, and President Park Chung Hee (1963–79) of South Korea, all under the authoritarian regimes.[8] However, the British case of an advanced industrial country democracy and the ongoing Indian experiment of a developing country democracy provide convincing counter-examples and in the latter case with non-charismatic, politically light-weight, minority reformist leadership! In our view, authoritarianism vs democracy is a red herring. A little thought would show that (i) reformist political leaders cannot be made to order with timely supply whether under democracy or an authoritarian regime – for every benevolent reformist leader, one can find large number of other dictators who destroyed the economy or polity of their country; (ii) even authoritarian ruler cannot operate for any length of time without deriving legitimacy to rule over the population – events in the erstwhile USSR and East European centrally planned economies in the 1980s provide eloquent testimony to the fact that one after another authoritarian leader gave up power without much fight after losing legitimacy to rule; and (iii) unfortunately, economic reforms that promise improved living standards constitute not the sole one but merely one of several means of legitimizing political power – readers can easily find contemporary examples of non-reformist but charismatic leaders with oratorical skills legitimizing their power by invoking other issues that capture people's imagination.

Our inference from the foregoing discussion is clear. Reform-oriented motivation and conviction of the leadership makes a decisive difference to the economic fortunes of a country and not the authoritarian or democratic character of polity.

CRISIS IN ECONOMIC REFORMS

In most successful cases of economic reforms, economic or political crisis is said to have opened up a window of opportunity for bringing about major economic change. It is important to emphasize that a serious crisis provides only a *necessary* and hence at best an *enabling condition* or environment by upsetting the existing equilibrium for undertaking reforms (Fanelli 2004). It is by no means a *sufficient* condition. Several possibilities are associated with the outcome of a crisis. In the specific context of economic reforms, it is possible that the opportunity may not be seized at all because of inertia, or may be seized half-heartedly so that reforms are not sustained, or may be botched by wrong diagnosis of the problem, or the crisis may be so serious or opposing interest groups so strong that reform measures get frustrated. The Indian experience discussed in the previous chapters brings out yet another facet of the role of crisis in the reform process. It was *not* the more serious fiscal-cum-structural crisis for which systemic reforms constituted a *medium-term* solution that enabled minority political leadership to undertake them. It was the *proximate* external payments crisis that shook the polity which regarded it as much more serious requiring emergency measures (Chapter 6). We argued that the proximate crisis-gripped atmosphere helped by forcing losers to lie low[9] in the face of losses involved in very sharp fiscal contraction (Chapter 6). Unlike in the case of the episode of 1980 involving the IMF loan *without* structural adjustment, it was the reformist conviction of the professionally trained Finance Minister that made it possible for him to look beyond stabilization and perceive the social benefits of structural adjustment. It was undoubtedly true that the success required the critical political backing of the Prime Minister to his politically lightweight Finance Minister.[10] Needless to add, both the Finance Minister and his reforming bureaucracy received positive reinforcement from the learning experience of the hesitant reforms in the 1980s to undertake a politically risky liberalization albeit with the helping hand of a crisis-gripped atmosphere that received fortuitous but much-needed support from normal agricultural harvests and favourable international trading environment.

The crisis also did not end up in a dictatorship like in Uzbekistan, state capture like in Ukraine, or populism like in Venezuela, as noted by Fanelli (2004). Obviously, it is not necessary that these outcomes in certain countries in specific and different contexts would repeat themselves elsewhere but they help us confirm our earlier observation above that any crisis, being an enabling condition, is capable of generating multiple outcomes, only one of which could possibly be successful reforms. Because of the critical role of contextuality highlighted by the North–Baumol framework, we make some India-specific observations with regard to these outcomes.

The unlikelihood of crisis leading to dictatorship in India is easy to explain. Given the diversities of the Indian society, it would be extremely difficult for a single authoritarian ruler to establish the social acceptability and legitimacy to rule without which, as we argued earlier in this chapter, even authoritarian regimes cannot be sustained. Long-established social acceptance of *democratic forms* (elections, orderly change of governments, impartial election commission) of governance in India would provide a strong element of path-dependence because of fourteen general elections since 1952 and many more at state level.[11] The nearest India came to dictatorship was when Mrs Indira Gandhi suspended constitutional rights and declared 'emergency' on 25 June 1975. This marked a climax to the increasing hiatus between progressively radical rhetoric and the inability of the political system to fulfil the rising expectations during the height of populist radicalism in the mid-1970s. While Mrs Gandhi succeeded in extending the constitutional term of the parliament by one year, even she felt compelled to establish legitimacy by announcing a general election in one-and-a-half years.

We turn finally to the possibility of populist policies whose presence is more prevalent in all low-income democracies as they help gain immediate popular support and where the persistent and widespread non-fulfilment of socially perceived pressing needs is also likely to cause social unrest. At central government level, these have very much been prevalent in India because of one-fourth of the population being below the poverty line and the still pervasive appeal of socialist goals. However, we interpret populist policies in a wider sense to mean not only those that are rationalized in the name of the poor[12] but also all those short-term policies entirely benefiting the non-poor that result in either a revenue loss or a rise in unproductive public expenditure or both. Such policies are populist in the sense that, given the fiscal constraint, they result in reduced public capital expenditure and tend to raise fiscal deficit, and potentially crowd out private investment. At the aggregate level, one direct approximation is provided by rising revenue deficits, which are financed by interest-bearing public borrowings. The central government has been incurring growing revenue deficits continuously since 1979–80 and a rising ratio of revenue deficit to fiscal deficit reaching the peak of 71 per cent in 2001–2 (see Appendix Table B3). How do reforming governments maintain some broad balance between populist policies, which are inescapable in coalition politics, and reform-induced growth-promoting policies? Revenue deficits are constrained at the upper end by their expected consequences for inflation given the past experience of double-digit inflation rates being associated with considerable social unrest as well as electoral defeats.[13] Growth-promoting specific reform measures of various kinds affect certain groups favourably and others adversely. If a reform initiative has adverse effects on the constituency outside the coalition, it usually does not create immediate problems. If it does have adverse impact on the intra-coalition constituency, then the support is conditional on the political clout of the concerned coalition partner or a complex trade-off between components of the social and economic agenda of the coalition partners. As we noted in our discussion, phenomenon of complex intra-coalition alliances between minority reformers and opportunistic elements in the regional parties with national party heavyweights remaining passive under the compulsions of coalition politics has also been observed. So far, the changing composition of coalition partners in different governments at the centre has helped maintain the broad direction of the reform process.

IDEOLOGICAL CHURNING IN POLITICAL PARTIES

We noted in our preceding discussion how the collapse of the erstwhile USSR and other centrally planned East European economies and the spectacular growth performance in China in the 1980s initiated a rethinking about the efficacy of the traditionally well-accepted ideological bases of socialism and economic nationalism underlying the earlier development strategy. The era of coalition politics over the last decade involved three different coalition governments (United Front, National Democratic Alliance, and United Progressive Alliance) ruling at the Centre with mostly different regional alliance partners. In this process, practically every major national party and almost all the regional parties have managed to taste and enjoy power at the national level for varying periods. This instant habit-forming experience had two consequences.

The first has already been noted in Chapter 7, namely, a welcome redefinition and restructuring of the 'national politics' in relation to the local and the regional levels so as to accommodate the needs of federal polity and multi-ethnic, multi-cultural, and multi-regional diversities of the Indian society (Sheth 2005).

Secondly, the trappings of power brought into open the conflicts between the requirements of governance dictated by liberalization and globalization and the earlier widely accepted ideological bases of socialism and economic nationalism that had permeated the mindsets of the leaders as well as their supporters. While in power, the leaders struck opportunistic ad hoc compromises with respect to individual reform initiatives involving often complex trade-off between their social, political, and economic agenda. While out of power, they performed their dharma of opposing every move of the ruling government. All this remained in the domain of elite politics. However, the shifting positions of leaders could not be kept away from their party cadres and supporters because of the wide reach of the audio-visual and print media and had to be 'explained' at the time of periodical elections whose frequency has increased. This has forced a fair amount of ideological churning at different organizational forums in major political parties. It has become all the more interesting because the reforms were introduced by stealth in 1991 and never publicly debated but have been proving politically convenient all the same. Only in the recent 2004 general elections, as mentioned in Chapter 7, they came to be claimed openly as part of competitive politics by the Congress and the Bharatiya Janata Party (BJP). The socialists and the Left parties still refuse to accept the legitimacy of liberalization and globalization calling them as 'Fund-Bank policies'—a good thirteen years after the Fund-Bank package of 1991 was successfully completed in 1993. This deserves some discussion[14] because, in our view, the ideological churning needs much deeper percolation so as to hopefully convert current reformers by convenience into those by conviction (Chapter 7) for the process to continue successfully.

We have argued that, so far, the coalition politics appears to have helped the forward march of the reform process. The stability of coalition government is clearly important in this context. In this connection, since the rise of BJP as a major party with its traditional advocacy of 'Hindutva' since 1991, the major division of the political parties has been along the hazy 'secular–non-secular' lines. This has posed an obvious ideological dilemma for the Communist Party of India (Marxist) CPI(M)—owing their ideological allegiance to secularism as well as socialism.[15] The CPI(M) practiced anti-Congress policy because of its bourgeois character in the 1980s and supported from outside the short-lived non-Congress – non-BJP minority Janata Party government of V.P. Singh after the General Elections in 1989 when the Congress Party had emerged as the largest single party in the hung parliament. During the post-reform period also, the 15th CPI(M) Congress in 1992 declared the policy of keeping equal distance from both the bourgeois parties, namely, the Congress and the BJP. However, seeing the bleak prospects of non-Congress-non-BJP third front after the 2004 General Elections, the all-powerful General Secretary H.K.S. Surjeet felt it necessary to justify the Party's stand at the 18th Party Congress in 2005. He argued that the BJP (being non-secular) was their 'Enemy number One' and despite it's known (bourgeois) class character and policies, the Congress, being the largest single (and secular) party, had the relevance to determine the secular character of the state 'at his juncture'.[16] The context of this intra-party discussion, which is equally important, came up around the time of passing the amended Patent Bill in order to keep the commitment made to the World Trade Organization. It is interesting to note that while the three major blocks – the National Democratic Alliance (NDA), the Left, and Socialist Party – launched into 'vociferous protests' against the patent legislation as being inimical to country's interests, '*they did not press for a division* (*of vote in the parliament*) *even when the numbers were clearly stacked in their favour*'.[17] The senior CPI(M) leader Jyoti Basu justified the Party stand saying it would be difficult for the government to insulate the country from 'the new inequitable global system' and claimed consolation that the 'Left has succeeded in making it (the Patent Bill) *less inequitable*'[18] (by insisting on certain amendments). This episode suggests two inferences. One, no opposition party wanted the government to fall even when an opportunity presented itself. Second, no party wanted the government to default on international commitments.

Another ideological issue which has been playing out within the CPI(M) is in the context of attracting private foreign investment. The Party has been ruling for 27 years continuously in the state of

West Bengal and has realized at last that its traditional opposition to private capital needed modification in the globalizing world and its traditional agitation-oriented approach needed to be replaced with constructive development. Approach to globalization had been discussed but could not be resolved in the 18th Party Congress in March 2005. It was taken up in the Central Committee meeting in August 2005, where it was resolved that 'in the era of globalization, it was not possible to prevent globalization of capital'.[19] Following this resolution, it appears that a pragmatic line is being advanced by the Party's senior leaders with regard to private foreign capital. Thus, maintaining the Party rhetoric that 'We will not surrender to the capitalists', the West Bengal state CPI(M) General Secretary, Anil Biswas, told a gathering of party supporters that development with the help of private capital needed to be looked at *in the context of the times and outside any ideological straitjacket.*[20] Before the recent state elections, the Chief Minister, Buddhadeb Bhattacharjee, admitted candidly that 'We are not doing socialism here, what we are doing is capitalism. Let us see how much we can do for workers from within this'.[21] He has been advocating responsible trade unionism and has been trying to discipline the Party trade union. More recently, veteran farmer leader and Party senior, Binoy Konar, presented an ideological argument for West Bengal's industrialization, quoting extensively from Marx and Lenin. He quoted Lenin to say that socialism was inconceivable without large-scale capitalist engineering based on latest discoveries in modern science. Defending Indonesia's Salim group's entry despite questions about its relationship with Indonesia's strong man Suharto, Konar says Marx was concerned about the *character of capital—and not the character of capitalists*—and asked a counter question: if Congressmen's hands were tainted with the blood of our comrades, would it be right to bring down the UPA government and let BJP come to power?[22] The foregoing pointers are indicative of percolation of pragmatism among the party ideologues at the state level. The central leadership of CPI(M) in the parliament is yet to exhibit this flexibility in practice.

We have already noted in Chapter 7 the smart shift in the interpretation of Hindu nationalism in the context of globalization in the vision document of the BJP for the 2004 General Elections.

The need for compromise in their traditional social agenda of Hindu nationalism was also reiterated by BJP after losing power in the 2004 elections. Its President, L.K. Advani, when asked whether the party made compromises with its ideology, replied with a counter question: 'Is it not a good idea that your government should be stable? Either you decide that you are going to be an ideological group, which will remain a pressure group in Indian politics, nothing more, nothing less. But if you aspire to become a ruling party and give good governance to the country, you have to compromise.'[23] The conservative Hindu nationalist organizations like the Vishwa Hindu Parishad (VHP) and the Rashtriya Swayamsevak Sangh (RSS) have registered strong objections against the pragmatic position of Advani who is currently the Leader of the Opposition in the Parliament.

Interestingly, the only major national party that has *not* undergone much ideological churning is paradoxically the Congress Party that was responsible for initiating reforms in 1991 and is currently continuing with them! The Party blamed economic reforms for their defeats in the state elections in 1995 and in the General Elections in 1996 when the (later) opinion polls showed that hardly 20 per cent of the voters had even heard of economic reforms. We also reported (Chapter 7) the Congress party's 'Introspection Committee' headed by A.K. Anthony.[24] This Committee, too, held the 1991–6 reforms responsible for the defeat in the 1999 parliamentary elections and argued for going back to pro-poor moorings and Nehruvian socialism. This report was approved by the Central Working Committee of the Party in the second week of December 1999. A similar ambivalent approach to reforms was advocated in an article in the year 2000 by P.V. Narasimha Rao, who is justly described in the title of the article as the 'the father of India's economic reforms'. Without mentioning explicitly, he was presumably reacting in the article to the strategic sale of non-strategic commercial public sector enterprises by the then ruling NDA government. After admitting all the ills afflicting the public sector, such as inefficiencies, chronic losses, deficiencies in management, etc., he declared: 'To put it bluntly, sale is certainly not the next generation of disinvestments. Let us not delude ourselves. Sale is expropriation of the nation, pure and simple', and added 'Liberalization did not mean total privatization, although it did mean massive addition to private investment.'[25] This reflected a 'half conviction, half exigency' attitude to reforms that were initiated during his tenure as the Prime Minister. It was only when, in the wake of 8.3 per cent GDP growth in 2003–4, the BJP, putting aside its Hindu nationalism, decided to claim credit for liberalizing and globalizing reforms and make them the centerpiece of their 2004 election campaign that the Congress Party felt compelled to (re)claim credit for being 'original reformers'! Commenting on the Party's economic 'Vision Document' released in the first week of April 2004 before the elections, one editorial in a leading national daily said that the Congress Party's 'relationship with economic reforms resembles that of a parent who doesn't want to acknowledge an illegitimate, if otherwise accomplished, child'.[26] Even the Congress President, Sonia Gandhi, in a pre-election televised interview, felt it necessary to reiterate repeatedly her Party's commitment to reforms, saying 'I know there are some reservations among people on our stand on reforms... economic reforms. There should be no worry whatsoever. The policy of continuing with economic reforms will carry on. Nobody should have any doubts on that.... We greatly admire our entrepreneurs, administrators, and business class because they have done a great deal. Business community going ahead, we are all for it. At the same time, we have to focus on the poor.'[27] It is thus indeed a matter of serious concern that at the party level, there has not been much open discussion nor awareness of the ideological implications of the reform programme that is being carried out by its government at the Centre. It should also be equally obvious that but for the political support of the then Prime Minister and the Party President, Narasimha Rao, during 1991–6 and the full backing of the current Party President now, Manmohan Singh and his handful cabinet colleagues, who are reformers by conviction, and their reform-minded bureaucracy would not have been able to carry out the economic reforms which, along with those implemented by the intervening governments, have made India one of the fastest growing economies of the world. It is hoped that the originality of reforms having legitimately been (re)claimed by the Congress Party since 2004, there would be more open discussions and debates.

RATIONALE FOR INDIGENOUS OWNERSHIP OF REFORMS

We turn to the all important issue of ownership of reforms. While at times reforms can be kick-started with external push or with a helping hand of (a usually avoidable) crisis or often both, it is tautology to say that they cannot be sustained without indigenous ownership. The reasons are not far to seek.

Liberalizing and globalizing reforms aim at improving economic growth performance of a given economy. This, in turn, enables improved living conditions and reduction in income poverty, and provides an important source of political legitimacy. While benefits of economic growth are readily accepted by all political parties, what is often not realized is that economic growth—whether in a closed or in an open economy—is not a socially painless process. It requires continuing adjustments in economic structure that involve pains of temporary unemployment, obsolescence, and rising earning disparities (Kuznets 1972). Let us elaborate.

Even in a closed economy, economic growth requires continuing structural adjustment to changing technologies and domestic demand structure, and involves the process of, what economist Schumpeter called, 'creative destruction'. In every growing economy, with continuing upgradation of technology, there are faster growing (usually described as sunrise) as well as technologically lagging (sunset) sectors, productive enterprises and skills or educational endowments with continually changing composition in response to changing domestic demand structure that takes place with rising per capita income. New productive opportunities emerge from technological upgradation while several old trades and skills get obsolete or experience declining demand. There are inevitable but temporary mismatches between locations, sectors, enterprises, and skills where new opportunities emerge and those where they are being phased out due to outmoded technologies. So long as the economy is growing rapidly, newly emerging opportunities outstrip those being phased out so that mobility of resources ensures that the resulting pains of unemployment, obsolescence, and rising earning disparities remain temporary. These are what are usually described as 'pains of structural adjustment' that are inherent in every economic growth process.

Societies differ in terms of pace adjustment to structural changes as also mechanisms they evolve for sharing and alleviating the inescapable pains of adjustment.

Opening up the economy to international trade and investment enables faster rate of growth by improving competitiveness of the economic structure and expanding opportunities for mutually beneficial exchange, but also makes the corresponding pains of adjustment sharper. International experience shows that rapid growth has been sustained, living standards improved, and poverty reduced only in open economies. No closed economy has sustained growth for long periods. Kuznets (1972) emphasized the institutional adjustments that are required in society and polity for ensuring mobility of resources and evolving mechanisms for equitable sharing and alleviation of the pains of structural adjustment in order to reap the benefits of economic growth. Historically, all the rapidly growing economies have been aggressively open economies and managed to bring about successful institutional adjustments. Many economies that found it difficult to carry out the necessary institutional adjustments did not manage to reap the benefits of new technologies and expanding opportunities for international trade and consequently experienced economic stagnation or slow growth.

Liberalizing and globalizing reforms seek to improve the growth performance of the economy by bringing about growth promoting adjustments in economic structure. Indigenous ownership of reforms and the associated consensus-building is clearly important for sustaining growth-promoting changes in economic structure as well as for evolving mechanisms for equitable sharing of both the inescapable pains of adjustment and potential benefits of economic growth.

CONSENSUS BUILDING FOR OWNERSHIP OF REFORMS, INDIAN STYLE

Ideally, ex ante *explicit* consensus building in society and polity is obviously desirable for a sustained and successful economic reform process. However, it is rarely obtained in practice. Charismatic reforming leaders, who are entrepreneurs in the social domain, manage to communicate their vision to the people and carry the polity with them—sometimes using available instrumentalities, sometimes devising novel ones. With opposition from the advocates of status quo, their path is never smooth. We have cited some examples earlier in the chapter without discussing the modalities adopted by the reforming leaders. We will now provide a brief discussion of our perceptions of the Indian reform process in this context.

Reform process generally involves major changes in the rules of the game and the associated incentive structure. The survival instinct of the Indian politicians does not permit them to own up the past mistakes and explicitly chart out a radically new strategy.

This came out clearly in the retrospective reflections of the reformist Prime Minister (1991–6) P.V. Narasimha Rao, who was then the President of the Congress Party as well. He admitted: 'what it (reform process) really entails is *a complete U-turn without seeming to be U-turn*'. Asked to explain what he meant, he said: 'If you understand that *where you are standing is itself in motion, the turning becomes easier.* You are not static.' He conceded the desperate external payments situation in 1991 ('we had come up against the wall. You had no money (foreign exchange), you were going to become defaulter (of foreign loan obligations) within two weeks. You can imagine *what it means for India to be a defaulter…*') and need for drastic changes ('you cannot possibly make do with clothes that you wore fifty years back.'). He, however, denied the big instinctive shift in strategy like Deng in China and referred to his (Congress Party) presidential speech at the All India Congress Committee in Tirupati in 1992 where 'I traced from Nehru to what I was doing and nobody could say that it was sudden shift', adding '*you cannot afford U-turns in this country*'.[28] His reformist Finance Minister and currently the Prime Minister of the UPA coalition government, Manmohan Singh (whom Rao described as 'expert in the job in which I didn't interfere … Behind him I stood like a rock') also paid tributes to the legacy of Nehru and Indira Gandhi in his first budget speech. His reformist colleague in the Commerce Ministry, P. Chidambaram, later recalled, 'when Dr Singh presented his first budget, several members of the Congress Working Committee (CWC) were outraged by the reversal of the Nehru–Indira policy line, Dr Singh offered to explain matters to the CWC. He took Congress manifesto released by Rajiv Gandhi (in 1984) and read chapter and verse from that document ... and many of his (Rajiv Gandhi's) politically inspired paragraphs fitted beautifully with his (Dr Singh's) budget announcements.'[29] Thus, the consensus in the Party was forged on the basis of the age-old line of 'continuity with change' where continuity was emphasized in rhetoric while much more drastic change was hidden in small print. For Rao, liberalization was not a major shift in the strategy but merely a change in the mix between the public and the private sectors in the existing mixed economy with massive investment by the private sector while keeping the public sector virtually untouched. A marginal variation of this formulation of the public sector policy was also reiterated by Dr Singh in an interview before the 2004 election, quoted earlier, and more recently by the Minister of State for Commerce, Jairam Ramesh, while replying to queries on disinvestments in profit-making public sector undertakings.[30]

Thus a massive change in the incentive structure that has been brought about by liberalization stood for merely a change in the mix in a continuum for the ruling Congress Party. It is, therefore, not surprising that reforms were described as being introduced 'by stealth'—without openly admitting the discontinuity with the past and without spelling out its consequences. Whether this drastic change was *really* what Dr Singh had visualized way back *in 1991* is a fascinating question only he would be able to answer. But, in retrospect, for a politically lightweight reformist and technocrat-cum-entrepreneur, it certainly appeared to be the only feasible course of action. By doing it, he certainly decisively changed the economic agenda before the nation for the better. It is, therefore, only apt that he took upon himself the task of interpreting consensus, Indian style:

> The *political consensus that has been the bedrock of the reform process since 1991* has been *implicit* rather than *explicit*. It is now well known that successive governments in the last fifteen years have *broadly followed this (liberalizing) policy orientation*. Many of the major issues of reform, ranging from tax and tariff cuts to changes in FDI ceilings have been the *subject of discreet consensus*. Such consensus is *rarely stated in public*, but has *often been displayed in the execution of policy*. This is important and essential.[31]

This characterization of the consensus being 'implicit, discreet, rarely stated in public but often displayed in the execution of policy' is consistent with our explanation that the directional convergence in economic reform initiatives in action rather than its open discussion for explicit political acceptance has been the result more of convenience than conviction—without sorting out its contradictions with accepted ideological positions. If we take the reform process to be an aggregation of individual reform initiatives, all the governments since 1991 have been carrying out individual reform measures that have either been within the jurisdiction of a government agency outside the central government (like the Reserve Bank of India) or within discretionary executive powers of the central government. Those requiring legislative amendments have often been avoided or deferred. It is not that *implicit* understanding on action on the floor of the house is not arrived at. We have already cited one example earlier in the chapter in the context of passing the Patent Bill in order to meet international commitment. This was one example of implicit rather than explicit consensus in permitting the legislation to pass without seeking a division of vote. Clearly, lengthy prior negotiations and bargaining must have preceded this action. It reflected the implicit consensus on the urgency to meet international commitment. Varshney (1995) cites similar instances while passing the first three central budgets after 1991.

The overall liberalizing direction might have been clear to the minority reformist leadership but not necessarily to its diverse opportunistic supporters with whom they established alliances whose motivating forces had little to do with reformist convictions and who were interested only in the potential outcome of their interest. In other words, the support was ad hoc to each individual reform measure with or without understanding its overall direction. Our surmise is that their support was possibly derived from their realization of the efficacy of the powerful instrumental role of rapid economic growth that may enable the effective pursuit of their sectional agenda as we pointed out in Chapter 7. However, the supporting contribution of two interrelated factors needs to be emphasized. One was the transformation of mass politics of the 1980s into organized party politics in the 1990s and the second was the consequential representation of diverse interest groups and ethnic and regional formations in the central government. These two factors made it possible to work out 'implicit and discreet consensus (in elite politics) that is rarely stated in public', as the Prime Minister has pointed out. Turnover of alliance partners and different coalition governments at the Centre has so far enabled the pursuit of different reform measures under different central governments depending on their political feasibility. For example, disinvestments by strategic sale route in non-strategic public sector enterprises was pushed by the last NDA coalition government[32] while the present UPA coalition has put them under the wraps not just because of the opposition from the Left parties supporting the government from outside but more importantly because, in the light of our discussion earlier in this chapter as well as in Chapter 8, the Congress Party's position on the public sector continues to be hazy, to say the least.

Flip-flops appear to be inherent in the uniquely Indian style implicit, discreet consensus process.[33] We have already stated the condition for such a consensus process to persist in Chapter 7, namely, implicit or explicit recognition by all the political parties of the powerful instrumental role of rapid economic growth (that individual reform initiatives seek to push) for resolving distributional conflicts in an orderly fashion. For the new distributional equilibrium to emerge, three more demanding conditions are required. One, the emergence of new political equilibrium consisting of two dominant coalitions (with stable or changing composition), each capable of ruling for a period of five years. Second, the interaction of mutually reinforcing reform initiatives result in a step-up in the growth rate from an average of a little over 6 per cent annually since 1992–3 by three percentage points or more while maintaining fiscal discipline and viable balance of payments. Three, the faster pace of collective 'learning by reforming' (Chapter 7) and deep (from its current shallow levels) and speedier percolation of the rationale, efficacy and desirability of the reform process at least in the mainstream political parties so that the breed of reformers by conviction expands and ultimately the consensus becomes explicit rather than implicit. We have stated what in our perception are an ex ante set of *sufficient* conditions. Needless to add, there are possibilities of substitution as well as interaction among these conditions and each one may or may not turn out to be *necessary* to the same extent for the new distributional equilibrium to emerge. We firmly believe, however, that responsible and responsive macroeconomic management would certainly remain an absolutely necessary and indispensable pre-condition.

We firmly believe that without explicit consensus and ownership of reforms, it would be difficult to work out the satisfactory mechanisms of equitable sharing of both the gains of rapid economic growth as well as the concomitant pains of continuing structural adjustment.

In conclusion, it is important to underline the fact that, just as during the earlier slow-growth phase (1950–80), the constraints on economic growth had been internal and policy-induced rather than external (Dhar 1990), the internal constraints imposed by the polity and the society and *not* the external factors continue to restrain the current faster growth trajectory as well and the attainment of the consequential societal goals of reducing poverty and improving living conditions. The original architect of the 1991 reforms and the present Prime Minister, Dr Singh, in his retrospective reflections on the reform process before the business leaders, felt compelled to amend his 1991 statement in the light of his 'field-level' experience of the Indian reform process. We cannot resist quoting extensively:

> Today, when I look back at the past two decades, I do feel a sense of vindication.
>
> Indian enterprise has proved doomsayers wrong.... Our industry and enterprise are far more confident, competitive and ambitious about their future and they feel they are second to none.... Yet, we still have the skeptics, the worriers and the critics. Today, when I look back, I am even more convinced that I was correct to observe in my first budget speech in 1991 *the idea of the emergence of India as a front ranking powerhouse of the world economy* was an idea whose time had indeed come. I had then added, quoting Victor Hugo that no power on earth can stop an idea whose time had come. *I must amend that to say that if there is any power that can still stop this idea of resurgent India, it is ourselves*. I believe that there are *no external constraints* now on India's growth and *whatever constraints there are, are internal*; constraints imposed by our polity, our social structures, our regional imbalances, our inability to handle inequity, and our ability to take hard, but essential decisions.[34]

NOTES

1. Notice that socialism and markets (identified with capitalism and private ownership of means of production) did not go together in the USSR and East European countries where public ownership of means of production was dominant and markets were supplanted by centralized commands which were driving the economy.
2. See Bhagwati and Srinivasan (1976), Dhar (2003), and Chaudhry et al. (2004) for cogent accounts.
3. An air of secrecy surrounding the IMF package also possibly contributed to the uproar as the package deal was made public by an investigative journalist.
4. Chaudhry et al. (2004) provide documentary evidence of debates in the IMF Board meetings.
5. Deng gave the pragmatic slogan: 'To grow rich is glorious' in a socialist country.
6. Interestingly, Singapore's legendary Prime Minister, Lee Kwan Yew, had reportedly anticipated this transition in China as early as 1974 in a meeting with the equally legendary Indian industrialist J.R.D. Tata. Critical of Mao's leadership that gave not only considerable political instability but punishingly low rate of growth, he said that all that the people of China would want after Mao's demise/retirement, would be a climate of political stability and economic incentives and leaders of China, after Mao, would dedicate themselves to economic growth. They would try to make up for almost a decade of economic chaos and move fast to rival not merely the city-states of Singapore and Hong Kong but even Japan. This account of the meeting between Lee and Tata was reported by Freddie Mehta in op-ed page article titled 'Free the Bottled Genie: Singapore's Lee Kwan Yew on Chinese and Indian Socialism', *Indian Express*, Pune, 29 May 2004, p. 9.
7. The Labour Party amended Clause 4 in its Constitution relating to the public sector.
8. See Pangariya (2002) for a convenient discussion of the role of these leaders in the growth process. We hasten to add that he is *not* discussing these cases in the context of authoritarianism vs democracy.
9. They would have lost more heavily had the growth process become unsustainable in the absence of reforms.
10. 'But I must say Mr Rao (the then Prime Minister) backed me to the hilt, I think in the first two years of our government.' Said the then Finance Minister Dr Singh in this connection. See the *Indian Express*, Pune, 23 May 2004, p. 7.
11. This is not to deny the still prevalent malpractices in certain parts of the country like large-scale rigging. On rigging Kaviraj (1995: 105) has an interesting observation: 'It could indicate blatant disregard of the democratic rules of the game but it could also show a certain *reluctant acceptance* of a flimsy hegemony of democratic language—that even the most powerful and entrenched groups gave sufficient importance to *democratic forms* to try to rig election in their own favour'.
12. Known to be a leaky bucket benefiting certain non-poor groups in the process who keep pressing for their continuation and expansion again invoking the name of the poor.
13. The first major episode of double-digit inflation followed the back-to-back droughts in 1965 and 1966 and resulted in a considerably reduced majority of the Congress Party at the centre and defeat in several assembly elections in 1967. The second

episode followed an indifferent harvest in 1971 followed by a severe drought in 1972, which also ended up in social unrest within three years of Indira Gandhi coming to power with a thumping majority on the '*Garibi Hatao*' (Eradicate Poverty) slogan and eventually resulted in the suspension of democracy on 25 June 1975 for one-and-a-half years. While other factors besides double-digit inflation rate contributed to social unrest, the prompt action of the succeeding government to rein in double-digit inflation seems to indicate the aversion that the Indian politicians have developed to high rates of inflation.

14. In our view, this issue is important enough to deserve in-depth discussion by political scientists. Our discussion here, which is subjectively selective, is to flag it on the basis of newspaper reports without claiming expertise.
15. It may be recalled that the CPI(M) is a dominant partner in the Left Front along with other left-leaning smaller political parties who share the same ideology. As already noted, the support of the Left Front from outside has been critical for the stability of the current United Progressive Alliance (UPA) coalition government.
16. See Akshay Mukul, 'Support to UPA Only to meet Exigencies of the Present,' the *Times of India*, Pune, 7 April 2005, p. 12, *Indian Express*, Pune, 8 April 2005 for excerpts from H.K.S. Surjeet's article from CPI(M)'s mouthpiece *People's Democracy* and Neerja Chowdhury: 'The CPI(M)'s Discovery of Bharat: the 18th Party Congress', *Indian Express*, Pune, 9 April 2005, op-ed p. 9.
17. See the Times News Network report titled 'Patent Bill Introduced amidst Protests', *Times of India*, New Delhi, 19 March 2005, p. 13.
18. See the Times New Network report titled 'CPM victorious, seven of its suggestions considered', *Times of India*, New Delhi, 19 March 2005, p. 13.
19. See 'The Left View on Reforms Changing?', the Times News Network report by Akshay Mukul, *Times of India*, New Delhi, 30 August 2005, p. 11.
20. See 'No capitalists, no development: Anil' by a staff reporter, *Daily Telegraph*, Calcutta, 18 October 2005, p. 13.
21. See 'We are not doing socialism in Bengal', Times News Network report, *Times of India*, New Delhi, 3 April 2006, p. 9.
22. See Ananda Majumdar: 'Marx in Motion', in the column 'A view from the Left' in *Indian Express*, posted online 11 October 2006.
23. See 'BJP has to compromise on Ideology', the Times News Network report, *Times of India*, New Delhi, 4 April 2005, p. 10.
24. See 'Anthony panel blamed Manmahanomics for '99 poll rout', report by P. Uday Kumar and A.R. Thiruwananthapuram, *Indian Express*, Pune, 24 May 2004, p. 5.
25. See 'Don't sell the house to pay the grocer's bills. It's too early to dismantle the public sector', says P.V. Narasimha Rao, *Times of India*, 5 March 2000.
26. See 'Congress Reforming, It's the fear of appearing Jurassic that has led the Party to finally endorse reforms', *Indian Express*, Vadodara, 9 April 2004, p. 6.
27. See *Indian Express*, Pune, 16 May 2004, p. 6–7. The interview took place some weeks before the publication.
28. See *Indian Express*, New Delhi, 11 May 2004, p. 7.
29. 'P. Chidambaram on Manmohan Singh', the Sunday Review titled 'Friends, Rivals, Contemporaries,' *Times of India*, New Delhi, 30 December 2001, p. 3.
30. 'NDA planned to divest 60 per cent of NALCO shares: Jairam Ramesh', Express News Service report in *Indian Express*, Pune, 3 July 2006.

31. Prime Minister's speech at the 30th Anniversary of *Business Standard*, 21 March 2005, downloaded from www.pmindia.nic.in
32. The then NDA Prime Minister, Mr Vajpayee clearly stated the primacy of governance reforms while addressing the full Planning Commission meeting. In the context of economic governance, he clearly stated: 'the primary aim...will have to be greater encouragement to private entrepreneurship, with the government strengthening its role in the formulation and implementation of policies, legislation, regulation and facilitation, and *exiting from direct participation in production and distribution*.' See the Press Release dated 5 October 2002 from the Prime Minister's Office.
33. We are calling it 'Indian style' because of our ignorance of what has been happening in other reforming economies. Our (decidedly shallow and casual) reading suggests that in Latin American countries too, a pre-election radical Left rhetoric is being followed by the centrist market-enhancing and globalizing policies in action when the same parties assume power. See 'Latin America's Leftist Mirage, Governments are opting for middle of the road' by former President of Uruguay, Julio Marma Sanguinetti in *Times of India*, New Delhi, 11 April 2006, p. 28; and 'Revolution, Shaken and Stirred, What Latin America has to teach Indian Left' by Swagato Ganguly in *Times of India*, New Delhi, 4 February 2006, p. 14.
34. Prime Minister's speech at the India Economic Summit, New Delhi, 29 November 2005, downloaded from www.pmindia.nic.in

Understanding Reforms: An Update

This year the post-1991 systemic reform process in India completes two decades. This is a good time to take both a fresh look at the entire process as also to bring up-to-date the major developments in the realms of economy, politics, and the political economy of reforms. Because of the predominantly, if not solely, growth-promoting focus of economic reforms as we viewed them, the distributional issues had been kept consciously outside our purview. This was not to regard economic growth as an end in itself but our firm belief that rapid growth could play a powerful instrumental role in realizing India's long-cherished goal of reducing poverty which is still pervasive in terms of absolute numbers though the share of the population below the official poverty line has shown a steady decline over the last two decades.

In the last five years after the first edition came out, the economy has been performing well in terms of growth without any big-ticket reforms; it came out of the global economic crisis with just a mild slowdown. The Congress Party proved its political management capabilities of coalition politics with continuously shifting political alignments and came to power for the second time in the 2009 general elections. However, rapid growth coupled with coalition politics seems to have made the United Progressive Alliance (UPA) governments lax on reforms and they are going in for populist welfare measures.

POLITICS AND POLITICAL ECONOMY

In the first edition, we had noted (Chapter 7) the convergence of the liberalizing and globalizing direction of economic actions by ideologically diverse ruling coalition governments at the Centre for pragmatic reasons evolved from what we called 'learning-by-reforming'. It was 'politically perceived indispensability of rapid economic growth (that reforms sought to promote) to sort out the distributional conflicts in a peaceful and orderly fashion' that prompted coalition governments, in which small regional parties got disproportionate bargaining powers in government formulation and policy execution and forced national parties to adjust their agendas—political, social, and economic, to continue reforms through learning-by-reforming. Coalition politics, especially with volatile political alignments, demand political management skills of the national party leading the coalition to continue in government. In this section we discuss coalition politics including the shifting political alignments and political management capabilities of the Congress Party that has been leading the coalition government at the Centre, and their impact on the functioning of coalition governments and on reforms in the last five years.

We are pleasantly surprised that the learning-by-reforming process came out stronger during the last five years. The Congress-led UPA despite not having any experience of coalition, not only completed its full five year term, but on the strength of rapid economic growth it also managed to beat the incumbency disadvantage and got re-elected in the 2009 general elections. A trust vote against the government on 22 July 2008 in the context of the nuclear agreement—one of the major political events before the 2009 general elections, is worth discussion. The Civilian Nuclear Cooperation Treaty (also called 123 Agreement) with the United States of America had been initiated by Prime Minister Manmohan Singh in July 2005 to ensure India's energy security by ending nuclear apartheid—the ban imposed (after India carried out test explosions of nuclear devices first in May 1974 and again in May 1998) by the existing nuclear powers on the supply of nuclear fission material to India to develop nuclear energy. The bilateral 123 Agreement was unveiled after prolonged negotiations in August 2007. The Left Front[1] that had been supporting the government from outside since 2004 with 59 Members of Parliament (MPs) opposed this treaty. The government tried to thrash out the differences with the Left Front with protracted negotiations between October 2007 and July 2008 without much success. On 8 July 2008 the Left Front announced a breakdown of talks and withdrew support to the UPA government leading to the trust vote. On 14 July 2008, the Bahujan Samaj Party (BSP) with 17 MPs also decided to vote against the UPA government in the event of a no-confidence motion.[2] On the eve of the trust vote on 22 July 2008, UPA had garnered support of 268 MPs in a house of 542 when it required 272 votes for a simple majority. Opposing the government were 263 MPs belonging to the BJP-led National Democratic Alliance (NDA) and the Left Front while 11 MPs were undecided. The trust was so critical that both the sides summoned MPs even from sick-beds. The Prime Minister and the ruling UPA coalition had to undertake major political manoeuvering and won the confidence vote with 275 votes to the opposition's 256 with 10 abstentions.[3] While substantive controversial issues underlying the trust vote are beyond our competence in political analysis, this brief discussion is meant to illustrate the shifting and unstable alignments in coalition politics that tested the political management capabilities of the Congress-led UPA coalition.

The next five yearly general parliamentary elections took place in May 2009. With seamless movements of small regional parties, the Congress (Indian National Congress) Party formed a UPA-II pre-poll alliance with 10 other parties. Half of the allies of UPA-I are absent in UPA-II. While the Rashtriya Janata Dal (RJD) and Lok Janshakti Samata Party (LJSP) from Bihar, Telangana Rashtriya Samiti (TRS) from Andhra Pradesh, Progressive Democratic Party (PDP) from Jammu and Kashmir, and two minor Dravida outfits PMK and MDMK from Tamil Nadu were all partners in the pre-poll UPA-I alliance, the Left Front and BSP supported it from outside after the polls. TRS, PMK, PDP, and MDMK left UPA-I and the Left Front and BSP withdrew support during the tenure of UPA-I[4] while the Samajwadi Party (SP) gave outside support to the UPA-I government since July 2008. After the 2009 general elections were announced, the Left Front and BSP along with some regional parties formed the Third Front and RJD and LSJP left the UPA-I alliance to fight the elections with SP. UPA, on the other hand tied up on 1 March 2009 with the West Bengal-based All India Trinamool Congress (AITC), which was earlier part of the BJP-led National Democratic Alliance (NDA). Seven other parties continued with NDA (see Table D5,

p. 222 and Box I in Appendix II for continuous shifts in political alignments since the 1990s).

With internal dissensions and leadership tussles, BJP was a divided house during this election to the central Parliament and the Congress Party (singly) increased its strength in the Lok Sabha (lower house of the directly elected representatives) from 145 in 2004 to 206 (Table 1, Appendix II) while that of BJP came down to 116 seats, 22 less than in 2004. The two Communist Parties lost heavily—as many as 33 out of 53 seats they held together in 2004 and RJD and LJSP were virtually routed. Another noticeable shift was a further reduction in the representation of regional parties from the highest number of 188 seats in 1999 to 171 in 2004 to 158 (Table 2, Appendix II) but a somewhat lower order of increase in favour of national parties from 354 to 364 and further to 376 respectively in the last three general elections. The underlying dynamics in terms of seat and vote shares (Table 3, Appendix II) indicate that the Congress Party gained by 11 percentage points (ppt) in seats but only 2 ppt in votes between 2004 and 2009. BJP lost more heavily in terms of seats (4 ppt) than in votes (3 ppt). Interestingly, the net loss in vote share of one ppt between the BJP and the Congress together accrued to the multi-state parties which, however, lost heavily (5 ppt) in terms of seats. What seems to be happening is that the recognized (non-national) multi-state regional parties lost out to either independents or other (as yet unrecognized and non-national) (single) state regional parties. The Congress-led UPA coalition returned to power with increased strength overcoming the incumbency disadvantage.

The new coalition government (UPA-II) came to power with 262 seats with pre-poll allies and outside support from several post-poll allies such as SP, RJD, and BSP. Although small regional parties such as DMK still play a critical role for the stability of the government, which can be seen from their disproportionately larger share in the government (Table 4, Appendix II), the UPA-II government was free from the support of the Left Front from outside that was deemed critical for the stability of the UPA-I coalition government. This gave the UPA-II government greater stability and freedom in case it wished to undertake economic reforms. However, two hurdles remain for undertaking reforms: (i) Although in clear majority in the Lok Sabha, the UPA-II coalition government does not enjoy similar strength in the Rajya Sabha (upper house of indirectly elected or nominated members). Any central legislation has to be passed in both the houses. (ii) Given that most of the political parties/ politicians continue to be reformers by convenience,[5] there is always uncertainty and the pace of reforms depends on a few reformers (by conviction) in the government and their political manoeuvrability. Added to these is that growth beyond some minimum (necessary to sustain distributional coalition) may make political parties lax on the reforms part. In such a situation, although the reform process is irreversible, it proceeds in a gradual fashion.

While the incumbent UPA-II coalition government differed in composition from its immediately preceding incarnation (UPA-I), it had to cope with the consequences of the most serious post-Second World War global financial crisis that had erupted during its previous regime. It also got engulfed in a variety of major scams (allocation of 2G spectrum and Commonwealth Games), embarrassment in the appointment of the Chief Vigilance Commissioner that was annulled by the Supreme Court with scathing remarks on the functioning of the Central Government, and the recent nation-wide protest led by Anna Hazare and his team against corruption and over drafting of the Lok Pal Bill. While the entire winter session (9 November-31 December 2010) of the Parliament was stalled by the adamant stand taken by both the government and the opposition parties on the issue of appointing a Joint Parliamentary Committee to investigate the 2G scam, the immediately following budget session was editorially lauded by a leading national newspaper for both 'engaged disagreement and principled co-operation between the two major political formations'.[6] The reference to 'engaged disagreement' was about the spirited and well-articulated attack by leaders of the BJP and the Left parties on the Prime Minister's role in the 2G scam during the debate in Parliament and the equally uncharacteristic but reasoned aggression shown by the technocrat Prime Minister and other Congress leaders in defending the government. The 'principled co-operation' came about the very next day (24 March 2011) after the spirited debate when the government was about to be embarrassed over the Left-sponsored vote on the introduction of the Pension Fund Regulation and Development Authority (PFRDA) Bill as the ruling coalition found itself short on attendance in the Lok Sabha on that day and the BJP, upon request, voted with the ruling UPA-II coalition for tabling the PFRDA Bill.[7] On critical reform-oriented policy issues, there seem to be no substantive differences between the UPA-II and NDA and the minor differences in detail appear to be capable of being ironed out in negotiations. Such pragmatic 'provisional coalition in action' (as the above-referred editorial puts it), if continued, augurs well both for the future of democracy as well as for political economy of reforms because several important legislative reform bills have been pending. Although the specific action relates only to the preliminary introduction of the PFRDA Bill, this action provides a hopeful portent while recalling the quote of the Prime Minister (Chapter 9, p. 171) about the political consensus on reforms in India being 'rarely stated in public, but often displayed in the execution of policy'.

POLICY REFORMS

In this section we provide a brief update of specific reform measures discussed in Chapter 8.

DOMESTIC AND FOREIGN PRIVATE INVESTMENT LIBERALIZATION

We noted (pp. 106–9) a wide-ranging liberalization of domestic private investment through the industrial policy statement dated 24 July 1991 by removing at one stroke the entry restrictions on private investors at the upper-end of the investment scale under the Industry (Development and Regulation) Act 1951 and Monopolies and Restrictive Trade Practices Act 1968 and also permitting entry of private sector in areas earlier reserved exclusively for the public sector. This facilitated the intensification of domestic competition among big players in the Indian industry. However, it took much longer to reverse the preferential treatment extended to small scale industries in competition with their large scale counterparts (including imports). A major policy instrument in this connection was reservation of certain items for exclusive production in the small scale industrial units defined by the original value of investment in machinery and equipment. The number of reserved items was as high as 836 from 1989 till 1997. This became increasingly inconsistent with the liberalizing and globalizing direction of the post-1991 reforms. However, with the entry of small scale industrialists and traders in the distributional coalition in the 1980s (Chapter 5, pp. 60–5), the political clout of this group could not be neutralized easily. In retrospect, a three-fold strategy emerged in this context. One, as part of international trade liberalization (Chapter 8, pp. 116–25), several items reserved for the small scale sector were put on the Open General License for imports, that is permission to import with customs duty. This introduced competition through imports for both the small scale and large units (Government of India 1997, pp. 175 and 179). Second, the investment limits for defining small scale industries were revised upwards. This was meant to induce existing small scale units to expand as also introduce limited competition from somewhat large scale and earlier ineligible domestic producers. Finally, there was a gradual pruning of the reserved list of industries. The process started very slowly with de-reservation of 24 products (1997–9) and picked pace with the addition of 141 products during the full tenure of the BJP-led NDA regime from 1999 to 2003. The de-reservation of as many as 116 products coincided (difficult to guess whether by design or accident) with the abolition of quantitative restrictions on imports of consumer goods during 2001–2 when India lost its case with the World Trade Organisation (pp. 118–19). It was successfully continued and accelerated by the subsequent UPA-I regime by further distinguishing ‘micro’, or ‘tiny’ and ‘medium’ units from ‘small’ scale and encompassing service enterprises along with manufacturing units under the Micro Small and Medium Enterprises Development (MSMED) Act, 2006. A separate ministry of MSME was also created at the Centre to look after the problems faced by this segment. As few as 20 products remained on the reserved list by July 2010.[8]

Turning now to private foreign investment, major changes have taken place since the first edition (pp. 110–16) in the face of accumulation of comfortable foreign exchange reserves and balance of payments. We noted that with its origin in the external payments crisis, the immediate post-1991 reform period was marked by increased emphasis on non-debt flows to finance the current account deficit in the balance of payments. However, given the resistance from domestic capitalists, the restrictive policy with regard to more stable foreign direct investment (FDI) kept FDI flows lower in absolute magnitude than the capital-gains-seeking private foreign portfolio investment (FPI) and both together dominating over the debt-creating inflows till 2005–6. The compulsions of balance of payments have changed considerably since then. Though capital account transactions continue to be subject to quantitative controls by the Reserve Bank of India, accumulation of comfortable foreign exchange reserves enabled these to be liberalized with respect to private inflows and outflows by Indian residents. In the presence of massive increase in FPI inflows till the recent financial crisis of 2008 as also exports of goods and services, the foreign exchange reserves increased from US$ 9.83 billion in 1993 to $ 38.04 billion by 2000 and jumped to the maximum of $ 309.72 billion at the end of March 2008 before coming down to $ 252.00 billion by the end of 2008–09 as result of the world financial crisis but rose further to $ 279.01 billion by end-March 2010.

Instead of updating since 2005–6, we note dramatic changes in the balance of payments between the 6-year regime each of the NDA (1998–9 to 2003–4) and the UPA (2004–5 to 2009–10) resulting mostly from progressive liberalization as both the regimes maintained the globalizing direction of reforms. While we use a short-hand description of 'NDA' and 'UPA' to denote 6-year periods each, an objective assessment demands a cautionary note that private capital flows are influenced not just by government policy but also by the fundamentals of the economy besides conditions in the real and financial markets abroad. It is important to note that the NDA regime was adversely affected by the Asian financial crisis in the second half of the 1990s and the dot.com burst in the early years of the first decade of the 21st century besides the slowdown in the pace of domestic growth. The UPA regime in contrast was helped by the resumption of growth in the global economy and financial markets besides the entry of the Indian economy on a higher growth trajectory that started in the final year of the NDA regime. But the sea change in magnitudes aggregated over the 6-year period each mentioned above for NDA and UPA regimes is obvious.

The aggregate debt-plus non-debt net capital inflows increased from $ 48.81 billion (NDA) to $ 310.91 billion (UPA). With comfortable foreign exchange reserves, the share of debt-flows (consisting of 60–5 per cent medium and long-term external commercial borrowings (ECBs) and the remaining short-term suppliers' credit) increased from 9.4 per cent to 28.3 per cent of the total (debt plus non-debt) net capital inflows. This is an indication of the increased involvement of the domestic (mostly private) corporate sector in international trade in goods and services which is financed from suppliers' credit and expanding domestic investment for which ECB permissions were given by the Indian government as part of capital account controls. Non-debt flows (FDI plus FPI) expanded from $ 44.24 billion (FDI including re-invested earnings and other capital [54.6 per cent] and the remaining FPI) to $ 222.88 billion, two-thirds of which was accounted by FDI. Among the components of FDI, there is a welcome decline in the share of discretionary SIA/FIPB route from 54.3 per cent to 13.7 per cent and rise in the share of automatic rule-based RBI route from 17.7 per cent to 59.8 per cent with the remainder consisting of investment by non-resident Indians (NRIs) and acquisition of shares of Indian companies by NRIs (see Table 5, in Appendix II). All these figures point out the progressive liberalization of private foreign investment.

In the context of liberalization of FDI, a recent change in policy is important. We had discussed (pp. 115–16) the resistance of domestic industrialists against FDI in competing areas as a factor in attracting greater flows of more volatile FPI rather than more stable FDI when some of the joint ventures went sore in the mid-1990s after the initial post-liberalization euphoria for joint ventures. In this context, to protect domestic industry, the government issued the controversial Press Note 18 dated 14 December 1998 that puts onerous conditions on a foreign partner making it mandatory to obtain a no objection certificate (NOC) from the domestic joint venture partner in case the foreign partner wants to start a fully-owned subsidiary in the same or allied fields. In an attempt to attract greater FDI, Press Notes 1 and 3 dated 25 March 2005 brought about some dilution in the rigorous conditions of Press Note 18 but continued the mandatory permission in the discretionary domain of the Foreign Investment Promotion Board (FIPB). A discussion paper was released by the Department of Industrial Promotion and Policy (DIPP) in 2010 on the need to review the condition of prior approval of an Indian joint venture partner. The DIPP Circular 1 of 2011 dated 1 April 2011 as part of the third edition of the Consolidated

FDI Policy, announced the government's decision to abolish the NOC condition in order to address the 'felt need to attract fresh investments and technology inflows as also to reduce state intervention in the commercial sphere'. This appears to be the result of two forces—either the government felt compelled to yield to pressures from foreign investors in view of the volatile nature of FPI or the domestic industry by now felt confident enough to face competition from foreign investors even though they reaped the incidental benefits from FPI inflows to domestic capital markets from which the domestic corporates managed to raise resources for investment. Either way, it is a welcome step toward raising the international competitiveness of domestic industry. However, as we note in the next section, the domestic industry continues to enjoy protection from import tariffs.

Liberalization of International Trade in Goods and Services

Our discussion (pp. 116–25) had pointed out a significant reduction in both tariff and non-tariff barriers till 2004–5 even though they remained higher in that year than their East and South Asian counterparts. Nevertheless, compared to the 1990s, the Indian Industry no longer clamoured for tariff protection and came to accept gradually, though reluctantly, the need for external competition. It would have been interesting to examine the progress in reducing a steep rise in weighted average tariffs (excluding countervailing duties) on consumer goods (Table 8.3, p. 121) from 2000–1 onwards with the forced removal of quantitative restrictions (QRs) on imports of consumer goods in two installments on losing the dispute with the US at WTO. Though showing some decline from the local peak of 66.2 per cent in 2000–1, the weighted average tariff on consumer goods still remained as high as 50.4 per cent in 2004–5 while it was a shade lower than 20 per cent on capital and intermediate goods. Further decline was clearly important for improving the competitiveness and efficiency in these segments. It is difficult to get comparable empirical updates for the period since then.

The inter-temporally consistent data set on tariffs (*including* countervailing duties and hence *not* comparable to those in Table 8.3) that we accessed provides simple and weighted (by product import shares of each partner country) average applied tariff rates for three categories of products, (i) all product lines; and two subgroups of (ii) primary products; and (iii) manufactured products (Table 6, in Appendix II). The three segments of our interest are aggregated in the manufactured products as a group. In the absence of data comparable to Table 8.3, we have chosen the following time points: The pre-reform year 1990, immediate post-reform year 1992 when savage import compression had to be resorted to because of the acute external payments crisis (Chapter 6); available pre-NDA (1998–2004) regime year (1997); two intermediate years, pre-dating (1999) and the year of removal of QRs on consumer goods (2001); the beginning of the UPA regime (2004); and the latest available year (2008). A weighted average is always expected to be lower than a simple unweighted mean because of the expected response of buyers to economize on imports of products with higher tariff rates. A significant reduction in tariff rates is apparent in 1992 despite savage import compression in a year of crisis of external payments. It reflects the pressure on the then minority government from international donors to establish credible seriousness of intention to undertake reforms. There was a decline in tariff rates from 1992 to 1997 before a rise in 1999 that is reflected in all the three categories of products whether simple or weighted averages. This increase was due to a uniform 8 per cent special additional countervailing duty on all imports imposed in 1998–99. There was a decline in tariff rates since 1999 including 2001 and 2005 (which is available but not included in the table). The decline is quite steep between 2004 and 2008.

The Finance Ministry's 'Economic Survey 2010–11' (Box 7.5, Table 1, p. 179) gives the tariff collection rates for selected import groups as well as all imports from 2003–04 to 2009–10. Tariff collection rates, it may be noted, provide a combined impact of both the reduction in rates of tariff and additional exemptions and in most cases, expected to be lower than corresponding weighted averages. The tariff collection rates for all imports showed a lower level as well as extent of reduction from 11.5 per cent (weighted average 22.9 per cent from our Table 6, in Appendix II) in 2004–5 to 6.9 per cent (weighted average 6.1 per cent) in 2008–9. On capital goods (consisting of electrical and non-electrical machinery and project imports) the collection rate remained at a higher level than that for all imports but declined from 15.8 per cent to 12.5 per cent during the same period. Since the weighted average tariff on capital goods is expected to be much higher than the collection rate on corresponding imports, the domestic capital goods industry has not been exposed to import competition. The continued inefficiencies in domestic capital goods are clearly undesirable for the competitiveness of the domestic manufacturing sector whose role in generating productive employment is significant.

Progressive liberalization of private foreign investment and reduction in import tariffs integrated the Indian economy increasingly with the world economy in the last two decades. Exports plus imports of goods, on an average, was around 19 per cent in the 1990s which increased to 30 per cent (2000s), and reached the maximum of 41 per cent of gross domestic production in 2008–9. Traded goods and services together increased, on an average, from 23 (1990s) to 39 per cent (2000s), and reached 54 per cent of GDP in the global financial crisis year of 2008–9. Current and capital receipts and payments together rose, at an average level, from around 42 (1990s) to 79 per cent (2000s), and reached the maximum of 111.5 per cent of GDP in 2008–9 (Table 7, Appendix II). To conclude, it is remarkable that in two decades since 1991, the Indian economy, while benefiting from progressively increasing openness, proved itself to be resilient to external shocks since the late 1990s and came out with a stronger external sector despite starting the post-1991 reforms in the face of acute external financing vulnerability (Chapter 6).

Privatization of Commercial Public Sector Enterprises

The rigid position of the Left parties against any disinvestment was a major though not the only reason for putting the disinvestment programme on the back burner during the UPA-I regime during 2004–9. The position of the Left parties in this context has its origin in their ideological belief in public sector but also carries shades of opportunism in protecting the interests of well-placed professional workers in these enterprises who have been averse to facing the rigours of competition after privatization. The tortuous path of disinvestment during the UPA-I regime has been narrated in Chapter 8 (pp. 125–38) where it is mentioned that the Congress Party had irrationally ruled out the modality of a strategic sale option of disinvestment. What the UPA-II has been doing is retail off-loading of shares of the central public sector undertakings (CPSUs) through initial public offers (IPOs) and follow-on public offers (FPOs) during 2010–11. This is clearly conditional on the situation in the stock markets and going to be a very restrictive modality of disinvestment. The incidental beneficial consequence of IPOs and FPOs has been the urgency generated in the resource-strapped CPSUs to list on the stock exchanges and subject themselves to the discipline of corporate governance standards. While listing was made mandatory for IPOs and FPOs, it was not done in the case of several CPSUs in 2010–11.

Turning to performance in terms of disinvestment proceeds, Table 8, (Appendix II) provides details of year-wise disinvestments since 2000–1 and Table 9, (Appendix II) summarizes the modality-wise proceeds during UPA (2004–5 to 2010–11), NDA (1998–9 to 2003–4), and all the pre-NDA regimes together that include the initial stint of the minority Congress government (1991–6). The last line in Table 9 indicates that out of the aggregate proceeds of Rs 997.39 billion from 1991–2 to 2009–10, nearly 55 per cent accrued during the last six years of UPA, a little over one-third during six years of NDA, and hardly 12 per cent during the initial period of disinvestment, that is, the pre-NDA years. Modality-wise, the last column shows that the lion's share (nearly 90 per cent) of the total proceeds is accounted by receipts (i) through the sale of minority shareholding (nearly 82 per cent) of the Central Public Sector Enterprises (CPSEs),[9] (ii) through the sale of residual shareholding (6.4 per cent) of already disinvested companies/CPSEs, and (iii) through the sale of majority shareholding (1.3 per cent) of one CPSE to another. UPA's hesitant approach comes through very clearly with nearly 93 per cent of the proceeds from the sale of minority shareholding. As discussed in Chapter 8, NDA experimented with different modalities including strategic sale (nearly 19 per cent of the proceeds) and sale of shares (nearly 12 per cent) to workers in a bold but not very successful attempt to win over public sector workers. The overall conclusion is that while the case for privatization of commercial CPSEs producing private goods and services is strong, not much progress has been achieved due either to the continued hold of the socialist ideology or political economy of unionized public sector workers or coalition politics.

The current position of CPSEs as ascertained from various sources is:

(1) The UPA-I government appointed the Bureau for Reconstruction of Public Sector Enterprises (BRPSE) in 2004 for revival/closure of CPSEs. As on 31 December 2010, 62 out of around 250 non-financial CPSEs were referred to BRPSE. BRPSE's recommendations were accepted for revival in the case of 40 and closure was approved in the case of two CPSEs. The government had spent Rs 236. 12 billion as on 31 December 2010 on the revival of CPSEs.[10]
(2) At the upper end, with a view to granting limited autonomy in terms of delegation of financial and operational powers in a graded fashion, a new 'Maharatna' (very precious jewel) or mega-Navratna status has been granted to four CPSUs (Indian Oil Company, Oil and Natural Gas Commission, National Thermal Power Corporation, and Steel Authority of India Limited), next grade 'Navratna' status to 16, and Miniratna' status to 65 CPSUs.[11]
(3) As of February 2011, total market capitalization of 47 non-financial CPSEs listed on the Bombay Stock Exchange accounted for a 22 per cent share of total market capitalization of 4,942 listed companies. Adding public sector banks and regional government-owned firms, the share goes up to 28.8 per cent.[12]
(4) Out of about 250 non-financial CPSEs, 55 CPSEs sold minority stakes between 1991 and 2009, some in multiple tranches. The BJP-led NDA government sold majority stakes and transferred the management control of 14 CPSEs (Gupta 2011).
(5) We report quantitative econometric results of Gupta (2011) based on annual financial data for 213 manufacturing and non-financial services for all privatization transactions from (April-March) 1987–8 to 2008–9. The two major sets of results discussed here hold *both* in terms of immediate impact in the following year *or* long-run impact in three years following partial or majority equity sales. It is important to caution that like all econometric results, they hold for pre-specified (partially or fully) CPSEs as a group in comparison with pre-specified control group of CPSEs on the average without ruling out deviations from average in individual

> cases. Compared to CPSEs that have been selected for privatization but have not been privatized, the share of privately owned equity in CPSEs has a positive impact on sales, ratio of profits before tax and depreciation to sales, net worth to sales, cash profits to sale, and borrowing and employment. Two, compared to partially privatized CPSEs whose shares are publicly traded, sale of majority equity stake and transfer of management control has an economically significant impact on sales, profitability, and employment.[13] These results only confirm that in the production of *private*[14] goods and services government ownership leads to underperformance in terms of operational efficiency. We have already elaborated the reasons (pp. 127–9) for underperformance.

Thus, both the entry of private sector in the areas earlier reserved for the public sector that has been introducing competition and privatization (even partial) of existing publicly owned units have succeeded in bringing about welcome improvements in the functioning of certain CPSEs. The ambivalent ideological position of the Congress Party leading the UPA-I and UPA-II coalition governments on disinvestment appears to be reflective of either its unwillingness to unburden the historical baggage of the socialist pattern of society of the 1950s or continued political hold of unionized public sector workers. Even non-Congress political parties which do not carry the ideological baggage of the public sector are cagey about even partial privatization before elections as some interesting quotes in Gupta (2011) indicate. For reasons clearly spelt out in Chapter 8, our argument for aggressive privatization and rapid disinvestment programme in *commercial non-strategic CPSUs producing private goods and services with a view to eventual full privatization*, if not found feasible for political reasons, is based on our judgment that full autonomy of CPSUs is not feasible in the Indian bureaucratic and political milieu. We have found no reason as yet to revise this judgment. Empirical evidence offered by Gupta leads us to reiterate this position.[15] This is important not only for efficiency gains but would also release scarce resources for public investment in making up deficiencies in physical infrastructure which have been holding back employment-oriented rapid growth in the manufacturing sector.

Labour Market Reforms

In the same context, not much progress is visible in the organized labour market reforms discussed in Chapter 8. The environment of informalization of labour market flexibility at the factory level in the face of formal legal rigidity in labour legislation still persists. Existing industrialists have also stopped raising this issue on political forums because of its near impossible political infeasibility although it is routinely and inconclusively discussed in the annual ritual of Indian Labour Conference where all the stakeholders—central trade unions, industrialists, and Government come together with inflexible positions. In our view, next to physical infrastructure, this is the second-most constraining factor for the employment-oriented manufacturing sector growth. It may not be a major problem for most of the existing producers who have reconciled themselves with and found formal and informal, legal and extra-legal ways of getting around rigid labour legislation mostly to carry on their existing businesses often at the cost of legitimate demands of blue-collar workers. But the existing labour laws continue to deter potential new investments in large scale labour-using industries which alone can provide *higher-than-average-productivity non-agricultural employment to unskilled and less educated workers* currently trapped in lower-than-average-labour-productivity agricultural and allied activities. The fact that it is also leading to rising inequalities and coming in the way of inclusive economic growth makes the matter worse.

ECONOMIC GROWTH PERFORMANCE

The economy has been performing well in terms of growth without any big-ticket reforms since 2004 when the UPA-I government took over.

Since we have presented in the first edition growth rates of GDP at constant 1993–4 prices (Table 4.1, p. 47 in the text and Appendix tables A1–A5), we provide in this edition the growth rates of sectoral GDP at constant 1999–2000 prices for 1991–2 to 2007–8 (Table 10, Appendix II) and at constant 2004–5 prices for 2005–6 to 2010–11 (Table 11, Appendix II). Although we have used GDP at constant 2004–5 prices for 2005–6, 2006–7, and 2007–8 in the discussion, we have calculated annual growth rates of sectoral GDP for these years at constant 1999–2000 prices as well as 2004–5 prices to have an idea about the difference between the two series. Although the differences are negligible at the aggregate GDP level, these are quite large at the sectoral level especially the industry sector. Table 12 in Appendix II provides averages of the reform period—1990s and 2000s, boom (2003–4 to 2007–8) and crisis period (2008–9 and 2009–10) of the 2000s. Table 13 in Appendix II provides quarterly growth rates of sectoral GDP at 2004–5 prices for 2006–7 to 2010–11.

Average annual growth rate of GDP was 5.7 per cent for the 1990s and 7.3 per cent in the 2000s. Average growth rate for the five years before the global economic crisis (2003–4 to 2007–8) was 8.9 per cent. Although, growth slowed down for the crisis years of 2008–9 (6.7 per cent) and 2009–10 (7.4 per cent) (Table 12, Appendix II), it was much higher than that of the pre-reform period. India remained the second fastest growing economy after China and together these economies are leading the recovery of the world economy.

The services sector followed by industry has been leading the growth of GDP. Within industry, manufacturing grew at an annual average rate of 5.6 per cent in the 1990s and 8.1 per cent in the 2000s. Average annual growth rate of the manufacturing sector was 10 per cent for 2003–4 to 2007–8 (Table 12, Appendix II). Growth rates of industry especially the manufacturing sector outperformed the services sector from the first quarter of 2006–7 to the third quarter of 2007–8 (Table 13, Appendix II). The growth performance of industry and manufacturing started slowing down from the last quarter of 2007–8 reaching their worst by the fourth quarter of 2008–9 before rising in the first quarter of 2009–10 (Table 13, Appendix II). The registered manufacturing segment grew, on an average at 6.29 per cent per annum in the 1990s and 7.55 per cent per annum for the 5-year period 2003–4 to 2007–8 (Table 10, Appendix II) and slowed down in the global financial crisis year of 2008–9 to 5.3 per cent (Table 11, Appendix II).

On the demand side, GDP growth was driven by the growth of gross fixed capital formation, which was 7.2 per cent in the 1990s, 10.3 per cent in the 2000s, and 15.5 per cent during the 5-year period 2003–4 to 2007–8 before coming down to 4 per cent in 2008–9 and rising again to 7.2 per cent in 2009–10. This can also be seen in the average growth of production of capital goods, which was 11.5 per cent per annum in the 2000s and went up to almost 16 per cent for the boom period of 2003–4 to 2007–8. The growth rate of capital goods production came down to 7.3 per cent in the crisis year of 2008–9 before rising to 19.2 per cent (2009–10) (Table 12, Appendix II).

The Indian economy experienced a slowdown in growth during 2008–9 and 2009–10 resulting from adjustment to a fast changing international environment. GDP growth rate slowed down to 6.8 (2008–9) from 9.3 per cent (2007–8). Growth of the manufacturing sector slowed down to 4.2 (2008–9) from 10.3 per cent (2007–8) (Table 11, Appendix II). The signs of slowdown are visible from the last quarter of 2007–8 (Table 13, Appendix II). The first half of 2008–9 was marked by an appreciating exchange rate resulting from foreign institutional investment (FII) inflows, rising international commodity and oil prices, and rising domestic inflation rate. The second half of 2008–9 witnessed rapid depreciation in the exchange rate resulting from heavy capital (FII) outflows, rapidly declining commodity and oil prices, and declining domestic inflation rates. While commodity producers gained and commodity users lost in the first half, the situation reversed in the second half of 2008–9. Unlike general and widespread employment and resulting decline in the purchasing power in the industrialized countries, it was only a slowdown in India in the earnings of different segments of the population in the two halves of 2008–9.

Possible reasons for the Indian economic growth performance since the first UPA government without any big-ticket reforms could be: (a) cumulative effects of the reforms undertaken earlier and the resulting improvements in corporate performance; and (b) rise in aggregate savings and investment. Liberalization of restrictions on both domestic and foreign (more hesitant) investment resulted in a spurt of new investment while rationalization of taxes and exemptions and steep reduction in import tariffs brought down the degree of distortions in resource allocations and enabled improvements in efficiency. Industrial output accelerated from 1992–3 to 1996–7 only to come down later (Table 10, Appendix II). It seemed that the industry initially overestimated the size of the middle class and (mis)took the suppressed demand during the import control regime to be normal demand and ended up with excess capacity. The years 1997–8 to 2002–3 was a period of adjustment for corporates to excess capacity and intensified competition—domestic as well as external, resulting in slow industrial growth (Table 10, Appendix II). Corporates cleaned up their balance sheets and expanded their internal resource base (Bhavani and Bhanumurthy 2012) by taking advantage of lower domestic and international interest rates.[16] The years 2003–4 to 2007–8 was a period of rapid industrial growth (Table 12, Appendix II) and high rates of corporate savings and investment (Table 15, Appendix II) approximating those in the East Asian countries. There was a rise in foreign direct investment and foreign portfolio investment inflows (Table 5, Appendix II) that gave boost to the capital markets enabling corporates to raise capital through IPOs and FPOs. Corporates could also raise capital through external sources such as ADRs and GDRs (Table 16, Appendix II). Apart from large scale enterprises, medium and small scale enterprises also had easier and cheaper access to technology due to tariff reductions, and have been competing on equal terms with corporates in certain domestic and international markets.

The private corporate sector displayed dynamism in terms of growth of their numbers, sales, and profits (Chari and Alfaro 2009), Tables 17 and 18, Appendix II). Growth rate of sales was, on an average, around 14 per cent through the 1990s and up till 2006–7 and it has been 20.2 per cent for the boom period of 2003–4 to 2007–8 (Table 17, Appendix II). Growth of sales of the corporate sector declined from 2007–8 (Table 18, Appendix II). But the quarterly results show that the growth of sales of the corporate sector came down from the third quarter of 2008–9 reaching negative levels in the first quarter of 2009–10 before rising to positive levels (Table 19, Appendix II).Gross profits grew at an annual average rate of 12.5 per cent during the 1990s and 20.4 per cent for the period of 2000–1 to 2006–7. In the boom period (2003–4 to 2007–8), it went up to 29.4 per cent, whereas net profits grew at higher rates in 2000s (Table 17, Appendix II). Growth of profits turned negative in 2008–9 (Table 18, Appendix II). Gross profits to sales went up in 2000s compared to that in the 1990s, whereas interest payments to sales as well as gross profits came down over time (Table 17, Appendix II). Although the financial performance of the corporate sector was sluggish during the global financial crisis, it recovered quickly. Manufacturing firms became more export oriented and technology intensive exports (engineering goods and chemicals) went up over the period (Reserve Bank of India 2010).

A dramatic rise in savings and investment made the growth process self-sustained. Gross domestic savings (GDS) rates increased from 23.7 (2000–1) to 36.9 per cent (2007–8). Gross domestic capital formation (GDCF) rose from 24.1 (2000–1) to 38.2 per cent (2009–10) (Tables 13 and 20, Appendix II).

However, uncertainties in the international environment and growing fiscal deficit and inflationary pressures will be a threat for the sustainability of growth. Fiscal and revenue deficits at the Centre have reached/crossed the deficits of the crisis year of 1990–1. Gross fiscal deficit (as a percentage of GDP) and revenue deficit (as a percentage of gross fiscal deficit) reached 6.64 and 79.52 respectively by 2009–10. Annual variations in the wholesale price indices were 8.3 per cent and consumer price indices for industrial workers were 9.1 per cent in the 2008–9 (Table 20, Appendix II). High inflation and fiscal deficits especially revenue deficits are not conducive for investment, which is highly sensitive to macroeconomic conditions, and thus influences future growth adversely. Adverse effects on growth will be compounded by the uncertainties in the world economy such as uncertain recovery of US and Europe and unrest in West Asia and North Africa and consequential fluctuations in crude oil prices.

All these uncertainties are reflected in declining business confidence. The recent business confidence surveys of the Federation of Indian Chambers of Commerce and Industry (FICCI) revealed that there has been a perceptible decline in the confidence levels of corporate India. Further, the surveys report that high inflation, slowdown of growth, continuous rise of interest rates, and incessant increase in raw material prices are some of the factors that have adversely affected business confidence. [17]

Apart from the immediate macroeconomic factors, the organized (corporate) segment of the economy, especially the manufacturing sector, is still to operate with the numerous regulations and cumbersome procedures, and infrastructure and other bottlenecks. The Heritage Foundation's 'Index of Economic Freedom' Report (2011) places India at 124 out of the 183 economies that it covered, just below Pakistan with the lowest points for freedom from corruption (34.0 out of 100) followed by investment freedom (35.0 out of 100), and business freedom (36.9 out of 100).[18]

The World Bank's 'Doing Business Survey' (2011) ranks India 134 out of the 183 economies covered. The survey results show that India ranks last but one (182) in enforcing contracts, which involves 46 procedures that take almost four years to complete and cost around 40 per cent of the claim. Further, closing a business in India takes seven years with a recovery rate of 16.3 cents to the dollar. Another difficult area for Indian business is construction permits that involve 37 procedures and take six-and-a-half months to obtain (the World Bank 2010). The same was confirmed by the Hong Kong based Political and Economic Risk Consultancy Private Limited (PERC) survey on 'Asian Business and Politics'. The PERC survey conducted in 2010 reveals that India tops the list of the most over-regulated countries in the world with a score of 9.16 out of 10. The survey reports that regulations in India are complex and non-transparent and there are regulations which are not enforced frequently raising a question about why at all these are in the books.[19] Apart from security risks, fragmented multi-party coalition governments, poor quality of infrastructure, and suffocating levels of bureaucracy show India in poor light.[20]

The economic reforms undertaken so far mainly relate to rules and regulations inhibiting entry moving slowly on rules and regulations regarding business operations (environment) and exit. Since the UPA government came into power in 2004, there have hardly been any big-ticket reforms. This is despite the fact that Prime Minister Manmohan Singh was very keen and concerned about reforms[21] and the Congress Party manifesto for the 2004 elections mentioned about 'broadening and deepening of reforms to have sustainable rapid growth'.[22] The UPA-I government developed cold feet in taking reforms further partly due to pressures of immediate coalition partners such as the Left parties and conservative ideologues within the Congress Party, and partly because most of the big-ticket reforms waiting to be undertaken such as labour market reforms require legislative amendments and thus broad-based political consensus, which is lacking.[23]

RISING POPULISM

Instead of removing hurdles to growth especially of manufacturing—a sector that can alone provide higher income employment to unskilled and less educated workers—such as infrastructure bottlenecks, cascading taxes, procedural delays, labour laws, and land acquisition and utilization laws through policy reforms, the UPA-I government resorted to populist social sector policies piggybacking on the record economic growth that the earlier reforms had enabled. It stepped up expenditure on social sectors such as education and health, and initiated a series of social welfare schemes such as the Mahatma Gandhi National Rural Employment Guarantee Scheme (MNREGA usually referred as NREGA or NREGS), social security for unorganized workers (SSUW), and waiving farm loans without paying much attention to their content and effective implementation.[24] The Congress Party that has always been for populist welfare measures since the radicalization of politics by Indira Gandhi in the mid-60s onwards exploiting the stronghold of the ideology of socialism (see the first edition, pp. 21–3), used these welfare schemes to improve the party's prospects in the 2009 elections after raising resources allocation to these programmes substantially in the interim budget presented in February 2009.[25] This can also be seen in the party highlighting its social welfare schemes in the 2009 election manifesto. The populist welfare strategy paid off and the Congress won more seats (than those in the 2004 elections) and came back to power with the support of smaller regional parties but without the support of the Left parties. The 2009 election results turned the most conservative naysayers in the Congress Party to these welfare schemes such as Manmohan Singh who raised concerns over the fiscal impact of funding, into supporters of these schemes[26] and encouraged the Congress-led UPA-II government to focus more on social sector policies including welfare measures keeping economic policy reforms aside proving wrong the expectations that the second UPA government would speed up reforms in the absence of pressures from the Left parties.

The UPA governments have raised public expenditure on social services and development in the name of 'inclusive development'. There has been a 5–7 percentage points hike in the central government's expenditure on social sector development during the UPA regime. Central government expenditure (plan and non-plan) on social services such as education and health increased from around 8 per cent (2000–1 to 2003–4) to 13 per cent (2008–9) of its total expenditure. If we add rural development,[27] public expenditure on social development was raised from about 11 per cent (2000–1 to 2003–4) to 18.32 per cent (2008–9) of the total central government expenditure (see Table 21, Appendix II). If subsidies such as food subsidy are included, social expenditure crosses 30 per cent of the total expenditure of the central government (Rajaraman 2010).

Expenditure on social development in India includes the provision of public services such as education, health, water supply, sanitation, roads and public transport, as well as transfer payments through welfare schemes such as rural employment and social security schemes, and subsidies to targeted groups. Provision of public services benefits all especially the poor who cannot afford these services on their own. Effective public services enable individuals (through skill and health improvements, and effective and easy movements) to get productive employment and thus enhanced incomes as well as contributing to growth. Whereas transfer payments and subsidies, if implemented effectively, take care of the immediate needs of the target groups, however, they do not improve their long term capabilities and income, making them dependents forever on the state. At the same time, transfer payments to large sections of the population, if continued for the long term, will be a fiscal strain and affect long term growth adversely. Provision of public services is always a superior alternative to transfer payments.

Notwithstanding, there has been a greater reliance in India on transfer payments and subsidies vis-à-vis provision of public services (Keefer and Khemani 2003, 2004). This is the consequence of the democratic political framework with universal adult franchise that India adopted in a low-income country with a significant proportion of an illiterate population and stupendous social diversity—religion, caste, region, and linguistic—where there exist competitive populist pressures for quick-fix solutions (see first edition, pp. 2–3). Electoral competition revolves around distribution of public resources as transfer payments and subsidies to individuals/ groups due to: (i) lack of information about politicians' performance; (ii) social fragmentation amongst voters; and (iii) lack of credibility of political promises to provide public goods (Keefer and Khemani 2003, 2004). Lack of credibility arises from the fact that 'there is a weak link between public expenditure and services delivering in India' (Saigal 2002). While a significant proportion of the population is yet to be provided with basic public services, even where these are provided their quality and reliability are far from satisfactory.[28] Some of the factors responsible for the current state of service delivery are corruption, absenteeism, low quality, and excessive costs. Without deep institutional reforms to strengthen capacity and impart accountability at all levels—politicians, policymakers, administration, and front line providers—allocation of huge budgets and better designated schemes remain ineffective in the delivery of public services (The World Bank 2006: 6). And effective implementation is the most important thing that needs to be focused on immediately.

Effective implementation is important even for welfare schemes such as rural employment guarantee schemes, social security for unorganized workers, and subsidized farm loans. However, evidence shows that effective implementation remains a serious concern in all these schemes. For instance, NREGS enacted in 2005 is one of the UPA's flagship welfare programmes. The Act provides 100 days of legally guaranteed employment to each rural household seeking employment in public work programmes. It was implemented in 200 districts in 2006–7 with a budget allocation of Rs 113,000 million and was later expanded to 619 districts with a budget allocation of Rs 391,000 million in 2009–10. However, the scheme came under severe criticism by many including important functionaries of UPA. Six sub-committees set up by the Central Employment Guarantee Council (CEGC) that was formed under the NREG Act, have raised questions on issues ranging from the utility of work done through NREGS to transparency and capacity building. The sub-committee on work said that the wage employment generated through NREGS was neither planned nor productive. Rather it was ad hoc and thrust on people.[29]

While UPA chairperson Sonia Gandhi and Prime Minister Manmohan Singh admitted that there are several problems in the implementation of NREGA such as delayed payments and unemployment allowances not being given,[30] Rural Development

Minister Jairam Ramesh expressed concerns over the leakage of funds meant for the scheme and serious shortcomings in its implementation.[31]

If NREGA was criticized on the implementation part, the Unorganized Workers Social Security Act 2008 (SSUW) has been criticized severely on the basic design itself. The main criticism relates to: (i) the definition of unorganized worker excludes many workers in the unorganized segment such as forest workers and fish workers; (ii) the concept of social security is not defined except mentioning a few possible schemes of social security; (iii) the Act does not confer any right to social security for unorganized workers; (iv) no nodal ministry or administrative mechanism is specified for implementation; (v) no grievance redressal machinery is specified; (vi) the national and state level social security boards do not have mandatory powers but only advisory role; and (vii) there was no financial memorandum to the Act providing for the creation of a social security fund. The central government has allocated Rs 10,000 million owing to mounting pressures to set up the National Security Fund only in the Union Budget 2010–11 to take care of specified workers such as weavers, toddy tappers, rickshaw pullers, and bidi workers.[32]

Subsidies to targeted groups in India are politically motivated and have always been misused and diverted to non-deserving groups for unintended purposes. Agricultural loans provide a good example in this respect. Agricultural loans are politically motivated in the sense that their amount is hiked 5–10 per cent in election years than in the years following an election and are costly as these are less likely to be repaid and do not reveal any measurable effect on agricultural output (Cole 2009). Concessional interest rates, interest subvention, and loan waiving schemes regarding farm loans have been a big source of misuse of public resources. A small percentage of marginal and small farmers, the main target group for subsidized loans and loan waiving, have access to formal financial institutions like banks despite numerous government policies (Bhavani and Bhanumurthy 2012). All these schemes mainly benefit large farmers with a possibility of diversion of these loans to unintended purposes. Farm loans in Delhi provide an idea in this regard. Delhi with 26,000 hectares of agricultural land is not a leading agricultural state but disburses more of concessional agricultural loans than that in agrarian states such as

Punjab, Haryana, and Uttar Pradesh. Since 2007–08, Delhi has disbursed more than Rs 570,000 million as farm loans and most of it has been given to the farmhouse owners, who have allegedly used these loans for real estate development purposes. A Task Force on Credit Flow headed by former Chairman of NABARD U. Sarangi mentioned that a big chunk of agricultural credit is being used for non-agricultural purposes in Delhi and Chandigarh (Chauhan 2011). Disregarding these facts, the UPA-I government waived farm loans worth Rs 720,000 million in 2008, the year preceding the general elections.

These illustrations point out that there is lack of genuine commitment on the part of the government. All the same, the UPA government (especially Congress Party) may most likely continue to focus on welfare schemes to come to power in the next elections (on its own without any coalition) by strengthening its electoral base through welfare schemes. How far it succeeds will depend on sustaining the growth momentum, which in turn depends on macroeconomic conditions (fiscal deficits, inflation, and international uncertainties) and further reforms, economic as well as institutional (judicial, administrative, etc.). Given coalition politics, lack of broad-based political consensus on big-ticket reforms, and an infirm government,[33] further reforms will be hesitant and episodic only when growth derails.

NOTES

1. Left Front includes the Communist Party of India (Marxist) (CPI-M), the Communist Party of India (CPI), the All India Forward Bloc (AIFB), and the Revolutionary Socialist Party (RSP).
2. BSP, another party supporting the UPA government from outside, withdrew its support to the government on 21 June 2008, accusing the government of failing to curb inflation and said 'in case of no-trust against the UPA government, we would decide on the basis of the issue' (http://www.hindustantimes.com/News-Feed/India/BSP-withdraws-support-UPA-in-fresh-crisis/, last accessed in August 2010.
3. http://en.wikipedia.org/wiki/2008_lOK_Sabha_vote_of_confidence, last accessed in August 2010.
4. TRS was the first one to leave the UPA-I government on 23 September 2006, over separate statehood for Telangana followed by PMK that left UPA-I on 16 March 2007 to tie up with AIDMK. While BSP withdrew support to the UPA-I government on 21 June 2008, citing inflation as the reason, the Left parties

withdrew support on 9 July 2008, as they did not want the nuclear deal to be signed by the government. PDP walked out of UPA-I on 4 January 2009; irked by the Congress coalition with the National Conference in the Jammu and Kashmir and PMK left on 26 March 2009, to join the AIDMK led front.

5. As mentioned in Chapter 7 (p. 92), regional parties like DMK and AITC with their flexible ideologies support/oppose reforms as per their convenience. If reforms are beneficial or not harmful to their constituencies, these parties support reform initiatives and oppose them if they go against their constituencies like the reversal of the stance of DMK in the case of privatization of Neyveli Lignite Corporation (NLC). Also, see 'Trinamool, DMK seek rollback of fuel hike', 27 February 2010, http://www.tribuneindia.com/2010/20100228/main1.htm, last accessed in September 2010.
6. *The Indian Express*, New Delhi, Saturday, 26 March 2011.
7. The Bill was passed with a division of 115 for and 43 against. If BJP had voted against the Bill, the potential 85–73 division was too close for comfort. See 'BJP helps government on bill after Left ambush', by the Telegraph correspondent, New Delhi, *The Telegraph*, Kolkata, 25 March 2011, p. 4.
8. http://www.dcmsme.gov.in/publications/reserveditems/respol.htm, last accessed in January 2011.
9. CPSUs and CPSEs are used interchangeably.
10. Ministry of Finance, *Economic Survey 2010–11*, para 9.60, p. 232–33.
11. Ministry of Finance, *Economic Survey 2010–11*, para 9.59, p. 232.
12. 'Bombay Stock Exchange Database', March 2011, quoted in Gupta (2011).
13. This result relates to totally privatized CPSEs as a group and does not rule out reduction of employment in individual overstaffed CPSEs. It is indicative of improved efficiency from private management.
14. Please see footnote 17, p. 37 for the distinction between private and public goods.
15. Even Manmohan Singh said in one of his interviews in 2001 that '... government will not be in the business of running industries and running trading enterprises', (http://www.pbs.org/wgbh/commandingheights/shared/minitextlo/int_manmohansingh.html, last accessed in December 2010) but once in government as Prime Minister, he talked of his inability because '... we are in a coalition government, and that limits our options in some ways. Privatization happens to be one such area....' PM's McKinsey Quarterly Interview held on 16 August 2005 "India's economic agenda: An interview with Manmohan Singh": http://pmindia.nic.in/, last accessed in December 2010. These quotes are elaborated later in footnotes 21 and 23.
16. See Table 14, Appendix II for the lending rates of scheduled commercial banks for the period 1996–2009.
17. FICCI: 'Business Confidence Surveys', February 2010; February 2011; and May 2011; Foreign Investment Survey 2010. See www.ficci.com/publication/surveys
18. The Heritage Foundation has been constructing the Index of Economic Freedom for 183 economies since 1995. *Economic freedom* is measured as a simple average of freedom in different areas of economics: business freedom, trade freedom, fiscal freedom, government spending, monetary freedom, investment freedom, financial freedom, property rights, freedom from corruption, and labour freedom. Each of these components is measured on a scale of 1 to 100. *Business freedom* is

taken as a quantitative measure of the ability to start, operate, and close a business and represents the overall burden of regulations as well as the efficiency of the government in the regulatory process. This is measured based on the World Bank's 'Doing Business Survey' data. *Investment freedom* refers to the freedom with which individuals and firms are allowed to move their resources into and out of specific activities both internally and across the country's borders. This index is constructed based on restrictions on land ownership, national treatment of foreign investment, foreign investment code, sectoral investment restrictions, expropriation of investment without fair compensation, and foreign exchange and capital controls. *Freedom from corruption* is derived primarily from the Transparency International's Corruption Perception Index. For the detailed methodology, refer to Heritage Foundation's Index of Economic Freedom at http://www.heritage.org/index/book/methodology, last accessed in July 2011.

19. 'India is Most Over-regulated Country in the World: Survey', *The Economic Times*, 27 January 2011.
20. 'Executive Summary of Major Risks in 2010', Political and Economic Risks Consultancy Private Limited, Hong Kong (http://www.asiarisk.com/), last accessed in August 2011.
21. Manmohan Singh stated in one of his interviews in 2001 that '... although the direction of economic policy reforms remains essentially what we laid out, the pace has not been to our liking. I think the pace has slowed down and that certainly worries me. If we had gotten another five years, I think we would have ensured that by the year 2010 or 2015, many of the dreams we had become reality.' 'The government will take a lot more interest in education and health... But the government will not be in the business of running industries and running trading enterprises'. Commanding Heights, Interview with Manmohan Singh conducted on 02/06/2001. http://www.pbs.org/wgbh/commandingheights/shared/minitextlo/int_manmohansingh.html, last accessed in December 2010.
22. www.congresssandesh.com. The manifesto of the Indian National Congress: Lok Sabha elections 2004 states that 'The Congress will broaden and deepen economic reforms. The over-riding objective will be to attain and sustain year after year 8–10 per cent rate of economic growth and to spread this growth over all sectors', last accessed in April 2011.
23. The Prime Minister Manmohan Singh stated in one of his interviews in 2005 that 'we are a coalition government, and that limits our options in some ways. Privatisation happens to be one such area ... so we have to make those compromises' (p. 2). 'Extreme rigidities in the labour market is not consistent in our achieving our goals in a world where demand conditions are changing so fast, technological conditions are changing so fast. But there are limitations for the time being' (p. 4). 'India's Economic Agenda: PM's Mckinsey Quarterly Interview' in the '*Mckinsey Quarterly 2005 Special Edition:* Fulfilling India's Promise', September 2005, http://pmindia.commandingheights/shared/nic.in, last accessed in December 2010).
24. The manifesto of the Indian National Congress: Lok Sabha Elections 2009 states (p. 7) that 'It has delivered five years of record economic growth. This has enabled an unprecedented step-up in government spending particularly on education and health', .

25. S. Narayan, 'Fine Speech but Little Else', *Mint*, 16 February 2009.
26. Siddharth Varadarajan, 'Political Logic of Budget is that Welfarism Pays', *The Hindu*, 7 July 2009.
27. Expenditure on rural development includes expenditure on various rural development schemes of the central government such as NREGS, Swarna Jayanti Swarojgar Yojana (SGSY), rural housing, the National Rural Drinking Water Programme, and rural sanitation.
28. Paul et al. (2004). Planning Commission Deputy Chairman, Montek Singh Ahluwalia told reporters that '.... Poor delivery of public services had frustrated many people. There is an issue of frustration that many people feel they are not able to access public services which are their right. It takes too long to take all those things which they should be getting on the table', *Business Standard*, 30 August 2011.
29. *Business Standard*, 19 September 2010.
30. 'PM, Sonia Admits Lapses in NREGA Implementation', *India Today*, 2 February 2010, http://indiatoday.intoday.in/, lst accessed in August 2011.
31. Ramesh Calls MREGA Execution Patchy" dated 2 October 2011 downloaded from http://ibnlivein.com/generalnewsfeed/news/ ramesh-calls-mnrega-execution.patchy on 23 October 2011.
32. John (2008); Ghosh (2009); 'Suggested Amendments to the Unorganised Workers' Social Security Act', National Convention on Social Security for Unorganised Workers, January 8–10 held in Patna, Bihar; Highlights of Central Plan 2010–11, 'Union Budget 2010–11', http://indiabudget.nic.in, last accessed in August 2011.
33. The ruling coalition is besieged by corruption scandals, Parliament paralysis, and bickering ministers, so the union cabinet managed to take just 112 decisions in 2010—the lowest single year tally since UPA assumed power in 2004. 'UPA: From Decisiveness to Total Disarray', Times of India, 17 January 2011.

REFERENCES

Bhavani, T.A. and N.R. Bhanumurthy (2012). *Financial Access in the Post-Reform India*. New Delhi: Oxford University Press.

Chari, Anusha and Laura Alfaro (2009). 'India Transformed? Insights from the Firm-Level 1988–2005', Working Paper No.10–030. Cambridge MA: Harvard Business School.

Chauhan, Madhavendra Singh (2011). 'Behind the Walls', *Agricultural Spectrum*, II (VII): 28–9.

Cole, Shawn A. (2009). 'Fixing Market Failures or Fixing Elections? Agricultural Credit in India', *American Economic Journal: Applied Economics*, 1 (1): 219–50

Ghosh, Pritam (2009). 'Unorganised Workers' Social Security Act 2008—A Critical Analysis', Available at: http://jurisonline.in/. Last accessed on 28 August 2009.

Government of India (1997). 'Report of the Expert Committee on Small Enterprises,' (Chairman: Abid Hussain), New Delhi: Industry Ministry, Government of India.

Gupta, Nandini (2011). 'Selling the Family Silver to Pay the Grocer's Bill? The Case of Privatization in India', Paper presented at the Columbia-NCAER Conference on Trade, Poverty, Inequality and Democracy, New Delhi, 31 March–1 April.

John, J. (2008). 'Social Security Act: The Great Indian Tamasha on Unorganised Workers', *Labour File*, 6 (6): 5–11. Available at: http://labourfile.org/. Last accessed in September 2010.

Keefer, Philip and Stuti Khemani (2003). 'The Political Economy of Public Expenditures', Background Paper for *World Development Report 2004: Making Services Work for Poor People*. Washington DC: The World Bank.

———. (2004). 'Why Do the Poor Receive Poor Services', *Economic and Political Weekly*, 39 (9): 935–43.

Ministry of Finance. 2010. *Economic Survey 2010–11*. New Delhi: Government of India.

Ministry of Finance. 2010. *Union Budget 2010–11*. New Delhi: Government of India.

Paul, Samuel, Suresh Balakrishnan, K. Gopakumar, Sita Sekhar, and M. Vivekananda (2004). 'State of India's Public Services: Benchmarks for the States', *Economic and Political Weekly*, 39 (9): 920–32.

Rajaraman, Indira (2010). 'Fiscal Federalism, Social Expenditure and Equity—India's Approach', Available at: www.indiapolicyforum.org. Last accessed in August 2011.

Reserve Bank of India (2010). *Report on Currency and Finance 2008–09: Global Financial Crisis and the Indian Economy*. Mumbai: Reserve Bank of India.

Saigal, Suraj (2002). 'Literature Review on Service Delivery in India', Background paper for *World Development Report 2004: Making Services Work for Poor People*. Washington DC: The World Bank.

The World Bank (2006). 'India—Inclusive Growth and Service Delivery: Building on India's Success', *Development Policy Review*, Washington DC: The World Bank.

———. (2010). *Doing Business 2011*. Washington DC: The World Bank.

Appendix I

APPENDIX A

Table A1: Annual Rate of Growth of GDP (FC) at Constant Prices by Industry 1951–2 to 1964–5

Year	Total	Agriculture and allied	Mining and quarrying	Industry	Manufacturing total	Manufacturing registered	Electricity, gas, and water	Construction	Services	Public administration and defence
1951–2	2.33	1.49	12.33	5.28	3.16	2.63	11.38	6.83	2.71	2.37
1952–3	2.84	3.15	2.31	0.38	3.48	0.46	4.52	–7.25	3.07	0.98
1953–4	6.09	7.70	1.50	5.86	7.74	4.40	7.89	3.09	2.97	4.37
1954–5	4.24	2.94	4.28	8.11	7.01	11.14	8.54	12.37	4.83	5.59
1955–6	2.56	–0.86	1.58	10.19	7.83	12.25	11.08	18.94	5.14	3.95
1956–7	5.69	5.44	5.09	8.44	7.50	11.14	8.96	11.50	4.90	7.19
1957–8	–1.21	–4.49	6.50	–0.29	3.86	4.67	15.12	–12.23	3.78	7.81
1958–9	7.59	10.08	3.12	6.74	4.95	2.88	12.79	11.75	4.28	6.14
1959–60	2.19	–1.01	5.15	6.91	6.79	10.09	15.02	6.86	5.09	6.48
1960–1	7.08	6.74	14.97	10.87	8.30	11.91	8.08	15.65	5.95	6.55
1961–2	3.10	0.08	5.76	7.05	8.54	9.12	14.22	3.51	5.48	6.40
1962–3	2.12	–1.99	11.87	6.92	7.28	9.74	12.23	3.72	5.78	12.96
1963–4	5.06	2.34	2.96	9.86	9.46	11.31	18.21	12.21	6.09	11.16
1964–5	7.58	9.22	1.44	6.80	6.92	8.25	9.16	8.03	5.87	10.74

Note: Industry includes manufacturing, mining and quarrying, construction, and electricity, gas and water supply.

Sources: National Accounts Statistics Back Series (1950–1 to 1992–3), Central Statistical Organization, Government of India, New Delhi; *National Accounts Statistics 2003*, Central Statistical Organization, Government of India, New Delhi.

Press note dated 7 Feb. 2003. Advanced Estimates of National Income, 2003–4.

Table A2: Annual Rate of Growth of GDP(FC) at Constant Prices by Industry 1965–6 to 1972–3

Year	Total	Agriculture and allied	Mining and quarrying	Industry	Manufacturing total	Manufacturing registered	Electricity, gas, and water	Construction	Services	Public administration and defence
1965–6	–3.65	–11.04	11.75	3.80	0.93	3.28	10.38	6.67	2.81	3.56
1966–7	1.02	–1.42	2.36	3.33	0.79	0.09	8.69	8.22	3.11	6.37
1967–8	8.14	14.87	3.03	3.08	0.39	–3.26	10.93	7.19	3.92	4.42
1968–9	2.61	–0.16	2.83	5.02	5.54	6.76	12.92	3.50	4.59	6.21
1969–70	6.52	6.43	4.94	7.84	10.73	17.37	8.96	3.11	5.22	8.73
1970–1	5.01	7.09	–6.85	1.00	2.35	2.38	6.22	–0.22	4.93	8.44
1971–2	1.01	–1.88	2.64	2.68	3.27	1.80	8.11	0.44	3.56	7.00
1972–3	–0.32	–5.02	5.91	3.69	3.92	3.19	4.65	2.35	2.99	3.65

Note: Same as Table A1.
Sources: Same as Table A1.

Table A3: Annual Rate of Growth of GDP(FC) at Constant Prices by Industry 1973–4 to 1979–80

Year	Total	Agriculture and allied	Mining and quarrying	Industry	Manufacturing total	Manufacturing registered	Electricity, gas, and water	Construction	Services	Public administration and defence
1973–4	4.55	7.20	1.26	1.08	4.45	4.93	2.22	–6.50	3.34	4.89
1974–5	1.16	–1.52	4.96	1.65	2.92	1.00	4.59	–3.18	4.49	3.89
1975–6	9.00	12.89	12.13	6.64	2.11	1.01	14.57	14.26	6.80	5.04
1976–7	1.25	–5.78	3.55	8.73	8.77	12.49	11.50	9.78	4.61	4.22
1977–8	7.47	10.04	3.13	6.87	6.23	6.71	4.77	10.12	4.95	4.16
1978–9	5.50	2.30	2.71	7.59	12.35	10.91	11.40	–2.23	6.74	7.38
1979–80	–5.20	–12.77	1.08	–3.08	–3.22	–2.10	1.24	–5.28	2.19	7.07

Note: Same as Table A1.
Sources: Same as Table A1.

Table A4: Annual Rate of Growth of GDP(FC) at Constant Prices by Industry 1980–1 to 1989–90

Year	Total	Agriculture and allied	Mining and quarrying	Industry	Manufacturing total	Manufacturing registered	Electricity, gas, and water	Construction	Services	Public adminis-tration and defence
1980–1	7.17	12.89	12.19	4.68	0.20	–1.61	5.98	13.18	4.50	6.59
1981–2	5.97	5.29	13.46	7.96	8.02	7.71	9.49	5.48	5.42	2.28
1982–3	3.06	–0.68	11.49	3.67	6.64	9.63	6.67	–7.02	6.71	9.58
1983–4	7.68	9.56	2.68	8.07	10.10	14.67	7.05	5.40	5.55	3.39
1984–5	4.31	1.47	1.43	5.77	6.57	8.43	11.71	3.46	6.32	9.08
1985–6	4.45	0.75	5.52	4.79	3.93	2.34	8.35	5.66	7.93	7.10
1986–7	4.33	–0.65	13.53	6.87	6.96	5.79	10.53	2.39	7.36	8.91
1987–8	3.83	–1.33	3.43	6.63	7.30	7.07	7.66	5.73	6.50	9.40
1988–9	10.47	15.46	15.00	9.22	8.83	10.64	10.93	7.03	7.28	6.08
1989–90	6.70	1.48	7.31	10.34	11.76	13.88	11.48	7.03	8.85	7.83

Note: Same as Table A1.
Sources: Same as Table A1.

Table A5: Annual Rate of Growth of GDP(FC) at Constant Prices by Industry 1990–1 to 2001–2

Year	Total	Agriculture and allied	Mining and quarrying	Industry	Manufacturing total	Manufacturing registered	Electricity, gas, and water	Construction	Services	Public adminis-tration and defence
1990–1	5.57	4.11	10.68	7.74	6.05	5.02	7.39	11.79	5.32	1.30
1991–2	1.30	–1.55	3.68	–0.55	–3.65	–2.29	10.39	2.06	4.80	2.11
1992–3	5.12	5.79	1.15	3.96	4.14	3.15	7.02	3.48	5.35	4.94
1993–4	5.90	4.12	1.38	5.21	8.49	11.47	–0.83	0.57	7.67	2.56
1994–5	7.25	5.01	9.29	10.18	11.95	14.43	9.41	5.51	7.08	1.28
1995–6	7.34	–0.87	5.93	11.64	14.90	14.70	6.77	6.22	10.46	6.76
1996–7	7.84	9.61	0.47	7.08	9.66	10.83	5.43	2.10	7.20	4.08
1997–8	4.79	–2.43	9.83	4.28	1.51	–1.04	7.87	10.24	9.83	14.52
1998–9	6.51	6.20	2.82	3.75	2.72	1.92	6.99	6.21	8.35	10.62
1999–2000	6.07	0.31	3.33	4.81	4.01	3.71	5.24	8.00	10.06	13.22
2000–1	4.37	–0.39	2.42	6.60	7.33	7.72	4.95	6.95	5.61	2.54
2001–2	5.77	5.66	2.21	3.33	3.70	4.71	2.97	2.77	6.64	2.75
2002–3	3.98	–4.19	8.77	6.44	6.25	6.62	3.81	7.30	7.14	5.25

Note: Same as Table A1.
Sources: Same as Table A1.

APPENDIX B

Table B1: Indicators of Macroeconomic Management of the Economy 1970–1 to 1980–1

S.No.		1970–1	1971–2	1972–3	1973–4	1974–5	1975–6	1976–7	1977–8	1978–9	1979–80	1980–1	Average of 1970–1 to 1979–80
Economy: Growth Performance and Macroeconomic Balances													
1	Growth rates of GDP(FC)	5.01	1.01	–0.32	4.55	1.16	9.00	1.25	7.47	5.50	–5.20	7.17	2.94
2	GDCF (current prices)	15.82	16.93	16.17	16.66	18.32	18.97	19.10	18.68	20.71	21.37	18.69	18.27
3	GDS (current prices)	14.56	15.06	14.59	16.76	15.98	17.23	19.40	19.83	21.50	20.12	18.88	17.50
4	Net inflow (current prices)	1.27	1.87	1.57	–0.11	2.34	1.75	–0.29	–1.14	–0.79	1.25	–0.19	0.77
5	GDCF (constant prices)	20.30	21.22	21.09	21.64	21.77	21.16	22.31	22.42	23.17	23.42	20.87	21.85
Government: Fiscal Management													
6	GFD/GDP centre	3.08	3.53	4.04	2.64	2.97	3.64	4.24	3.62	5.18	5.29	5.77	3.82
7	GFD/GDP states	1.97	2.15	2.5	2.24	1.6	1.32	1.69	2.01	2.4	2.38	2.58	2.03
8	GFD/GDP combined												
9	RD/GFD centre	–11.69	5.67	0.74	–13.64	–33.33	–29.12	–7.78	–11.60	–5.21	10.78	24.61	–9.52
10	RD/GFD states	2.03	–0.47	5.20	8.04	–31.88	–88.64	–72.19	–49.75	–42.92	–53.78	–39.92	–32.43
Key Variables Reflecting Macroeconomic Management													
Rate of inflation (percentage change year to year basis)													
11	WPI	5.48	5.60	10.04	20.22	25.20	–1.09	2.08	5.21	0.00	17.12	18.24	8.99
12	CPIIW	5.08	3.23	7.81	20.77	26.80	–1.26	–3.83	7.64	2.16	8.76	11.39	7.72
13	GDP deflator (perentage change)	1.30	5.33	10.35	17.22	16.36	–2.56	6.16	6.20	1.87	15.11	11.51	7.73
Exchange rate (percentage change)													
14	NEER		–6.09	–5.20	–7.02	–3.54	–1.83	–1.96	0.31	0.06	0.79	4.52	–2.72
15	REER		–6.67	–2.80	–1.30	6.95	–9.88	–12.20	–0.85	–6.62	3.03	10.95	–3.37
Prime lending rate													
16	IDBI	8.5	8.5	8.5	9	10.25	11	11	11	11	11	14	9.98
17	ICICI	8.5	8.5	8.5	9	10.25	11	11	11	11	11	14	9.98
18	Net international terms of trade (percentage change)	1.92	9.96	6.78	–15.03	–27.44	–8.23	9.56	22.84	–12.28	–7.60	–12.55	–1.95

Table B1 (contd.)

S.No.	1970–1	1971–2	1972–3	1973–4	1974–5	1975–6	1976–7	1977–8	1978–9	1979–80	1980–1	Average of 1970–1 to 1979–80

Notation in Order of Serial Number:

1. GDP(FC): Gross Domestic Product at Factor Cost at 1993–4 prices (NAS 2003: Table1).
2. GDCF(curr): Gross Domestic Capital Formation (% of GDP at current market prices), (NAS 2003).
3. GDS(curr): Gross Domestic Savings (% of GDP at current market prices) (NAS 2003).
4. NetInflow(curr): Net Capital Inflow (% of GDP at current market prices) equals the difference between GDCF(curr) and GDS(curr) (NAS 2003).
5. GDCF(const): GDCF (% of GDP at market prices) at 1993–4 prices (NAS 2003).

6, 7, 8. GFD/GDP: Gross Fiscal Deficit as percentage of GDP at market prices (RBI 2002: Table 221, 222, 223).
For the Central government they relate to the old definition without adjustment of the states' share in small savings.

9, 10. RD/GFD: Revenue Deficit as % of Gross Fiscal Deficit (RBI 2002–3).

11. WPI: Wholesale Price Index (average of the weeks for all commodities, (RBI 2002–3: Table 34).
Rate of inflation based on WPI for the year 1970–1 is from handbook of industrial policy and statistics 2001, ch. XIV, Table 177, p. 589.
12. CPIIW: Consumer Price Index for Industrial Workers, (average of the months) (RBI 2003: Table 35).
Rate of inflation based on CPIIW for the year 1970–1 is from Report on Currency and Finance 1975–6, volume II, statement 17, p. 38.
13. GDP deflator is GDP(FC) at current prices divided by GDP(FC) at constant prices, (NAS 2003).

14, 15. NEER: Nominal Effective Exchange Rate (thirty-six country bilateral export weights) change in annual average index(1985=100) (negative for depreciation) (RBI 2002–3: Table 141).
REER: Real Effective Exchange Rate (thirty-six country bilateral export weights) change in annual average index (1985=100) (negative for depreciation) (RBI 2002–3: Table 141).
NEER and REER indices are based on calendar year

16, 17. Prime Lending rates IDBI Industrial Development Bank of India,
ICICI Industrial Credit and Investment Corporation of India
RBI 2002–3: Table 63. The mid-point of the range is used for the period average in the last column

18. Net Terms of Trade are given by unit value Index of Exports expressed as percentage of unit value Index of Imports, Base Year=1978–9, Net terms of trade for the year 1970–1 are from Report on Currency and Finance 1975–6, volume II, statement 90, p.145.

Sources: National Accounts Statistics 2003, Central Statistical Organization, Government of India, New Delhi
National Accounts Statistics Back Series (1950–1 to 1992–3), Central Statistical Organization, Government of India, New Delhi
RBI, *Handbook of Statistics on Indian Economy 2002–3*, Reserve Bank of India, Mumbai.

Table B2: Indicators of Macroeconomic Management of the Economy 1980–1 to 1990–1

S.No.	1980–1	1981–2	1982–3	1983–4	1984–5	1985–6	1986–7	1987–8	1988–9	1989–90	1990–1	Average of 1980–1 to 1989–90
Economy: Growth Performance and Macroeconomic Balances												
1 Growth rates of GDP(FC)	7.17	5.97	3.06	7.68	4.31	4.45	4.33	3.83	10.47	6.70	5.57	5.80
2 GDCF(current prices)	18.69	22.41	21.66	19.68	21.60	23.67	23.20	22.11	23.69	23.66	24.07	22.04
3 GDS(current prices)	18.88	18.60	18.26	17.58	18.76	19.49	18.94	20.58	20.85	22.00	23.10	19.39
4 Net inflow (current prices)	–0.19	3.81	3.41	2.10	2.84	4.19	4.26	1.54	2.84	1.66	0.97	2.64
5 GDCF(constant prices)	20.87	23.99	22.91	21.04	22.42	23.53	22.85	22.41	23.39	22.77	23.22	22.62
Government: Fiscal Management												
6 GFD/GDP centre	5.77	5.14	5.64	5.94	7.09	7.86	8.47	7.63	7.34	7.33	7.85	6.82
7 GFD/GDP states	2.58	2.41	2.65	2.9	3.34	2.71	2.98	3.17	2.77	3.17	3.3	2.87
8 GFD/GDP combined	7.50	6.30	5.90	7.30	9.00	8.00	9.90	9.20	8.50	8.90	9.40	8.05
9 RD/GFD centre	24.61	4.47	12.23	19.53	24.26	26.97	29.52	33.81	33.92	33.42	41.53	24.28
10 RD/GFD states	–39.92	–34.02	–17.74	–3.45	11.38	–8.86	–1.68	9.78	15.52	23.97	28.18	–4.50
Key Variables Reflecting Macroeconomic Management												
Rate of inflation (percentage change year to year basis)												
11 WPI	18.24	9.33	4.90	7.53	6.47	4.41	5.82	8.14	7.46	7.46	10.26	7.98
12 CPIIW	11.39	12.47	7.76	11.00	6.31	6.78	8.73	8.76	9.40	6.13	11.56	8.87
13 GDP deflator (per– centage change)	11.51	10.23	8.18	8.81	7.49	7.28	6.88	9.38	8.42	8.46	10.50	8.66
Exchange rate (Percentage change)												
14 NEER	4.52	0.38	1.07	–0.43	–3.80	–2.75	–11.47	–7.57	–6.09	–6.23	–5.19	–3.24
15 REER	10.95	–1.30	–3.88	1.26	–2.20	–1.63	–7.99	–7.12	–3.94	–5.45	–3.97	–2.13
Prime lending rate												
16 IDBI	14	14	14	14	14	14	14	14	14	14	14.00 –15.00	14.00
17 ICICI	14	14	14	14	14	14	14	14	14	14	14.00 –15.01	14.00
18 Net international terms of trade (percentage change)	–12.55	15.35	3.86	23.97	–12.50	2.48	19.61	–5.13	2.54	–3.27	–9.74	3.43

Notation in Order of Serial Numbers: Same as Table B1.
Source: Same as Table B1.

Table B3: Indicators of Macroeconomic Management of the Economy 1990–1 to 2001–2

S.No.		1990–1	1991–2	1992–3	1993–4	1994–5	1995–6	1996–7	1997–8	1998–9	1999–2000	2000–1	2001–2	Average of 1992–3 to 2001–2
Economy: Growth Performance and Macroeconomic Balances														
1	Growth rates of GDP(FC)	5.57	1.30	5.12	5.90	7.25	7.34	7.84	4.76	6.57	6.04	4.37	5.57	6.08
2	GDCF(current prices)	24.07	21.93	23.79	21.25	23.38	26.53	21.77	22.57	21.38	23.66	22.51	22.43	22.93
3	GDS(current prices)	23.10	22.03	21.77	22.53	24.83	25.10	23.21	23.13	21.54	24.09	23.37	23.95	23.35
4	Net inflow (current prices)	0.97	–0.10	2.02	–1.28	–1.45	1.43	–1.44	–0.56	–0.16	–0.43	–0.86	–1.52	–0.43
5	GDCF(constant prices)	23.22	21.44	23.05	21.25	23.72	26.85	22.36	23.79	23.31	25.93	24.61	24.22	23.91
Government: Fiscal Management														
6	GFD/GDP centre	7.85	5.56	5.37	7.01	5.7	5.07	4.88	5.84	6.51	5.41	5.65	6.14	5.76
7	GFD/GDP states	3.3	2.89	2.79	2.4	2.73	2.65	2.72	2.9	4.27	4.72	4.25	4.64	3.41
8	GFD/GDP combined	9.40	7.00	7.00	8.30	7.10	6.50	6.40	7.30	9.00	9.50	9.50	10.30	8.09
9	RD/GFD centre	41.53	44.78	46.18	54.35	53.68	49.31	48.98	52.23	59.14	64.51	71.68	71.01	57.11
10	RD/GFD states	28.18	30.10	24.37	18.33	22.34	26.04	43.38	36.90	58.78	58.90	59.76	56.90	40.57
Key Variables Reflecting Macroeconomic Management														
Rate of inflation (percentage change year to year basis)														
11	WPI	10.26	13.74	10.06	8.35	12.50	8.09	4.61	4.40	5.95	3.27	7.16	3.60	6.80
12	CPIIW	11.56	13.47	9.59	7.50	10.08	10.21	9.27	7.02	13.11	3.38	3.74	4.28	7.82
13	GDP deflator (percentage change)	10.50	13.81	8.72	9.59	9.43	9.03	7.44	6.71	7.87	3.97	4.28	3.43	7.05
Exchange rate (percentage change)														
14	NEER	–5.19	–19.38	–14.31	–8.26	–0.97	–7.25	–5.18	3.58	–7.17	–5.27	–0.15	–0.09	–4.51
15	REER	–3.97	–13.40	–6.23	–4.41	8.43	–0.83	–3.38	5.89	–4.07	–2.67	3.82	3.39	–0.01
Prime lending rate														
16	IDBI	14.00–15.00	18.00–20.00	17.00–19.00	14.50–17.50	15	16.00–19.00	16.2	13.3	13.5	13.60–17.10	14	11.5	15.04
17	ICICI	14.00–15.00	18.00–20.00	17.00–19.00	14.50–17.50	14.00–17.50	14	16.5	14.00–14.50	13	12.5	12.5	12.5	14.53
18	Net international terms of trade (percentage change)	–9.74	9.33	6.53	13.83	5.18	–9.51	–8.48	15.53	2.88	–10.53	–4.55	–2.11	0.88

Table B4: Indicators of Macroeconomic Management of the Economy (1970–1 to 2001–2)

S.No.	Average of 1970–1 to 1979–80	1980–1	Average of 1980–1 to 1989–90	1990–1	1991–2	Average of 1992–3 to 2001–2	2001–2
Economy: Growth Performance and Macroeconomic Balances							
1 Growth rates of GDP(FC)	2.94	7.17	5.80	5.57	1.30	6.08	5.57
2 GDCF(current prices)	18.27	18.69	22.04	24.07	21.93	22.93	22.43
3 GDS(current prices)	17.50	18.88	19.39	23.10	22.03	23.35	23.95
4 Net inflow (current prices)	0.77	–0.19	2.64	0.97	–0.10	–0.43	–1.52
5 GDCF(constant prices)	21.85	20.87	22.62	23.22	21.44	23.91	24.22
Government: Fiscal Management							
6 GFD/GDP centre	3.82	5.77	6.82	7.85	5.56	5.76	6.14
7 GFD/GDP states	2.03	2.58	2.87	3.30	2.89	3.41	4.64
8 GFD/GDP combined		7.50	8.05	9.40	7.00	8.09	10.30
9 RD/GFD centre	–9.52	24.61	24.28	41.53	44.78	57.11	71.01
10 RD/GFD states	–32.43	–39.92	–4.50	28.18	30.10	40.57	56.90
Key Variables Reflecting Macroeconomic Management							
Rate of inflation (percentage change year to year basis)							
11 WPI	8.99	18.24	7.98	10.26	13.74	6.80	3.60
12 CPIIW	7.72	11.39	8.87	11.56	13.47	7.82	4.28
13 GDP deflator (percentage change)	7.73	11.51	8.66	10.50	13.81	7.05	3.43
Exchange rate (percentage change)							
14 NEER	–2.72	4.52	–3.24	–5.19	–19.38	–4.51	–0.09
15 REER	–3.37	10.95	–2.13	–3.97	–13.40	–0.01	3.39
Prime lending rate							
16 IDBI	9.98	14.00	14.00	14.00–15.00	18.00–20.00	15.04	11.50
17 ICICI	9.98	14.00	14.00	14.00–15.00	18.00–20.00	14.53	12.50
18 Net international terms of trade (percentage change)	–1.95	–12.55	3.43	–9.74	9.33	0.88	–2.11

Notation in Order of Serial Numbers: Same as Table B1.
Source: Same as Table B1.

APPENDIX C

Table C1: Selected Indicators of External Sector: 1980–1 to 1990–1

S.No.	Item/years	1980–1	1981–2	1982–3	1983–4	1984–5	1985–6	1986–7	1987–8	1988–9	1989–90	1990–1
1	Growth of exports	7.0	2.6	4.6	3.8	4.5	–9.9	9.4	24.1	15.6	18.9	9.2
2	Growth of imports	40.5	–4.4	–2.5	3.5	–5.9	11.5	–2.1	9.1	13.6	8.8	13.5
	a. of which non-POL	27.0	1.9	–4.4	18.6	–7.3	21.6	12.8	3.8	17.5	5.8	3.4
3	Exports/imports – (Bop %)	51.8	54.5	57.6	59.5	64.0	54.7	58.7	63.8	60.4	69.5	66.2
4	Import cover of FER (No. of months)	5.0	3.3	3.6	4.1	4.5	4.5	4.4	3.8	2.4	1.9	2.5
5	Growth rate of volume index of total exports	1.8	1.9	6.0	–3.2	6.9	–7.9	9.0	15.4	8.6	15.0	11
6	Growth rate of volume index of total imports	18.5	9.2	2.7	19.9	–15.8	16.8	16.5	–3.5	9.5	1.6	4.4
7	Growth rate of vol. index of imports of machinery and transport equipment	N.A.	28.4	25.1	36.9	–33.4	22.5	24.1	1.2	2.0	36.5	–9.3
8	Short-term debt/ FER (%)	N.A.	N.A.	N.A.	N.A.	N.A.	4.2	2.6	3.6	5.3	23.1	146.5
9	Debt service payments as % of current receipts	9.1	10.1	12.5	15.7	17.4	22.2	31.2	28.8	27.3	28.4	31.6
As per cent of GDP(MP)												
10	Exports	4.6	4.6	4.9	4.6	4.9	4.2	4.3	4.6	4.9	5.8	5.8
11	Imports	9.0	8.5	8.4	7.8	7.6	7.6	7.3	7.3	8.1	8.4	8.8
12	Trade balance	–4.3	–3.9	–3.6	–3.2	–2.7	–3.4	–3.0	–2.6	–3.2	–2.6	–3
13	Invisibles balance (net)	2.8	2.2	1.8	1.6	1.6	1.3	1.1	0.8	0.5	0.2	–0.1
14	Current account balance	–1.5	–1.7	–1.7	–1.5	–1.2	–2.1	–1.9	–1.8	–2.7	–2.3	–3.1
15	External debt	11.7	12.5	14.5	15.6	17.1	18.1	19.9	20.2	21.3	22.3	28.7
16	Debt service payments	0.8	0.8	1.0	1.2	1.4	1.5	2.1	2.0	2.1	2.2	2.8

Notes: 1. FER: Foreign Exchange Reserves; GDP (MP): Gross Domestic Product at current market prices.

2. Rupee equivalents of BOP components are used to arrive at GDP ratios. Percentages and growth rates shown in the upper panel are based on US dollar values except rows 5 to 7 which are based on quantum indices published by the DGCI&S
3. Stock of External Debt in US dollars has been converted into rupees using end–of–the–financial–year exchange rate (RBI 2002–3)
4. Debt service payments in US dollars has been converted into rupees using average exchange rate for the financial year (RBI 2002–3).
5. Lines 8, 9, 15, and 16 are based on World Debt Tables.

Sources: 1. *RBI Handbook of statistics on the Indian Economy* (2002–3), Reserve Bank of India, Mumbai.

2. *Economic Survey* (2002–3).
3. *RBI Annual Report 2002–3*, Reserve Bank of India, Mumbai.
4. World Debt Tables, World Bank (1989–90, 1990–1).

Table C2: Selected Indicators of External Sector 1981–90, 1990–1 to 2002–3

S.No	Item/Years	1981–90	1990–1	1991–2	1992–3	1993–4	1994–5	1995–6	1996–7	1997–8	1998–9	1999–2000	2000–1	2001–2	2002–3 (P)
1	Growth of exports	8.1	9.2	–1.5	3.8	20	18.4	20.8	5.3	4.6	–5.1	10.8	21	–1.6	17.9
2	Growth of imports	7.2	13.5	–19.4	12.7	6.5	23	28	6.7	6	2.2	17.2	1.7	1.7	15.5
	a. of which non-POL	9.7	3.4	–21.9	12	11.2	29.5	28.3	–0.2	15.5	8	3	–5.9	7.2	13.3
3	Exports/imports – (BOP %)	59.4	66.2	86.7	77.6	84.8	74.8	74	69.7	69.7	72.1	67.8	75.8	78	86.9
4	Import cover of FER (No. of months)	3.8	2.5	5.3	4.9	8.6	8.4	6	6.5	6.9	8.2	8.2	8.6	11.3	N.A.
5	Growth rate of volume index of total exports	5.4	11	7.5	6.9	15.5	13.7	31.3	7.2	–6.3	3.4	15.5	23.9	3.9	N.A.
6	Growth rate of volume index of total imports	7.5	4.4	4.1	23.7	16.7	24.1	26.1	–0.6	9.8	14.6	9.5	–1.0	5.0	N.A.
7	Growth rate of vol. index of imports of machinery and transport equipment	15.9	–9.3	–3.6	34.6	25	130.1	15.2	–13.6	–21.3	1.6	7.9	3.6	17.2	N.A.
8	Short-term debt/ FER (%)	7.7	146.5	76.7	64.5	18.8	16.9	23.2	25.5	17.2	13.2	10.3	8.2	5.1	N.A.
9	Debt service payments as % of current receipts	20.3	35.3	30.2	27.5	25.6	26.2	24.3	21.2	19	17.8	16.2	17.2	13.9	14.7
As percent of GDP(MP)															
10	Exports	4.7	5.8	6.7	7.1	8.3	8.4	9.1	8.9	8.7	8.3	8.4	9.8	9.4	10.4
11	Imports	8.0	8.8	7.7	9.4	9.8	11.1	12.3	12.7	12.5	11.5	12.4	13	12	12.8
12	Trade balance	–3.2	–3	–1	–2.3	–1.5	–2.8	–3.2	–3.8	–3.8	–3.2	–4	–3.1	–2.6	–2.4
13	Invisibles balance (net)	1.4	–0.1	0.6	0.6	1.1	1.8	1.6	2.7	2.4	2.2	3	2.6	2.9	3.2
14	Current account balance	–1.9	–3.1	–0.3	–1.7	–0.4	–1	–1.7	–1.2	–1.4	–1	–1.1	–0.8	0.2	0.7
15	External debt	17.3	28.7	37.7	36.6	33.8	30.9	27	24.5	24.3	23.6	22.1	22.4	21	20
16	Debt service payments	1.5	2.8	3	2.9	3.1	3.4	3.4	3.2	2.7	2.6	2.5	2.9	2.4	N.A.

Notes: 1. FER: Foreign Exchange Reserves; GDP (MP): Gross Domestic Product at current market prices.

2. Rupee equivalents of BOP components are used to arrive at GDP ratios. Percentages and growth rates shown in the upper panel are based on US dollar values except rows 5 to 7 which are based on quantum indices published by the DGCI&S.

3. Column 1 refers to the average values for the years 1980–1 to 1990–1.

4. Figures in Line 8, 9, 15, and 16 in the average for the period from 1980–1 to 1989–90 are based on the World Debt Tables of the World Bank. From 1990–1 onwards, these lines are based on the Economic Survey, various issues. Those based on the World Debt tables presumably exclude debt service payments on non-civilian credits as well as accrued interest on NRI deposits and relate to the calendar year. Hence they are not strictly comparable.

Sources: Same as Table C1.

Table C3: Different Types of NTBs Imposed on India's Imports 1996 to 2001
(Number of Tariff lines, 10-digit level*)

Type of NTB	As on 1.4.1996		As on 1.4.1997		As on 1.4.1998		As on 1.4.1999		As on 1.4.2000		As on 1.4.2001	
	No. of lines	Per cent share	No. of lines	Per cent share	No. of lines	Per cent share	No. of lines	Per cent share	No. of lines	Per cent share	No. of lines	Per cent share
Prohibited	59	0.6	59	0.6	59	0.6	59	0.6	59	0.6	59	0.5
Restricted	2984	29.6	2322	22.8	2314	22.7	1183	11.5	968	9.5	479	4.7
Canalized	127	1.2	129	1.3	129	1.3	37	0.4	34	0.3	-	-
SIL	765	7.6	1043	10.2	919	9.0	886	8.7	226	2.2	-	-
Free	6161	61.0	6649	65.1	6781	66.4	8055	78.8	8854	87.3	9611**	94.7
Total	10096	100.0	10202	100.0	10202	100.0	10220	100.0	10141	100	10149	100

Notes: *As per Harmonisec System of India Trade Classification, HS-ITC classification of export and import.
** Including 29 tariff lines shifted to State Trading.
Source: GOI-MOF (2002a), *Economic Survey 2001–2*, Box 6.3, p. 142.

APPENDIX D

Table D1: Abbreviated Political Party Names

AIADMK	= All India Anna Dravid Munnetra Kazhagam	KC	= Kerala Congress
AGP	= Asom Gan Parishad	LJSP	= Lok Jana Shakti Party
AIFB	= All India Forward Bloc	MDMK	= Marumalarchi DMK
BJP	= Bharatiya Janata Party	ML	= Muslim League
BJD	= Biju Janata Dal	MSCP	= Manipur State Congress Party
BSP	= Bahujan Samaj Party	NC	= National Conference
Congress (S)	= Congress (Socialist)	NCP	= Nationalist Congress Party
CPI	= Communist Party of India	NDA	= National Democratic Alliance
CPM	= Communist Party of India (Marxist)	NF	= National Front
CPI (ML)	= Communist Party of India (Marxist-Leninist)	PDP	= People's Democratic Party
DMK	= Dravida Munnetra Kazhagam	PMK	= Pattali Makkal Kachi
HVC	= Himachal Vikas Congress	RJD	= Rashtriya Janata Dal
HVP	= Haryana Vikas Party	RSP	= Revolutionary Socialist Party
INC	= Indian National Congress	SJP	= Samajwadi Janata Party
IUML	= Indian Union Muslim League	SDP	= Sikkim Democratic Party
JD(G)	= Janata Dal (Gujarat)	SP	= Samajwadi Party
JD(S)	= Janata Dal (Secular)	SSP	= Sikkim Sangram Parishad
JD(U)	= Janata Dal (United)	TDP	= Telugu Desam Party
JMM	= Jharkhand Mukti Morch	TRC	= Tamilnadu Rajiv Congress
		TRS	= Telangana Rashtra Samiti
		UF	= United Front

Table D2: Definitions of National and State Political Parties

If a political party is a recognized political party in four or more states, it is treated as a 'National Party'. If a political party is a recognized party in less than four states, it is taken to be a 'State Party' in the states it is so recognized.

A political party is treated as a recognized political party if it has been engaged in political activity for a continuous period of five years; *and* has returned, at the last general election, with at least 4 per cent of members to the Lok Sabha from that state or at least 3.33 per cent of members to the legislative assembly of the state as the case may be; *or* its candidates have together polled at least 6 per cent of the total number of valid votes cast in the last general election in the state to the Lok Sabha or state assembly as the case may be.

A political party is recognized as long as it fulfils the required conditions.

Source: www.eci.gov.in/ FAQ/ Registration of Political Parties.

Table D3: Growing Importance of Regional Parties

1977:	Regional parties first shared power at national level. The Akali Dal and DMK were partners in the Janata Party (which was a pre-poll coalition of all anti-Congress Parties including the breakaway groups from the Congress Party opposed to Mrs Gandhi) government. Although the JP had a clear majority, the government fell in 1980 because of internal dissensions.
1989:	Non-Congressism brought many emerging regional parties (TDP, DMK, AGP, Congress [S]) together with the Janata Dal to form the National Front in 1988, which came to power in 1989 with outside support from the BJP and Left parties. Withdrawal of support by the BJP led to its fall. The short-lived Chandra Shekhar government was supported by the Congress from outside and fell because the withdrawal of its support.
1991:	The AIADMK, JD (G), IUML, SSP, KC, supported the Congress government of Narasimha Rao from outside.
1996:	Regional parties became indispensable in the formation of the central government at national level. Out of a total of 137 MPs (Members of Parliament) belonging to regional parties, ninety-five were part of the United Front coalition government in a post-poll alliance. This government was supported by the Congress Party from outside and defeated by the withdrawal of support by the Congress.
1998:	The regional parties accounted for 161 MPs in all. Of whom ninety-two (belonging to fifteen parties) were part of the ruling National Democratic Alliance (NDA). The TDP chose to join the NDA after the polls and its support proved crucial for the survival of the NDA government. The AIADMK decided to break from the pre-poll alliance and played a decisive role in defeating the first NDA government.
1999:	There were 168 MPs belonging to the regional parties in all. Of whom 109 (belonging to nineteen parties) remained part of ruling NDA through the full-term till 2004.
2004:	Of the total of 171 MPs belonging to regional parties, seventy-four formed part of ruling United Progressive Alliance (UPA) government led by the Congress Party. Left parties support this government from outside.

Note: For party name abbreviations, see Appendix Table D1.
Source: Palshikar (2003); Newspaper reports for the recent election year.

Table D4: Congress-Led UPA Government 2004

Party	No. of MPs	No. of ministers		
		Cabinet rank	State rank	Total
Congress	145	19	24	43
DMK	16	3	4	7
RJD	24	2	6	8
NCP	9	1	2	3
LJSP	3	1	0	1
TRS	5	1	1	2
PMK	6	1	1	2
JMM	5	1	0	1
ML	1	-	1	1
Total	214	29	39	68

Source: Compiled from the newspaper reports and subject to final corrections. For party name abbreviations, see the Appendix Table D1.

Table D5: Pre-Poll Alliances of the 1990s

1996 Elections:
INC+ = INC + AIADMK
BJP+ = BJP + Samata + Shiv Sena + Haryana Vikas Party
NF = Janata Dal + Samajwadi Party
LF = CPM + CPI + RSP + FBL

1998 Elections:
BJP+ = BJP + Samata + Shiv Sena + Haryana Vikas Party + AIADMK + Akali Dal + Trinamool Congress + Lok Shakti + Biju Janata Dal + TDP (NTR) (*10 parties*)
UF = Janata Dal + SP (Mulayam) + TDP + AGP + TMC + DMK + MGP + CPI + CPM + RSP + FBL (*11 parties*)

1999 Elections:
INC+ = INC + RJD + AIADMK + Muslim League + Rashtriya Lok Dal + Kerala Congress (Mani) (*6 parties*)
BJP+ = BJP + JD(U) + Trinamool Congress + TDP + BJD + Loktantrik Congress + Shiv Sena + Janatantrik Congress + DMK + PMK + MDMK + Lok Dal Rashtriya + Himachal Vikas Congress + Akali Dal + Sikkim Democratic Front + Tamizhaga Rajiv Congress + Democratic Bahujana Samaj Morcha + MGR-ADMK + MGR-Kazhagam + Arunachal Congress + Manipur State Congress Party (*21 parties*)

2004 Elections:
INC+ = INC + RJD + DMK + PMK + MDMK + NCP + TRS + JMM + LJSP + PDP + RPI + ML
BJP+ = BJP + Shiv Sena + BJD + SAD + JD(U) + TDP + Trinamool Congress + NPF + MNF + IFDP + AIADMK

Note: Party name abbreviations are given in Appendix Table D1.
Source: Prakash, Amit (2003). 'Social, Cultural and Economic Dimensions of the Party System', in Ajay K. Mehra, D.D. Khanna, and Gert W. Kueck (eds). *Political Parties and Party Systems*. Sage, New Delhi, pp. 129–61. Newspaper reports for the year 2004.

Table D6: BJP-Led NDA Coalition Government 1999

Party	No. of MPs	No. of ministers		
		Cabinet rank	State rank	Total
BJP	182	14	32	46
JD(U)	20	4	2	6
Shiv Sena	15	2	–	2
DMK	12	2	1	3
BJD	10	1	1	2
Tinamul Congress	8	1	1	2
PMK	5	–	2	2
MDMK	4	–	2	2
National Conference	4	–	1	1
Independent (Maneka Gandhi)	–	–	1	1
MSCP	1	–	1	1
Total No. of ministers	25	44	69	

Source: Fadia B.L. (2003), *Indian Government and Politics*. Sahitya Bhawan Publications, Agra, p. 420. For party name abbreviations, see the Appendix Table D1.

Appendix II

Box 1: Pre-Poll Alliances of General Election 2009

United Progressive Alliance (UPA)
Indian National Congress (INC) + All India Trinamool Congress (AITC) + Dravida Munnetra Kazhagam (DMK) + Nationalist Congress Party (NCP) + Jharkhand Mukti Morcha (JMM) + Jammu Kashmir National Conference (JKNC) + Indian Union Muslim League (IUML) + Viduthalai Chiruthaigal Katchi (VCK) + Kerala Congress (Mani) (KC (M)) + Republican Party of India (Athvale) (RPI(A)) + All-India Majlis-e-Ittehadul Muslimeen (AIMIM)

National Democratic Alliance (NDA)
Bharatiya Janata Party (BJP) + Janata Dal (United) (JD–U) + Shiv Sena + Rashtriya Lok Dal (RLD) + Shiromani Akali Dal (SAD) + Telangana Rashtra Samiti (TRS) + Asom Gana Parishad (AGP) + Indian National Lok Dal (INLD)

Third Front
Communist Party of India (Marxist) (CPM) + Communist Party of India (CPI) + Revolutionary Socialist Party (RSP) + All India Forward Bloc (AIFB) + Bahujan Samaj Party (BSP) + Biju Janata Dal (BJD) + All India Anna Dravida Munnetra Kazhagam (AIADMK) + Telugu Desam Party (TDP) + Janata Dal (Secular) (JD –S) + Marumalarchi Dravida Munnetra Kazhagam (MDMK) + Haryana Janhit Congress (HJC) + Pattali Makkal Katchi (PMK)

Fourth Front
Samajwadi Party (SP) + Rashtriya Janata Dal (RJD) + Lok Janshakti Party (LJP)

Source: http://en.wikipedia.org/wiki, last accessed in July 2010.

Table 1: Lok Sabha (Lower House of Parliament) Seats of National Parties 1984–2009

Political Party	Election Year							
	1984	1989	1991	1996	1998	1999	2004	2009
Total no. of seats*	542	529	511	543	543	543	541	543
Indian National Congress (INC)	415	197	227	140	141	114	145	206
Bharatiya Janata Party (BJP)	2	85	119	161	182	182	138	116
Janata Party (JP)/ Janata Dal (JD)/ Rashtriya Janata Dal (RJD)	10	143	56	46	6	21**	–	4***
Communist Party Marxist (CPM)	22	33	35	32	32	33	43	16
Communist Party of India (CPI)	6	12	13	12	9	4	10	4
Bahujan Samaj Party (BSP)	–	–	–	–	–	–	19	21
Nationalist Congress Party (NCP)	–	–	–	–	–	–	9	9
Total of national parties (seats)	455	470	450	391	370	354	364	376
Total of national parties (%)	84.0	88.9	88.1	72.0	68.1	65.2	67.03	69.24

Notes: *Number of Lok Sabha seats had become 543 from the earlier 542. Number less than that indicates the number of seats for which elections were held; **JD (U) includes Samata and Lokshakti; *** RJD was considered a national party in the 2009 general elections; definitions of national party and state party are given in Table 2. Following the definitions, the composition of national parties kept changing over time.

Source: Balveer, Arora (2003). 'Federalisation of India's Party System', in Ajay K. Mehra, D.D. Khanna and Gert W. Kueck (eds.), *Political Parties and Party Systems*. Sage Publications, New Delhi, ch. 3, pp. 83–99; www.eci.gov.in, last accessed in August 2010.

Table 2: Importance of Regional Parties in the Lok Sabha (Lower House of Parliament)

	Election Year								
	1980	1984	1989	1991	1996	1998	1999	2004	2009
No. of regional parties*	23	23	23	49	49	49	49	36	34
No. of Lok Sabha seats	36	76	89	56	137	161	188	171	158
% Share in total Lok Sabha seats	6.8	14.0	16.8	11.0	25.2	29.7	34.6	31.3	29.1

Notes: Total number of Lok Sabha seats are 543.

*These are recognized state parties. Other than recognized 'National' and 'State' parties, we have a number of registered but unrecognized parties; 230 and 332 such parties participated in the general elections in 2004 and 2009 respectively. Number of seats reported here include the seats of unrecognized parties along with that of recognized state parties.

If a political party is a recognized political party in four or more states, it is treated as a 'National Party'. If a political party is a recognized party in less than four states, it is taken to be a 'State Party' in the states it is so recognized.

A political party is treated as a recognized political party if it has been engaged in political activity for a continuous period of five years and has returned, at the last general elections, with at least 4 per cent of the members to the Lok Sabha from that state or at least 3.33 per cent of members to the Legislative Assembly of the state as the case may be; or its candidates have together polled at least 6 per cent of the total number of valid votes cast in the last general elections in the state to the Lok Sabha or State Assembly as the case may be. A political party is recognized as long as it fulfils these conditions (www.eci.gov.in/FAQ).

Source: Palshikar, Suhas (2003). 'The Regional Parties and Democracy', in Ajay K. Mehra, D.D. Khanna and Gert W. Kueck (eds), *Political Parties and Party Systems*. Sage Publications, New Delhi, ch.13, pp. 306–35.

Table 3: Seats and Votes (%) Won by Categories of Parties in the Lok Sabha

Political Party	1996		1998		1999		2004		2009	
	Seats	Votes	Seats	Votes	Seats	Votes	Seats	Votes	Seats	Votes
Indian National Congress (INC)	25.8	28.8	26.0	25.8	21.0	28.3	26.9	26.7	37.9	28.6
Bharatiya Janata Party (BJP)	29.6	20.3	33.6	25.6	33.5	23.8	25.6	22.2	21.4	18.8
Sub-total	55.4	49.1	59.5	51.4	54.5	52.1	52.5	48.9	59.3	47.4
Multi-state parties	18.8	20.0	11.8	16.6	13.3	15.0	15.0	14.2	9.9	16.3
State parties and independents	25.8	30.9	28.7	32.0	32.2	32.9	32.5	36.9	30.8	36.4
Sub-total	44.6	50.9	40.5	48.6	45.5	47.9	47.5	51.1	40.7	52.7

Source: Balveer, Arora (2003). 'Federalisation of India's Party System', in Ajay K. Mehra, D.D. Khanna and Gert W. Kueck (eds.), *Political Parties and Party Systems*. Sage Publications, New Delhi, ch. 3, pp. 83–99; www.eci.gov.in, last accessed in August 2010.

Table 4: Congress-led United Progressive Alliance (UPA) Coalition Government 2009
(As on 29 May 2009)

Party	No. of MPs	No. of Ministers		
		Cabinet Rank	State Rank	Total
Indian National Congress (INC)	206	24	35	59
All-India Trinamool Congress (AITC)	19	1	5	6
Dravida Munnetra Kazhagam (DMK)	18	3	5	8
Nationalist Congress Party (NCP)	9	1	2	3
J&K National Conference	3	1	-	1
Indian Union Muslim League (IUML)	2	-	1	1
Total	257	30	48	78

Notes: If we include other pre-poll alliance parties, namely, Jharkhand Mukti Morcha (JMM, 2), Viduthalai Chiruthaigal Katchi (VCK, 1), Kerala Congress (Mani, 1), and All-India Majlis-e-Ittehadul Muslimeen (AIMIM, 1), UPA had 262 Lok Sabha seats. In addition, the UPA government had unconditional outside support from the Samajwadi Party (SP, 23), the Bahujan Samaj Party (BSP, 21), the Rashtriya Janata Dal (RJD, 4), Janata Dal Secular (JD (S), 3), and independents and other parties (3) making its strength 322 Members of Parliament.

Source: Compiled from newspaper reports.

Table 5: Foreign Investment Inflows by Different Categories 1998–99 to 2009–10

(in Million US Dollars)

	1998–9	1999–2000	2000–1	2001–2	2002–3	2003–4	1998–9 to 2003–4	2004–5	2005–6	2006–7	2007–8	2008–9	2009–10	2004–5 to 2009–10
A. Direct investment	2,462	2,155	2,400	4,095	2,764	2,229	16,105	3,778	5,975	16,481	26,864	28,031	27,149	1,08,278
a. RBI automatic route	179	171	454	767	739	534	2,844	1,258	2,233	7,151	17,127	17,998	18,990	64,757
b. SIA/FIPB route	1,821	1,410	1,456	2,221	919	928	8,755	1,062	1,126	2,156	2,298	4,699	3,471	14,812
c. NRI	62	84	67	35	–	–	248	–	–	–	–	–	–	–
d. Acquisition of shares	400	490	362	881	916	735	3,784	930	2,181	6,278	5,148	4,632	3,148	22,317
e. Equity capital of unincorporated bodies	–	–	61	191	190	32	474	528	435	896	2,291	702	1,540	6,392
B. Portfolio investment	–61	3,026	2,760	2,021	979	11,377	20,102	9,315	12,492	7,003	27,271	–13,855	32,376	74,602
a. FIIs	–390	2,135	1,847	1,505	377	10,918	16,392	8,686	9,926	3,225	20,328	–15,017	29,048	56,196
b.GDRs/ADRs	270	768	831	477	600	459	3,405	613	2,552	3,776	6,645	1,162	3,328	18,076
c. Offshore funds and others	59	123	82	39	2	–	305	16	14	2	298	–	–	330
Total A+B	2,401	5,181	5,160	6,116	3,743	13,606	36,207	13,093	18,467	23,484	54,135	14,176	59,525	1,82,880
% Share of SIA/FIPB in FDI	73.96	65.43	60.67	54.24	33.25	41.63	54.36	28.11	18.85	13.08	8.55	16.76	12.79	13.68
% Share of FDI in total	102.50	41.59	35.35	50.24	45.96	14.20	36.41	24.59	27.85	55.25	43.26	116.88	38.71	48.58
C. Other investment flows	–	–	1,629	2,035	2,271	2,093	8,028	2,273	2,986	6,345	7971	9,807	10,614	39,996
a. Re-invested earnings	–	–	1,350	1,645	1,833	1,460	6,288	1,904	2,760	5,828	7679	9,030	8,669	35,870
b. Other capital	–	–	279	390	438	633	1,740	369	226	517	292	777	1,945	4,126
Total A+B+C	2,401	5,181	6,789	8,151	6,014	15,699	44,235	15,366	21,453	29,829	62,106	23,983	70,139	2,22,876

Notes: (1) Data for 2009–10 are estimated as average of the previous two years.

(2) Acquisition of shares in direct investment relates to the acquisition of shares of Indian companies by non-residents under section 6 of FEMA 1999. Data on such acquisitions have been included as part of FDI since January 1996.

(3) FII portfolio investment represents fresh inflow/outflow of funds by foreign institutional investors.

(4) GDRs/ADRs figures represent the amounts raised abroad by the Indian corporates through GDRs/ADRs.

(5) Data on FDI have been revised since 2000–01 with expanded coverage to approach international best practices.

(6) Other capital pertains to inter-company debt transactions of FDI entities.

(7) Abbreviations: SIA: Secretariat for Industrial Approval; FIPB: Foreign Investment Promotion Board; NRI: Non-Resident Indian; GDR: Global Depository Receipts; ADR: American Depository Receipts.

Sources: Central Statistical Office, *National Accounts Statistics* (2007, 2008, and 2009), Statement 11.2, New Delhi: CSO, for manufacturing–registered and public administration & defence; Reserve Bank of India (2010), *Handbook of Statistics on Indian Economy 2009–10*, tables 3 & 224, Mumbai: RBI, for all other sectors; RBI (2011); *RBI Monthly Bulletin*, February 2011, Table No. 44, p. S188, Mumbai: RBI.

Table 6: World Bank Indicators, India—Tariffs

	1990	1992	1997	1999	2001	2004	2008
Applied tariff rates							
All products: simple mean	81.56	56.41	28.90	32.47	31.86	28.98	9.74
All products: weighted mean	53.95	27.47	20.13	28.55	26.50	22.89	6.09
Manufactured products: simple mean	83.06	57.06	29.03	32.75	31.78	28.73	8.38
Manufactured products: weighted mean	76.29	42.91	20.71	31.52	28.56	25.27	5.86
Primary products: simple mean	71.25	51.76	27.87	30.70	32.35	30.66	19.47
Primary products: weighted mean	27.12	9.15	15.81	23.12	22.77	18.60	7.25

Notes: 1. Simple mean: simple average of effectively applied rates for products subject to tariffs.
2. Weighted mean: average of effectively applied tariff rates weighted by product import shares corresponding to each partner country.
Source: http://www.tradingeconomics.com/india/tariff-rate-applied-simple-mean-all-products-percent-wb-data.html, last accessed in August 2010.

Table 7: Openness Indicators of Indian Economy

	1990–1 to 1999–2000	2000–1 to 2009–10	2003–4 to 2007–8	2008–9	2009–10
% of GDP at market prices					
A. Exports plus imports of goods	18.8	29.7	30.5	41.0	36.7
B. Exports plus imports of goods and services	22.9	39.4	40.0	53.7	48.4
C. Current receipts plus current payments	26.8	45.4	46.7	60.5	55.2
D. Gross capital a/c receipts plus capital a/c payments	15.1	33.8	36.9	51.0	48.3
E. Current receipts & payments plus capital receipts & payments	41.9	79.2	83.6	111.5	103.5

Source: Reserve Bank of India (2010). 'Macroeconomic and Financial Indicators', *Annexure IV, Annual Report 2009–10*, p. 181, Mumbai: RBI.

Table 8: Budgeted and Actual Receipts and Modalities of Disinvestment 2000–1 to 2010–11 (Rs Crores)

Year	Budgeted Receipt for the Year	Actual Receipts	Modality
2000–1	10,000	1,871.26	Sale of KRL, CPCL, and BRPL to CPSEs; strategic sale of BALCO and LJMC
2001–2	12,000	5,657.69	Strategic sale of CMC, HTL, VSNL, IBP, PPL, hotel properties of ITDC and HCI, slump sale of Hotel Centaur Juhu Beach, Mumbai, and leasing of Ashok Bangalore; special dividend from VSNL, STC and MMTC; sale of shares to VSNL employees
2002–3	12,000	3,347.98	Strategic sale of HZL, IPCL, hotel properties of ITDC, slump sale of Centaur Hotel Mumbai Airport, Mumbai; premium for renunciation of rights issue in favour of SMC; put option of MFIL; sale of shares to employees of HZL and CMC.
2003–4	14,500	15,547.41	Strategic sale of JCL; call option of HZL; offer for sale of MUL, IBP, IPCL, CMC, DCI, GAIL and ONGC; sale of shares to ICI Ltd.
2004–5	4,000	2,764.87	Offer for sale of NTPC and spill over of ONGC; sale of shares to IPCL employees
2005–6	No target fixed	1,569.68	Sale of MUL shares to Indian public sector financial institutions & banks and employees
2006–7	No target fixed	–	
2007–8	No target fixed	4,181.39	Sale of MUL shares to public sector financial institutions, banks, and Indian mutual funds and sale of PGCIL and RGC shares through offer for sale
2008–9	No target fixed	–	
2009–10	No target fixed	4,259.90	NHPC and OIL
2010–11 (up to 22.12.2010)	40,00	22,762.96	Rs 1062.74 SJVN, EIL 959.65, COAL INDIA 15199.44 CR; PGCIL 3721.17; MOIL 1,237.51; SCI 582.45

Source: Disinvestment Commission Onsite, available at www.divest.nic.in/summarysale.asp, last accessed in January 2011.

Table 9: Disinvestment by Different Modalities by UPA, NDA and Other Regimes

(Rs crore)

	UPA 2004–5 to 2010–11	NDA 1998–9 to 2003–4	Others (1991–2 to 1997–8)	Total 1991–2 to 2010–11 (till 22.12.2010)
1. Receipts through sale of minority shareholding of CPSEs	50,830.40 (92.70)	19,592.06 (58.21)	11,251.50 (100.00)	81,673.90 (81.89)
2. Receipts through sale of majority shareholding of one CPSE to another	–	1,317.23 (3.91)	–	1,317.23 (1.32)
3. Receipts through strategic sale	–	6,344.35 (18.85)	–	6,344.35 (6.36)
4. Receipts through other related transactions	66.89 (0.12)	3,938.28 (11.70)	–	4,005.17 (4.02)
5. Receipts through sale of residual shareholding in disinvested CPSEs/companies	3,934.54 (7.18)	2,463.73 (7.32)	–	6,398.27 (6.42)
6. Total: all modalities	54,831.83 (54.98)	33,655.59 (33.74)	11,251.50 (11.28)	99,738.92 (100.00)

Notes: 1. Figures in parentheses for the rows 1 to 5 are percentage shares of different modalities in the total disinvestment receipts during the specified period.

2. Figures in parentheses for row 6 (last row) are percentage share of disinvestment in the specified regime in the total disinvestment receipts till 22.12.2010.

3. UPA: United Progressive Alliance, 2004–5 to 2010–11; NDA: National Democratic Alliance 1998–9 to 2003–4.

Source: Disinvestment Commission Onsite, available at www.divest.nic.in/summarysale.asp, last accessed in January 2011.

Table 10: Annual Rates of Growth of GDP (FC) at 1999–2000 Prices by Industry (%)

Year	Total	Agriculture & Allied Activities	Mining & Quarrying	Industry	Manufac-turing	Manufacturing–registered	Electricity, Gas, & Water Supply	Construction	Services	Public Administration & Defence
1990–1										
1991–2	1.43	–1.95	3.36	–0.29	–2.40	–1.26	9.69	2.06	4.30	2.11
1992–3	5.36	6.65	0.92	3.25	3.09	2.06	6.94	3.48	5.41	4.96
1993–4	5.68	3.32	1.39	7.47	8.59	11.24	7.50	0.57	6.44	2.56
1994–5	6.39	4.72	9.29	10.44	10.82	13.04	9.37	5.38	5.84	1.29
1995–6	7.29	–0.70	5.87	13.16	15.46	15.93	6.80	5.98	9.62	6.75
1996–7	7.97	9.92	0.55	7.96	9.50	10.74	5.44	1.87	6.95	4.09
1997–8	4.30	–2.55	9.81	2.02	0.05	–2.61	7.72	10.47	9.00	14.48
1998–9	6.68	6.32	2.83	3.57	3.13	3.47	7.03	6.27	8.08	10.62
1999–2000	6.44	2.67	3.19	3.51	3.22	4.01	5.54	8.39	9.35	13.28
2000–1	4.35	–0.25	2.39	6.39	7.75	7.84	2.05	6.23	5.71	1.89
2001–2	5.81	6.25	1.75	2.35	2.54	4.58	1.74	4.00	6.85	2.93
2002–3	3.84	–7.24	8.85	6.79	6.81	7.59	4.75	7.95	7.52	1.60
2003–4	8.52	9.96	3.09	6.00	6.63	7.15	4.77	11.98	8.84	2.59
2004–5	7.47	0.05	8.15	8.51	8.65	9.08	7.90	16.14	9.86	6.47
2005–6	9.50	5.80	4.90	10.17	9.10	9.30	5.10	16.20	10.59	4.90
2006–7	9.70	4.00	8.80	11.00	11.80	11.60	5.30	11.80	11.23	4.00
2007–8	9.10	4.90	3.30	8.10	8.20	7.60	5.30	10.10	10.85	4.20

Note: Industry includes manufacturing, mining and quarrying, construction, and electricity, gas, and water supply.
Sources: Central Statistical Office (various years), *National Accounts Statistics* (2007, 2008, and 2009), Statement 11.2, CSO, New Delhi, for manufacturing–registered and public administration & defence; RBI (2010), *Handbook of Statistics on Indian Economy 2009–10*, Tables 3 & 224, Mumbai: RBI, for all other sectors.

Table 11: Annual Rates of Growth of GDP (FC) at 2004–5 Prices by Industry (%)

Year	Total	Agriculture & Allied Activities	Mining & Quarrying	Industry	Manufac-turing	Manufacturing–registered	Electricity, Gas, & Water Supply	Construction	Services	Public Administration & Defence
2004–5										
2005–6	9.5	5.1	1.3	8.08	10.1	12.1	7.1	12.8	11.27	4.2
2006–7	9.6	4.2	7.5	13.62	14.3	15.8	9.3	10.3	10.22	2.0
2007–8	9.3	5.8	3.7	9.21	10.3	10.1	8.3	10.7	10.44	7.6
2008–9	6.8	–0.1	1.3	3.08	4.2	5.3	4.9	5.4	9.26	20.2
2009–10	8.0	0.4	6.9	10.37	8.8	9.4	6.4	7.0	8.28	13.0
2010–11	8.6	5.4	6.2	–	8.8	–	5.1	8.0	–	–

Note: Data for 2008–9 are provisional estimates and for 2009–10 are quick estimates.

Sources: Central Statistical Office (2011), *Press Note on Quick Estimates of National Income, Consumption Expenditure, Saving and Capital Formation, 2009–10* dated 31 January 2011, Statement 3, New Delhi: Press Information Bureau, Government of India, for all the columns except for industry and services and for the years 2005–6 to 2009–10; CSO (2011), *Press Note on Advance Estimates of National Income 2010–11* dated 7 February 2011, Statement 3, New Delhi: Press Information Bureau, Government of India, for the year 2010–11; and Reserve Bank of India (2010), *Handbook of Statistics on Indian Economy 2009–10*, Table 3, Mumbai: RBI, for the industry and services sectors.

Table 12: Indicators of Faster Growth Trajectory from 2003–4 to 2007–8 in Perspective

	Average of 1990–1 to 1999–2000	Average of 2000–1 to 2009–10 (10 years)	Average of 2003–4 to 2007–8 (5 years)	2008–9	2009–10
% Change					
1. Overall GDP (FC)	5.7	7.3	8.9	6.7	7.4
(a) Agriculture	3.2	2.4	4.7	1.6	0.2
(b) Industry	5.7	7.4	9.1	3.1	10.4
Of which, manufacturing	(5.6)	(8.1)	(10.0)	(3.2)	(10.8)
(c) Services	7.1	8.8	10.1	9.3	8.3
2. Demand-side aggregates					
(d) Private final consumption expenditure	4.8	6.2	7.6	6.8	4.3
(e) Gross fixed capital formation	7.2	10.3	15.5	4.0	7.2
3. Index of industrial production					
(f) Manufacturing	6.5	7.5	9.4	2.8	10.9
(g) Capital goods	5.5	11.5	15.9	7.3	19.2

Source: Reserve Bank of India (2010). 'Macroeconomic and Financial Indicators', Annexure IV, *Annual Report 2009–10*, p. 178, Mumbai: RBI.

Table 13: Quarterly Growth Rates of GDP (FC) at 2004–5 Prices by Industry (%)

Year	Overall	Agriculture & Allied Activities	Industry	Manufacturing	Services
2006–7					
Q1	9.8	3.1	12.9	14.68	10.8
Q2	10.1	3.0	13.7	15.12	10.6
Q3	9.4	3.8	13.3	14.18	10.1
Q4	9.6	4.7	14.5	15.75	9.4
2007–8					
Q1	9.3	3.1	10.5	12.07	10.7
Q2	9.4	3.9	9.5	10.32	10.5
Q3	9.7	8.7	9.5	10.71	10.2
Q4	8.5	2.1	7.8	8.31	10.4
2008–9					
Q1	7.3	3.2	4.9	5.41	9.2
Q2	7.2	2.4	4.8	5.27	9.0
Q3	6.1	–1.4	1.7	1.31	10.0
Q4	5.8	3.3	0.8	0.56	8.0
2009–10					
Q1	6.3	1.8	4.6	2.0	8.0
Q2	8.6	1.2	8.5	6.1	10.2
Q3	7.3	–1.6	12.3	11.4	7.3
Q4	8.6	0.7	15.1	–	8.5
2010–11					
Q1	8.9	2.5	11.7	13.0	9.4
Q2	8.9	4.4	9.0	9.8	9.7
Q3	8.2	8.9	–	5.6	–
Q4	–	–	–	–	–

Sources: 1. For the overall GDP, agricultural & allied activities, and manufacturing for the first three quarters of 2009–10 and 2010–11, Central Statistical Office (2011), *Press Note on Gross Domestic Product for the Third Quarter (Oct–Dec) of 2011*, 28 February 2011, Statement 1, New Delhi: Press Information Bureau, Government of India.
2. Remaining estimates are obtained from the RBI through email.

Table 14: Lending Rates of Scheduled Commercial Banks

As on 1 April	Share (%) of total credit in interest range			Total credit outstanding (Rs crore)	Median range of interest
	Upto 10%	10%–15%	15% & higher		
1996	2.4	20.7	77.2	2184.39	17% to 18%
1997	1.6	23.0	75.4	2469.28 (13.0)	16% to 17%
1998	1.4	30.4	68.2	2591.70 (5.0)	16% to 17%
1999	4.0	33.3	62.7	2605.04 (neg.)	15% to 16%
2000	1.2	46.2	52.6	3198.51 (22.8)	14% to 15%
2001	0.8	58.2	41.0	4287.86 (34.1)	13% to 14%
2002	3.3	61.1	35.6	4830.97 (12.7)	-do-
2003	5.5	67.4	27.1	5597.40 (15.9)	-do-
2004	14.0	58.0	28.0	6678.38 (19.3)	-do-
2005	19.9	56.5	23.6	8847.83 (32.5)	-do-
2006	25.7	59.7	14.6	11940.38 (35.0)	12% to 13%
2007	22.1	68.0	9.9	15918.09 (33.3)	-do-
2008	9.6	81.5	8.9	19828.03 (24.6)	-do-
2009	24.1	69.7	6.2	24072.94 (21.4)	10% to 12%

Note: Figures in parentheses are year-on-year growth rates; neg. = negligible.
Source: Reserve Bank of India, *Basic Statistical Returns of Scheduled Commercial Banks of India*, Mumbai: RBI, Annual issues of the respective years.
Table 1.14 for years 1996 to 1998; Table 1.13 for the remaining years.

Table 15: Rates of Gross Domestic Savings, Gross Domestic Capital Formation and Gross Fixed Capital Formation with Shares of Corporate Sector (%)

Year	GDS Rate	Share of Corporate Sector	GDCF Rate (current prices)	Share of Corporate Sector	GFCF Rate (current prices)	Share of Corporate Sector	GDCF Rate (constant prices)	Share of Corporate Sector	GFCF Rate (constant prices)	Share of Corporate Sector
NAS 1999–2000 Prices										
1999–2000	24.8	18.0	25.9	28.3	23.3	27.9	25.9	28.3	23.4	27.9
2000–1	23.7	16.2	24.3	21.3	22.7	25.1	24.1	21.1	22.5	24.8
2001–2	23.5	14.4	22.8	23.7	23.6	24.1	23.5	23.5	22.9	24.0
2002–3	26.3	15.3	25.2	23.5	23.8	23.2	25.0	23.6	23.6	23.2
2003–4	29.8	15.5	27.6	24.8	25.0	25.1	27.1	25.0	24.7	25.2
NAS 2004–5 Prices										
2004–5	32.4	20.2	32.8	31.5	28.7	31.8	32.8	31.5	28.7	31.8
	(31.7)	(21.2)	(32.7)	(33.5)	(28.4)	(33.5)	(30.5)	(34.5)	(27.2)	(34.2)
2005–6	33.5	22.4	34.7	39.1	30.3	39.0	34.9	39.2	30.5	39.1
	(34.2)	(22.5)	(35.5)	(38.7)	(31.0)	(38.4)	(33.3)	(39.3)	(29.2)	(39.3)
2006–7	34.6	22.8	35.7	40.8	31.3	39.9	36.2	41.2	31.8	40.5
	(35.7)	(23.2)	(36.9)	(40.2)	(32.5)	(39.4)	(34.4)	(41.1)	(30.5)	(40.6)
2007–8	36.9	25.5	38.1	45.4	32.9	43.3	39.0	46.3	33.6	44.5
	(37.7)	(23.4)	(39.1)	(40.6)	(34.0)	(39.4)	(36.2)	(41.7)	(31.6)	(40.8)
2008–9	32.2	24.4	34.5	33.3	32.0	32.4	35.1	34.9	32.6	34.2
2009–10	33.7	24.1	36.5	32.0	30.8	35.2	38.2	37.9	32.6	37.3

Notes: Figures in bracket from 2004–5 onwards are from 1999–2000 price series; GDS rate = gross domestic savings as % of GDP at current market prices; GDCF rate (current prices) = gross domestic capital formation as % of GDP at current market prices; GDCF rate (constant prices) = gross domestic capital formation as % of GDP at constant (1999–2000/2004–5) market prices; GFCF rate (current prices) = gross fixed capital formation as % of GDP at market prices; GFCF rate (constant prices) = gross fixed capital formation as % of GDP at constant (1999–2000/2004–5) market prices.

Sources: Central Statistical Office (2009), *National Accounts Statistics 2009*, New Delhi: Press Information Bureau, Government of India, for series at 1999–2000 prices; Central Statistical Office (2011), *Press Note on Quick Estimates of National Income, Consumption, Saving and Capital Formation 2009–10*, 31 January 2011, Statements 6 and 7.1, New Delhi: Press Information Bureau, Government of India, for the remaining figures.

Table 16: Indicators of Wider Availability of Finance for Private Corporate Sector

	Average of				
	1992–3 to 1996–7	1997–8 to 2002–3	2003–4 to 2007–8	2008–9	2009–10
1.Gross medium and long-term external commercial borrowings ($billion)	4.011	5.599	15.539	13.248	13.700
2. Gross suppliers' credit ($billion)	4.476	6.768	25.778	41.841	53.565
3. Gross portfolio flows ($billion)	3.403	8.410	96.481	128.512	159.897
4. New capital issues by non-Government public ltd. companies (Rs Crore)	18,392	4,449	26,439	14,671	25,479
5. Resource mobilisation in the private placement market (Rs Crore)	-NA-	20,401	61,452	95,689	234,100

Notes: Data for 2009–10 are preliminary estimates and for 2008–9 are partially revised for the first three rows; data for 2009–10 are provisional for the fourth and fifth rows.
Sources: Reserve Bank of India (2009), *Handbook of Statistics on Indian Economy 2008–9*, Table 142, pp. 236–41, Mumbai: RBI, for the first three variables for the years up to 2007–8; Reserve Bank of India (2010), *Handbook of Statistics on Indian Economy 2009–10*, Table 140, p. 250 Mumbai: RBI, for the years 2008–9 and 2009–10 for the first three variables, Table 76, p.159 for all the years of the fourth variable; and Table 81, p. 163 for all the years of the fifth variable.

Table 17: Corporate Financial Performance in the Post-Reform Period

	Average of 1991–2 to 1999–2000	Average 2000–1 to 2006–7	Average 2003–4 to 2007–8
	(1)	(2)	
Growth Rates (%)			
Sales	14.0	14.2	20.3
Expenditure	14.1	13.6	19.4
Gross profits	12.5	20.4	29.4
Interest payments	15.8	–1.4	5.3
Profits after tax	11.8	36.5	43.0
Select Ratios (%)			
Gross profits to sales	10.5(Min)–14.2(Max)	10.1(Min)–15.5(Max)	11.1(Min)–16.3(Max)
Profits after tax to sales	3.3(Min)–7.8(Max)	2.6(Min)–10.7(Max)	5.9(Min)–11.8(Max)
Interest to sales	5.3(Min)–6.9(Max)	2.1(Min)–6.1(Max)	2.1(Min)–3.4(Max)
Interest to gross profits	36.9(Min)–62.7(Max)	13.0(Min)–60.1(Max)	13.4 (Min)–30.7(Max)
Debt to equity	58.7(Min)–99.5(Max)	43.0(Min)–70.5*(Max)	43.0(Min)–58.6**(Max)
Internal sources of funds	26.1(Min)–40.3(Max)	43.6(Min)–65.3*(Max)	43.6(Min)–55.5**(Max)
Bank borrowings to total borrowings	27.5(Min)–35.0(Max)	34.4(Min)–58.2*(Max)	48.0(Min)–58.2**(Max)

Notes: *Data pertain to the period 2000–1 to 2005–6; **data pertain to the period 2003–4 to 2005–6.
Source: Reserve Bank of India (2008), *Annual Report 2007–08*, Table 2.18, p. 68, Mumbai: RBI.

Table 18: Annual Performance of the Corporate Sector

	2002–3	2003–4	2004–5	2005–6	2006–7	2007–8	2008–9	2009–10
	(1)	(2)	(3)	(4)	(5)	(6)	(7)	(8)
Growth Rates (%)								
Sales	8.	16.0	24.1	16.9	26.2	18.6	17.2	11.7
Expenditure	10.2	14.9	23.6	16.4	23.5	19.4	19.5	9.6
Gross profits	9.8	25.0	32.5	20.3	41.5	24.9	–4.2	24.9
Net profits	76.2	59.8	51.2	24.2	45.2	26.0	–18.4	28.8
% of Sales								
Interest	4.9	3.4	2.6	2.0	2.1	2.5	3.1	2.7
Gross profits	10.3	11.1	11.9	13.0	15.6	14.9	13.3	14.8
Net profits	4.2	5.9	7.2	8.7	10.7	9.8	8.1	9.4

Sources: Reserve Bank of India (2007), *Annual Report 2006–07*, Table 1.16, p. 30, Mumbai: RBI, for column (1); Reserve Bank of India (2008), *Annual Report 2007–08*, Table 2.18, p. 68, Mumbai: RBI, for columns (2)–(5); Reserve Bank of India (2010), *Report on Currency and Finance 2008–09*, Box VI.8 Table 1, p. 286, Mumbai: RBI, for columns (6)–(8).

Table 19: Quarterly Performance of the Corporate Sector

	2006–7				2007–8				2008–9				2009–10			
	Q1	Q2	Q3	Q4	Q1	Q2	Q3	Q4	Q1	Q2	Q3	Q4	Q1	Q2	Q3	Q4
	(1)	(2)	(3)	(4)	(5)	(6)	(7)	(8)	(9)	(10)	(11)	(12)	(13)	(14)	(15)	(16)
Growth Rates (%)																
Sales	25.6	29.2	30.2	22.5	19.2	16.0	18.0	20.6	29.3	31.8	9.5	1.9	–0.9	0.1	22.5	29.1
Expenditure	24.6	26.6	26.9	19.5	18.0	15.3	18.9	23.3	33.5	37.5	12.6	–0.5	–4.4	–2.5	20.6	30.7
Gross profits	33.9	45.9	51.8	39.2	31.3	22.5	20.4	16.8	11.7	8.7	–26.7	–8.8	5.8	10.9	60.0	336.7
Net profits	34.7	49.4	59.5	39.6	33.9	22.7	29.4	14.1	6.9	–2.7	–53.4	–19.9	5.8	12.1	99.3	44.0
% of Sales																
Interest	2.2	2.0	2.0	2.0	2.0	2.1	2.5	2.2	2.4	2.9	3.8	3.2	2.8	3.1	2.7	2.4
Gross profits	15.6	15.9	15.8	15.3	16.7	16.3	16.2	15.0	14.5	13.5	11.0	13.2	15.7	14.9	14.3	14.5
Net profits	10.6	11.0	11.0	10.6	11.6	11.5	12.2	10.3	9.7	8.6	5.3	8.1	10.2	9.4	8.8	9.0

Sources: Reserve Bank of India (2007), *Annual Report 2006–07*, Table 1.16, p. 30, Mumbai: RBI, for columns (1)–(4); Reserve Bank of India (2008), *Annual Report 2007–08*, Table 2.18, p. 68, Mumbai: RBI, for columns (5)–(8); Reserve Bank of India (2010), *Report on Currency and Finance 2008–09*, Box VI.8, Table 1, p. 286, Mumbai: RBI, for columns (9)–(16).

Table 20: Indicators of Macroeconomic Management of the Economy 2000–1 to 2010–11

	2000–1	2001–2	2002–3	2003–4	2004–5	2005–6	2006–7	2007–8	2008–9	2009–10	2010–11
	1999–2000 Prices							2004–5 Prices			
Economy: Growth Performance and Macroeconomic Balances											
Growth rates GDP (FC)[1]	4.4	5.8	3.8	8.5	(7.5)	9.5 (9.5)	9.6 (9.7)	9.3 (9.1)	6.8	8.0	8.6
GDCF (current prices)[2]	24.3	22.8	25.2	27.6	32.8 (32.7)	34.3 (35.5)	35.5 (36.9)	37.7 (39.1)	34.9	36.5	
GDS (current prices)	23.7	23.5	26.3	29.8	32.4 (31.7)	33.1 (34.2)	34.4 (35.7)	36.9* (37.7)	32.2*	33.7*	
Net capital inflow (current prices)	0.6	–0.7	–1.1	–2.2	0. 4 (1.0)	1.2 (1.3)	1.1 (1.2)	1.2 (1.4)	2.3	2.8*	
GDCF (constant prices)	24.1	23.5	25.0	27.1	32.8 (30.5)	34.2 (33.3)	38.2 (34.4)	39.0 (36.2)	35.1	38.2	
Government: Fiscal Management											
GFD/GDP centre	5.65	6.19	5.91	4.48	3.88	3.95	3.33	2.56	6.05	6.64	
GFD/GDP states	4.18	4.14	4.06	4.38	3.33	2.43	1.81	1.53	2.63	3.2	
GFD/GDP combined	9.43	9.86	9.48	8.42	7.20	6.46	5.38	4.12	8.50	9.59	
RD/GFD centre	0.72	0.71	0.74	0.80	0.62	0.63	0.56	0.41	0.75	0.80	
RD/GFD states	0.63	0.64	0.57	0.53	0.36	0.08	–0.32	–0.57	–0.07	0.16	

Key Variables Reflecting Macroeconomic Management										
Rate of inflation										
WPI	7.2#	3.6#	3.4	5.5	6.5	4.4	5.4	4.7	8.3	3.8
CPI–IW	3.8#	4.3#	4.0	3.9	3.8	4.4	6.7	6.2	9.1	12.4
GDP deflator (% change)	3.3	3.0	3.8	3.4	5.5	4.7 (4.2)	5.6 (4.9)	5.5 (4.9)	7.9	4.5

Notes: Figures in parentheses from 2004–5 onwards are from the 1999–2000 price series;
Growth rates of GDP (FC) for 2000–1 to 2004–5 are based on 1999–2000 prices and for later years, these are based on 2004–5 prices;
GDCF (current prices): gross domestic capital formation as % of GDP at current market prices;
GDS (current prices): gross domestic savings as % of GDP at current market prices;
GDCF (constant prices): gross domestic capital formation as % of GDP at constant (1999–2000/2004–5) market prices;
GFD/GDP: gross fiscal deficit as % of GDP at market prices;
RD/GDP: revenue deficit as % of GDP at market prices;
WPI: Wholesale price index (average of the weeks for all commodities) – annual variation; Base 1993–4 = 100;
CPI–IW: Consumer price index for industrial workers (average of months) – annual variation; Base: 1980=100 for 2002–3 to 2006–7 and 2001=100 for 2007–8 onwards;
GDP deflator is GDP (FC) at current prices divided by GDP (FC) at constant prices (1999–2000 and 2004–5).
**Statement 1*, *Press Note 31 January, 2011*. # Figures are taken from RBI *Handbook of Statistics on the Indian Economy 2007–8*.

Sources: Reserve Bank of India (2010), *Handbook of Statistics on Indian Economy 2009–10*, Tables 1, 2, 223, 224, 232, 233, 234, and 236, Mumbai: RBI; Central Statistical Office (2011), *Press Note on Advance Estimates of National Income 2010–11*, 7 February 2011, New Delhi: Press Information Bureau, Government of India; Central Statistical Office (2009), *National Account Statistics 2009*, Statements S1.1 and 1.2, New Delhi: Press Information Bureau, Government of India; Central Statistical Office (2011), *Press Note on Quick Estimates of National Income, Consumption, Saving and Capital Formation 2009–10*, 31 January 2011, Statement 1, New Delhi: Press Information Bureau, Government of India, for the figures marked with *; Reserve Bank of India (2008), *Handbook of Statistics on Indian Economy 2007–08*, Mumbai: RBI, for the figures marked with #.

Table 21: Central Government Expenditure (Plan and Non-Plan) on Social Services and Development

	2000–1	2001–2	2002–3	2003–4	2004–5	2005–6	2006–7	2007–8	2008–9	2009–10
I. Social Services										
1. Education, sports & youth affairs	2.36	2.39	2.39	2.32	2.81	3.71	4.28	4.02	4.04	3.96
2. Health & family welfare	1.63	1.65	1.56	1.53	1.64	1.89	1.87	2.05	1.91	1.90
3. Water supply, housing, etc.	1.51	1.65	1.65	1.67	1.81	2.08	1.72	2.02	2.31	2.20
4. Information & broadcasting	0.40	0.35	0.34	0.28	0.26	0.30	0.25	0.22	0.22	0.20
5. Welfare of SC/ST & OBC	0.30	0.30	0.28	0.24	0.27	0.33	0.34	0.36	0.35	0.41
6. Labour & employment	0.27	0.23	0.19	0.18	0.20	0.25	0.32	0.27	0.27	0.22
7. Social welfare & nutrition	0.74	0.72	0.57	0.50	0.52	0.84	0.85	0.82	0.72	0.79
8. North-Eastern states	0.00	0.00	0.00	0.00	0.00	0.00	0.00	0.00	1.56	1.50
9. Other social services	0.53	0.55	0.11	0.15	0.34	0.40	-0.17	1.29	1.55	1.87
Total of 1 – 9	7.75	7.86	7.10	7.48	7.85	9.79	9.47	11.06	12.94	13.06
II Rural Development	2.09	2.42	3.52	3.10	2.47	3.12	2.84	2.80	4.50	4.27
III Pradhan Mantri Gram Sadak Yojana (PMGSY)	0.77	0.69	0.60	0.49	0.49	0.83	1.08	0.91	0.88	1.11
Total of I, II and III	10.60	10.97	11.00	10.46	10.81	13.35	13.38	14.77	18.32	18.44

Note: All figures are percentages of the total central government expenditure.

Sources: Ministry of Finance (2011), *Economic Survey 2010–11*, Table 12.3, p. 293, New Delhi: Government of India; Ministry of Finance (2010), *Economic Survey 2009–10*, Table 11.3, p. 272, New Delhi: Government of India; Ministry of Finance (2006), *Economic Survey 2005-06*, Table 2.2, p. 21, Table 10.2, p. 204, New Delhi: Government of India.

Bibliography

Acharya, Shankar (2006). 'Macroeconomic Management in the Nineties', in Shankar Acharya, *Essays on Macroeconomic Policy and Growth in India*, Oxford University Press, New Delhi.

Ahluwalia, I.J. (1994). 'The Role of Trade Policy in Indian Industrialisation', in G.K. Helleiner (ed.), *Trade Policy and Industrialisation in Turbulent Times*. Routledge, New York, pp. 292–316.

Ahluwalia, M.S. (1978). 'Rural Poverty and Agricultural Performance in India', *Journal of Development Studies*, vol. 14, no. 3 (April), pp. 298–323.

Arora, Balveer (2003). 'Federalisation of India's Party System', in Ajay K. Mehra, D.D. Khanna, and Gert W. Kueck (eds), *Political Parties and Party Systems*. Sage Publications, New Delhi, ch. 3, pp. 83–99.

Bator, Francis M. (1958). 'The Anatomy Of Market Failure', *Quarterly Journal of Economics*, vol. 72, no. 3 (August), pp. 351–79.

Baumol, William J. (1990). 'Entrepreneurship: Productive, Unproductive and Destructive', *Journal of Political Economy*, vol. 98, no. 5, part 1(October), pp. 893–921.

Bhagwati, J.N. and Padma Desai (1970). *India: Planning for Industrialization*. Oxford University Press, Delhi.

Bhagwati, J.N., K. Sundaram, and T.N. Srinivasan (1972). 'The Political Response to 1966 Devaluation—I', *Economic and Political Weekly*, vol. 7, no. 36 (2 September), pp. 1835–6.

Bhagwati, J.N. and T.N. Srinivasan (1976). *Foreign Trade Regimes in Economic Development, India*. Macmillan, New Delhi.

Bhavani, T.A. (2001). *Technological Change in the Indian Small Scale Industries: Its Causes and Consequences*. IDPAD Project Report, Institute of Economic Growth, Delhi.

——— (2006). *Globalisation and Indian Small Scale Industries: Technology and Competitiveness*. Ane Books India, Delhi.

Bhavani, T.A. and Suresh D. Tendulkar (2000). 'Determinants of Firm-level Export Performance: A Case Study of Indian Textile Garment Industry', *Journal of International Trade and Development*, vol. 10, no.1, pp. 65–92.

Bhoothalingam, S. (1968). 'Private Industry in a Mixed Economy - 3: Reconciling Efficiency with Social Justice', *Asian Review*, vol. 2 (1 October), pp. 20–34.

Brus, W. Wlodzimierz and Kazimierz Laski (1989). *From Marx to the Market: Socialism in Search of an Economic System*. Clarendon Press, Oxford.

Cerra, Valerie and Sweta Chaman Saxena (2002). 'What Caused the 1991 Currency Crisis in India?', *IMF Staff Papers*, vol. 49, no. 3, pp. 395–425.

Chaudhry, Praveen, Vijay Kelkar, and Vikash Yadav (2004). 'The Evolution of "Homegrown Conditionality" in India – IMF "Relations"', Version 4.0. Final Copy email vikash1@ssc.upenn.edu

Chenery, Hollis B. and Alan M. Strout (1966). 'Foreign Assistance and Economic Development', *American Economic Review*, vol. 56, no. 3 (June), pp. 679–733.

de Alessi, Louis (1988). 'How Markets Alleviate Scarcity', in Vincent Ostram, David Feeny, and Harmut Picht (eds), *Rethinking Institutional Analysis and Development: Issues, Alternatives and Choices*. International Centre for Economic Growth, San Francisco.

Deaton, Angus (2003). 'Adjusted Poverty Estimates for 1999–2000', *Economic and Political Weekly*, vol. 38, no. 4 (25 January), pp. 322–6.

Deaton, Angus and Jean Dreze (2002). 'Poverty and Inequality in India: A Re-Examination', *Economic and Political Weekly*, vol. 37, no. 36 (7 September), pp. 3729–49.

Desai, Ashok V. (1999). *Transition to an Open Market Economy: The Politics of Economic Reforms*. OECD, Paris.

Dhar, P.N. (1990). *Constraints on Growth*. Oxford University Press, New Delhi.

——— (2000). *Indira Gandhi, the 'Emergency', and Indian Democracy*. Oxford University Press, New Delhi.

——— (2003). *The Evolution of Economic Policy in India: Selected Essays*. Oxford University Press, New Delhi.

Economic and Political Weekly (2004), 'State Parties, National Ambitions', a set of special articles, Vol. XXXIX, nos. 14 & 15, 3–9/10–15 April 2004, pp. 1477–1537.

Fadia, B.L. (2003). *Indian Government and Politics*. Sahitya Bhavan Publications, Agra.

Fanelli, Jose Maria (2004). 'Understanding Reform: A Global GDN Project', Draft Paper prepared for the Fifth Annual Global Development Conference 'Understanding Reform', organized by the Global Development Network (GDN), New Delhi, India, 28–30 January.

Gadgil, D.R. (1968, 1973). 'Towards self-Reliance' Speech delivered at Bangalore on 4 September 1968. Reprinted in A.R. Kamat, (ed.) (1973), *Selected Writings and Speeches of Professor D.R. Gadgil on Planning and Development*, Orient Longman, New Delhi, pp. 247–61.

Garg, Charu, S.K. Sanyal, S.T. Nagarathinam, and K.R. Pandit (1996). *Central Fiscal Incentives and Concessions to Small Scale Industries: Impact on*

Growth and Structure. National Institute of Public Finance and Policy, New Delhi.

GOI-DCSSI (1997). *Report of the Expert Committee on Small Enterprises* (Chairman: Abid Hussain), Department of Small-Scale and Agro and Related Industries, Ministry of Industry, New Delhi.

GOI-MID (1974). *Guidelines for Industries 1974–5*, Ministry of Industrial Development, Government of India, New Delhi.

GOI-MOF (1970). *Economic Survey 1969–70*.

GOI-MOF (2002). *Economic Survey 2001–02*, Department of Economic Affairs, Ministry of Finance, Government of India, New Delhi.

GOI-MOF (2005). *Economic Survey 2004–05*, Department of Economic Affairs, Ministry of Finance, Government of India, New Delhi.

Goswami, Omkar (1996). *Corporate Bankruptcy in India: A Comparative Perspective*. Development Centre Studies, OECD, Paris.

Goyal, S.K., K.S. Chalapati Rao, and Nagesh Kumar (1984). *Small Scale Sector and Big Business*. The Corporate Study Group, The Indian Institute of Public Administration, New Delhi.

Gulati, Ashok and Sudha Narayanan (2000). *Subsidy Syndrome in Indian Agriculture*, Institute of Economic Growth, Delhi (December).

Hye, Hasnat Abdul (2001). 'Good Governance: A Social Contract for the New Millennium', in Hasnat Abdul Hye (ed.), *Governance: South Asian Perspectives*. Manohar, New Delhi, pp. 1–32.

Jenkins, Rob (1999). *Democratic Politics and Economic Reforms in India*. Cambridge University Press, Cambridge.

Jha, L.K. (1985). *India's Development Strategy in 1980s*. New Delhi.

Joshi, Vijay and I.M.D. Little (1996). *India's Economic Reforms: 1991–2001*. Oxford University Press, New Delhi.

Kaviraj, Sudipto (1995). 'Democracy and Development in India', in A.K. Bagchi (ed.), *Democracy and Development*, St. Martin Press in association with the International Economic Association, London, ch. 4, pp. 92–130.

Kohli, Atul (2006). 'Politics of Economic Growth in India 1980–2005' Parts I & II in *Economic and Political Weekly*, vol. 41, nos. 13 & 14 (April).

Krishna, Sridhar (2001). 'Phasing Out of Import Licensing: Impact on Small-Scale Industries', *Economic and Political Weekly*, vol. 36, no. 27 (7 July), pp. 2545–50.

Kumar, Sanjay (2004). 'Impact of Economic Reforms on Indian Electorate', *Economic and Political Weekly*, vol. 39, no.18, 17–23 April, pp. 1621–30.

Kuznets, Simon (1972). 'Innovations and Adjustments in Economic Growth', *Swedish Journal of Economics*, vol. 74, no. 4, pp. 432–51.

Lakha, Salim (2002). 'From Swadeshi to Globalisation: The Bharatiya Janata Party Shifting Economic Agenda', *South Asia*, vol. 25, no. 3 (December), pp. 83–104.

Lall, D. (1988). *Cultural Stability and Economic Stagnation: India, 1500 BC–AD 1980*. Oxford University Press, New York.

Mahalanobis, P.C. (1955). 'The Approach of Operational Research to Planning in India', *Sankhya, The Indian Journal of Statistics*, vol. 16, parts 1 and 2, pp. 3–130.

Marathe, Sharad S. (1986). *Regulation and Development: India's Policy Experience Of Controls Over Industry*. Sage, New Delhi.

Mathur, Archana S. and Arvinder S. Sachdeva (2005). 'Customs Tariff Structure in India', *Economic and Political Weekly*, vol. XL(16), 5–11 February, pp. 535–9.

Mayer, Peter (2002). 'The Hindu Rate of Reform: Privatisation under the BJP—Still Waiting for that *BADA KADAM*', *South Asia*, new series, vol. 25, no. 3 (December), pp. 105–30.

Millikan, M.F. and D.L.M. Blackner (1961). *The Emerging Nations: Their Growth and the United States*. Little, Brown and Company, Boston.

Minhas, B.S. (1991). 'Public Versus Private Sector: Neglect of Lessons of Economics in Indian Policy Formulation', *Artha Vijnana*, vol. 33, no. 1 (March), pp. 1–11.

Mitra, P. and Suresh D. Tendulkar (1994). 'Adjustment with Growth or Stagnation? India, 1973/74 to 1983/84', in Pradeep K. Mitra (ed.), *Adjustment in Oil-Importing Developing Countries: A Comparative Economic Analysis*. Cambridge University Press, Cambridge, UK, ch. 6, pp. 146–92.

Mohan, Rakesh (1992). 'Industrial Policy and Controls', in Bimal Jalan (ed.), *The Indian Economy: Problems and Prospects*. Vikings, New Delhi, pp. 85–115.

——— (2002). 'Small-Scale Industry Policy in India: A Critical Evaluation' in Anne O. Krueger (ed.), *Economic Policy Reforms and the Indian Economy*, Oxford University Press, New Delhi, pp. 213–302.

Morris, M.D. (1983). 'The Growth of Large-Scale Industry', in D. Kumar (ed.), *The Cambridge Economic History of India*. Cambridge University Press, Cambridge, UK.

Myint, H. (1971). 'Market Mechanism and Planning—The Functional Approach', in H. Myint, *Economic Theory and Underdeveloped Countries*. Oxford University Press, London, ch. 13, pp. 291–324.

Myrdal, G. (1968). *Asian Drama: An Inquiry in to the Poverty of Nations*, vol. 2. The Penguin Press, Allan Lane.

Nayar, Baldev Raj (1997). 'National Planning for Autarky and State Hegemony: Development Strategy Under Nehru', *The Indian Economic Review*, vol. 32, no. 1 (January–June), pp. 13–38.

——— (2001). *Globalisation and Nationalism: The Changing Balance in India's Economic Policy, 1950–2000*. Sage Publications, New Delhi.

Nehru, Jawaharlal (1946). *The Discovery of India*. The John Day Company, New York.

North, Douglass C. (1990). *Institutions, Institutional Change and Economic Performance*. Cambridge University Press, Cambridge.

——— (1994). 'Economic Performance through Time', *American Economic Review*, vol. 84, no. 3 (June), pp. 359–68.

——— (1997). *The Contribution of the New Institutional Economics to an Understanding of the Transition Problem*. WIDER Annual Lectures 1, World Institute for Development Economics Research, United Nations University, March.

North, D.C. and J.J. Wallis (1994). 'Integrating Institutional Change and Technical Change in Economic History: A Transaction Cost Approach', *Journal of Institutional and Theoretical Economics*, vol. 150, no. 4 (December), pp. 609–24.

Palshikar, Suhas (2003). 'The Regional Parties and Democracy', in Ajay K. Mehra, D.D. Khanna, and Gert W. Kueck (eds), *Political Parties and Party Systems*. Sage Publications, New Delhi, ch. 13, pp. 306–35.

Panagariya, Arvind (1999). 'Trade Policy in South Asia', *The World Economy*, vol. 22, no. 3 (May), pp. 353–78.

——— (2002). 'Trade Liberalisation in Asia', ch. 8, pp. 219–302 in J. Bhagawati (ed.), *Going Alone, The Case for Relaxed Reciprocity in Foreign Trade*. MIT Press, Cambridge, MA.

——— (2004). 'Growth and Reforms during 1980s and 1990s', *Economic and Political Weekly*, vol. 39, no. 25 (19–25 June), pp. 2581–94.

Paranjape, H.K. (1985). 'New Lamps for Old! A Critique of the "New Economic Policy"', *Economic and Political Weekly*, vol. 20, no. 36 (7 September), pp. 1513–22.

Prakash, Amit (2003). 'Social, Cultural and Economic Dimensions of the Party System', in Ajay K. Mehra, D.D. Khanna, and Gert W. Kueck (eds), *Political Parties and Party Systems*. Sage, New Delhi, pp. 129–61.

Pursell, Gary and Ashok Gulati (1993). '*Liberalising Indian Agriculture: An Agenda for Reform*', Policy Research Working Paper, Trade Policy, World Bank, Washington, D.C.

Reserve Bank of India (2003a). *Handbook of Statistics on the Indian Economy 2003–4*. Mumbai.

———(2006). *Annual Credit Policy Statement 2006–7*, Mumbai.

Rodrik, Dani (1996). 'Understanding Economic Policy Reforms', *The Journal of Economic Literature*, vol. 34, no. 1(March), pp. 9–41.

Rudolph, Lloyd L. and Susanne H. Rudolph (1987). *In Pursuit of Lakshmi: The Political Economy of the Indian State*. University of Chicago Press, Chicago and London.

Sachs, Jeffrey D., Ashutosh Varshney, and Nirupam Bajpai (eds) (1999). *India in the Era of Economic Reforms*. Oxford India Paperback, New Delhi.

Sheth, D.L. (2005). 'The Change of 2004', *Seminar* (Annual Number, January), pp. 34–9.

Srivastava, D.K. and C. Bhujanga Rao (2004). 'Government Subsidies in India: Issues and Approach', in Edgardo M. Favaro and Ashok K. Lahiri (eds). *Fiscal Policies and Sustainable Growth in India.* Oxford University Press, New Delhi, 2004, ch. 6, pp. 148–50.

Srivastava, D.K. and Tapas K. Sen (1997). *Government Subsidies in India.* National Institute of Public Finance and Policy, New Delhi

Srinivasan, T.N. (1991). 'Reform of Industrial and Trade Policies', *Economic and Political Weekly*, vol. 26, no. 37 (14 September), pp. 2143–5.

——— (1996). 'Liberalisation and Economic Development: India', *Journal of Asian Economics*, vol. 7, no. 2, pp. 203–16.

——— (2003). 'Foreign Trade Policies And India's Development', in Uma Kapila (ed.), *Indian Economy since Independence*, 14th edition, Academic Foundation, New Delhi.

——— (2005). *Information Technology Enabled Services and India's Growth Prospects*, (May 06), processed.

Srinivasan, T.N. and Suresh D. Tendulkar (2003). *Reintegrating India with the World Economy*. Institute for International Economics, Washington, D.C. and Oxford University Press, New Delhi.

Sundaram, K. (1972a). 'Political Response to 1966 Devaluation–II, Politicians and Parties', *Economic and Political Weekly*, vol. 7, no. 37 (9 September), pp. 1883–92.

——— (1972b). 'Political Response to 1966 Devaluation–III, Politicians and Parties', *Economic and Political Weekly*, vol. 7, no. 38 (16 September), pp. 1929–33.

Sundaram, K. and Suresh D. Tendulkar (2003a). 'Poverty Has Declined in 1990s: A Resolution of Comparability in NSS Consumer Expenditure Data', *Economic and Political Weekly*, vol. 38, no. 4, (25 January), pp. 327–37.

——— (2003b). 'Poverty in India in the 1990s: An Analysis of Changes in 15 Major States', *Economic and Political Weekly*, vol. 38, no. 14 (5 April), pp. 1385–94.

——— (2003c). 'Poverty among Social and Economic Groups in India in 1990s', *Economic and Political Weekly*, vol. 38, no. 50, (13 December), pp. 5263–76.

Tamarajakshi, R. (1990). 'Intersectoral Terms of Trade Revisited', *Economic and Political Weekly*, vol. 25, no. 13 (31 March), A48–A52.

Tendulkar, Suresh D. (1991). 'The Role of Policy Research in the Formulation and Implementation of Macroeconomic Strategies and Policies in India', in *Institutional Relations in Development*. Development Papers, no. 8, UN-ESCAP, Bangkok, pp. 31–50.

——— (1993). 'Industrial Planning in India: Institutional Environment and Regulatory Regime', in Kanta Ahuja, Hubb Coppens, and Herman van de Wusten (eds), *Regime Transformations and Global Realignments: Indo-*

European Dialogues on the Post-Cold War World. Sage Publications, New Delhi, ch. 16, pp. 279–94.

Tendulkar, Suresh D. (1997). 'India's Economic Policy Reforms and Poverty', in I.J. Ahluwalia and I.M.D. Little (eds), *Indian Economic Reforms and Development, Essays for Manmohan Singh*. Oxford University Press, New Delhi, ch. 12, pp. 280–309.

——— (2004). 'Organised Labour Market in India: Pre and Post Reform', paper presented at the Conference on Anti Poverty and Social Policy in India organized by the Mac Arthur Research Network on Inequality and Economic Performance at the Neemrana Fort Palace, Alwar, Rajasthan, 2–4 January 2004.

Tendulkar, Suresh D. and L.R. Jain (1995). 'Economic Growth, Relative Inequality and Equity: The Case of India', *Asian Development Review*, vol. 13, no. 2, pp. 138–68.

Tendulkar, Suresh D. and T.A. Bhavani (1997). 'Policy on Modern Small Scale Industries: A Case of Government Failure', *Indian Economic Review*, vol. 32, no. 1 (January–June), pp. 85–110.

Tendulkar, Suresh D. and Binayak Sen (2003). 'Markets and Long-term Economic Growth in South Asia, 1950–1997', in I.J. Ahluwalia and John Williams (eds), *The South Asian Experience with Growth*. Oxford University Press, New Delhi, ch. 4, pp. 146–218.

Thorner, Daniel (1980). *Shaping of Modern India*. Allied Publishers, New Delhi.

Varshney, Ashutosh (1995). *Democracy, Development and the Countryside: Urban-Rural Struggles in India*. Cambridge University Press, Cambridge, UK.

——— (1999). 'Mass Politics or Elite Politics? India's Economic Reforms in Comparative Perspective', in Jeffrey D. Sachs, Ashutosh Varshney, and Nirupam Bajpai (eds), *India in the Era of Economic Reforms*. Oxford India Paperback, New Delhi, ch. 7, pp. 222–60.

World Bank (1992). *India: Stabilising and Reforming Economy*, Country Operations, Industry and Finance Division, India Country Department, South Asia Region, Report No. 10489 (18 May).

———['] (2004). *Trade Policies in South Asia: An Overview*, Three volumes (prepared by Gary Pursell and Zaidi Sattar), Poverty Reduction and Economic Management Sector Unit, Document of the World Bank, Report No. 29949 (7 September).

Zagha, R. (1999). 'Labour and India's Economic Reforms', in Jeffrey D. Sachs, Ashutosh Varshney, and Nirupam Bajpai (eds), *India in the Era of Economic Reforms*. Oxford India Paperback, New Delhi, ch. 5, pp. 160–85.

Index